The Making, Breaking, and Renewal of a Surgeon-Scientist:
A Personal Perspective of the Physician Crisis in America

Steven E. Wilson, MD

Steven E. Wilson, MD

The Making, Breaking, and Renewal of a Surgeon-Scientist: A Personal Perspective of the Physician Crisis in America

Copyright © 2019 by Steven E. Wilson

Published in the United States by H-G Books. Website: H-G-Books.com   SAN: 255–2434

First H-G Books Edition: 2019

Library of Congress Control Number: 2019900195

Kindle Book ISBN: 978-1-7329151-3-8

Paperback ISBN: 978-1-7329151-4-5

Audiobook ISN: 978-1-7329151-5-2

Editor: Janice Phelps Williams

Caduceus and the stick © Shutterstock

MANUFACTURED IN THE UNITED STATES OF AMERICA

Wilson, Steven E. (Steven Eugene), 1951–
The Making, Breaking, and Renewal of a Surgeon-Scientist: A Personal Perspective of the
Physician Crisis in America/ Steven E. Wilson.—
Cleveland, Ohio: H-G Books, c2019.
p.; cm.1. Medicine—21st century—Nonfiction. 2. Legal. 3. Autobiographical. 3. Malpractice. 4. Scandal.

Dedicated to Nicholas A. Halasz, MD, Professor of Surgery and Head of the Division of Anatomy at UCSD School of Medicine. Dr. Halasz was also the founding Director of the UCSD Transplantation Program, one of the founding fathers of USCD School of Medicine, and my greatest teacher ever.

Other books by Steven E. Wilson

The Stone Waverly Trilogy
Winter in Kandahar
Benjamin Franklin Award Finalist, Best New Voice in Fiction, 2004
Ascent from Darkness
Next Generation Indie Book Award Finalist, Action-Adventure, 2008
The Benghazi Affair
2018

The Ghosts of Anatolia: An Epic Journey to Forgiveness
Foreword Reviews Book of the Year Gold Award Fiction (multicultural), 2010

Table of Contents

Prologue

Abraham Flexner issued his famous report that changed the course of medical education in the United States in 1910. Now, over one hundred years later, the medical profession, including its practitioners, teachers, and institutions, finds itself engaged in a deepening struggle of uncertainty, foreboding, and cynicism. The outcome of this struggle will likely determine the quality of medical care obtainable in the United States during the twenty-first century and beyond.

Medicine is a profession under siege from seemingly every direction. Many of its greatest institutions are on the brink of bankruptcy due to spiraling costs, declining reimbursements, increasing governmental and payor intrusion, and mismanagement. Practitioners are buckling under the burden of layer upon layer of regulation, much of which changes from year to year, or even month to month. Clinician–scientists are abandoning their laboratories under the crush of decreasing funding and increasing regulatory demands, and claims on their time related to the practice of medicine. They also face diminishing availability of American trainees interested in research and frustration in dealing with institutional, state and federal bureaucracy. Physicians and surgeons are under legal attack by ever-increasing legions of plaintiffs' attorneys trolling the airways, phone directories, and newspapers for clients using slogans like "make them pay." Many illustrious careers that took decades to build have disintegrated under the weight of a legal and governmental onslaught.

It's obvious—even to the uninitiated layperson—the medical profession in America has sunk into crisis. Newspapers, airwaves, and blogs are filled with missives concerning assaults on the profession, addressing the ills of its institutions and the plight of individual physicians. What is often not clear, however—even to many medical professionals themselves—is the impact that these events have had on the lives and careers of real people. It is my sincere hope that the telling of my personal journey, from wide-eyed youth to shell-shocked physician–scientist to embattled department chairperson of one of the great medical schools in America, will increase understanding of the human costs of the turmoil that has invaded our glorious profession and stimulate concrete measures to halt this downward vortex.

I have no illusions of there being a consensus on remedies that I propose in the pages to follow, and hopefully even better remedies can be orchestrated. At the least, however, I hope the telling of my story, as well as those of some of my maligned colleagues, will stimulate discussion and efforts to address the concerns of those who, like me, truly love the medical profession and are deeply troubled by the signs of its demise.

Chapter 1
The Long, Hard Road—
Not Unlike that Traveled by Many Others Who Longed to Take the Oath

I remember the first time I felt medicine's tug on my heart and soul. I was a mischievous and impressionable sixth-grade boy growing up in the Southern California suburb of Whittier (YES, where former president Richard Nixon grew up!). Sitting anxiously on an examination table, I watched tearfully as kindly old Dr. Bradford mixed a batch of plaster and prepared to apply a cast to the leg I'd broken two hours earlier in a skateboarding mishap. The doctor pulled on one of his gloves and, with a twinkle in his benevolent eyes, roughed my hair with his fingertips. "Well, Steven, I guess it's about time you got rid of that skateboard," he said with a chuckle and a smile, as he patted the weathered and ink-marked cast on my left arm—that I'd broken two weeks earlier jumping off the roof playing commando. "Don't you think?"

"Yes, sir," I muttered, nodding my head.

And I kept my word, at least until three years later, when once again Dr. Bradford was called into the emergency room of Whittier Hospital to examine my compound-fractured right arm.

"I thought you were going to get rid of that skateboard, Steven," he quipped with a wide grin, as he walked into the exam room carrying my X-rays.

"I did, Dr. Bradford," I replied awkwardly. "This was a new one."

"Well," he laughed, "you'd better get rid of that one, too!"

Dr. Bradford was off call when I had another childhood accident that came close to ending my future eye surgery career, if not my life. My parents scraped up money to go watch a musical, *The Sound of Music,* at The Music Center in Los Angeles—a venue nineteen miles and thirty minutes from our house—as I recall for one of their few major outings alone. I had just turned seventeen and was a junior in high school, and I was left under the loose supervision of the next-door neighbors, the Browns. A group of neighborhood teenagers were out in the street in front of their house, playing with a homemade, makeshift go-cart that required a push to start.

Well, this go-cart had a sheet metal frame with sharp corners that was an accident waiting to happen. At some point, along with several other boys, I was push-starting the go-cart for another neighbor boy, when I was accidentally tripped onto the tail end of the go-cart. I still remember the shocked look on the other boys' faces when I got up from the pavement and a huge L-shaped chunk of the underside of my right upper arm nearly five inches long was dangling out, with blood spurting across my chest and the street. I ran to the Brown's front door—with the other boys right behind me—and rang the doorbell. Mrs. Brown and her teenage daughter answered the door, and promptly fainted in the doorway at the sight of my arm. Mr. Brown stepped over them, took off his belt and used it as a tourniquet to apply to my arm above the laceration. While two other teenage daughters cared for their mother and sister, Mr. Brown loaded me up in his car and rushed me to Whittier Hospital. Surgeons and nurses at the hospital stabilized me, while the Whittier police called The Music Center to stop the performance and page my parents out of the theatre audience to obtain their permission to operate. By the time mom and dad reached the hospital, I was already anesthetized and in surgery. Three hours later, the surgeon came out to update them in the waiting room outside the operating suite. It had taken ninety-six sutures in two layers to close the laceration. According to my parents, the surgeon—whose name I don't recall—said, "Steven must be the luckiest boy alive. The deep laceration narrowly missed the main nerve (*ulnar nerve*) and nicked, but did not sever, the main brachial artery in his right upper arm. I think there's a good chance he'll regain full use of the arm." And regain full use of it I did. It took several months—after Dr. Bradford removed the external sutures—for my arm to function normally—except for a numbness of the skin in the area I felt for years—but, thank God, I could throw a baseball nine months later, and the injury never seriously affected my future activities.

I remember Dr. Bradford smiling at me when I went to see him for my first follow-up visit. "Well, Steven, I guess you better get rid of that go-cart, too!"

It's doubtful Dr. Bradford realized the impression his gentle, but firm, bedside manner had on me, but he influenced choices I made during the formative years of my life. By the time I was a junior in high school, I knew I wanted to be a doctor. Many clinicians I've known had similar early experiences with doctors—in some cases, doctors who were also their parents—who stimulated childhood dreams of one day becoming a physician.

I was born on December 28, 1951, in a hospital in Oklahoma City, the firstborn of parents who'd been raised on farms in the small agricultural community of Altus, Oklahoma. My father, Gilford Eugene Wilson, though not yet thirty, had served as a Boson's Mate aboard the battleship *USS Mississippi* (BB-41) during World War II, where he earned eight battle stars in engagements at the Aleutian Islands, the invasion of the Gilbert Islands, Leyte Gulf, and Okinawa. On June 5, 1945, just off the coast of Okinawa, a kamikaze smashed into the bridge on the huge ship's starboard side and killed my father's closest friend. It was an event that would haunt him for years to come, and I'm certain, would leave its mark on the remainder of his life. I still own the Boson's whistle he carried in his pocket when the *Mississippi* sailed into Tokyo Bay with Admiral Halsey's Task Force 31 to witness the Japanese surrender on the second day of September 1945.

My father married my mother, Margie Francis Wheeler, in 1948, and began to master the "new-fangled" computers in college courses and on the job at Tinker Air Force Base outside of Oklahoma City. In 1955, the family moved to Ft. Worth, Texas. My brother Lex was born shortly thereafter in nearby Dallas. Two years later, in 1957, the family moved to California to join my Grandfather Fred and Uncle Gordon, living for a short time in Bell, and eventually settling in a small three-bedroom home on Lambert Road in Whittier in 1958. Over the next few years, Dad moved from Revlon to Cannon Electric and, finally, to Stuart Pharmaceuticals in Pasadena, the manufacturer of Mylanta and other medical products. There, he became the supervisor of data processing.

My father was a stern but highly-positive influence on my early life, as he instilled into me the value of education and the importance of hard work. On the other hand, along with golden-voiced Vin Scully, longtime announcer for the Los Angeles Dodgers, he cultivated in me a lifelong love of sports, especially baseball. My loving and highly-religious mother worked as a homemaker and made sure that my brother and I were involved in character-building activities like Cub Scouts, Indian Guides, and Little League Baseball.

I always did well in school when I was younger but also found time for sports and playing with neighborhood friends. Encouraged by my parents, I worked at mowing lawns and doing other chores for neighbors to earn spending money. I got my first real job working at the mom-and-pop grocery store down the street on Colima Road at the age of twelve. My responsibility was to sort pop bottles returned for deposit for an hour a day after school, until I was promoted to bag boy at the checkout stand the following year. This was followed by a two-year stint as a paperboy for the *Whittier Daily News*. I believe I had a normal, middle-class upbringing—at least into high school.

Then, seemingly overnight, and much to my parent's horror, I developed behavioral and motivational problems, to the point that I nearly flunked out of my freshman year at California High School. I went from being an A student to flunking algebra and German, getting D's in English and the rest of my classes, and finding myself spending more time in the vice principal's office than in class. It got so bad that my freshman algebra teacher told me I should avoid career choices that in anyway involved math because I "didn't have the aptitude for it." To this day, I'm not sure what led to these tribulations, just as I'm unsure why the problems faded away. Maybe it was just one of those restless and rebellious phases that many young people go through at some point in their life. Perhaps my resurgence was attributable to increased self-confidence after I shot up to over six feet of height and lost baby fat between my freshman and sophomore years. Whatever the reasons, my grades went from C's and B's in my sophomore year to A's and B's in my junior year to straight A's in my senior year, as I set my sights on becoming a doctor. Late in my senior year of high school, the vice principal, the same one who'd disciplined me dozens of times during my tumultuous freshman year, called me to the administration building, a place I hadn't visited in three years. He welcomed me into his office, and spreading my four-year transcript across his desk, ran his finger down the page. "Steven. I'd really like you to tell me what happened here. What brought about this change?"

"I don't know, sir," I replied respectfully. "I guess I just grew up."

It was also during my senior year in high school I met my lifelong friend Dan Everts—who helped me through hard times to come during college, just by being my best friend. Dan now lives with his family in Texas.

Despite the upswing in academic performance, however, my goal of attending medical school had already been dreadfully muddled far more than I could appreciate at the time. Admission to college is, for the most part, determined by grades from the first three years of high school. Even though I scored high on the SAT exams, with my dismal academic showing as a freshman, the only real choice was to begin higher education at Rio Hondo Community College in Whittier. At "Rio," I took two years of premed courses, with majors in biology and chemistry, culminating in my being selected "Biology Major of the Year" in my second year. Everything seemed to be coming together just fine; at least those were my rather naïve thoughts at the time.

During these high school years, I worked for spending money for two years, first as a dish washer, then waiter, then salad maker, then cook at Sir George's Smorgasbord, owned by Lou Greashammer. Mr. Greashammer begged me to stay, and offered a big raise, when I finally left late in my senior year of high school to work as a waiter and cook at the much "cooler" Farrell's Ice Cream Parlor—also in Whittier. I was fired from that job after only a few months, when I teasingly put ice down the cashier's back, not knowing she was secretly dating the manager. At that point, I decided to focus on college classes and didn't work for a year or so. My parents helped me with gas and spending money during that period—and I didn't do much beyond studying.

I was hired to be a ride operator at Disneyland in Anaheim, California, early in my sophomore year of college and worked in Tomorrowland on the Matterhorn, Submarines, Autopia Cars, People Mover, and Monsanto rides. I was promoted to permanent part-time after my first summer, and worked weekends, holidays, and summer vacations for the next five years while attending college and graduate school. Working with the public and thousands of other young people at this celebrated Southern California institution was the perfect confidence builder for a somewhat shy young man who played on the Tomorrowland Friday night softball team, and with liberal use of styling gel, was always testing the strict hair length regulations of one of America's most conservative institutions—earning me a bit of a reputation for being a rebel among my peers. I remember the night that an affable supervisor hid me deep inside the Matterhorn in a secret room until executives from the corporate office finished their park inspection—out of fear that a few strands of my hair that clearly touched the tops of my ears would earn us all black marks. I still have copies of a Disneyland employee newsletter that pictured me in the iconic Matterhorn costume—with an interview in which I proclaimed my goal was to become a physician-scientist. Little did I know at the time just what that would entail.

The time came for transfer to a four-year university and I decided to apply to only two institutions—Revelle College at the University of California, San Diego, and California State University, Fullerton. I was accepted to both and, after visiting the campuses, and settled on UCSD in picturesque La Jolla. As I prepared to leave Orange County, however, my family was suddenly and unexpectedly hit with a gut-wrenching crisis. My father, after many years as data processing supervisor at Stuart Pharmaceuticals, quit his job following a disagreement with one of his superiors—"Frosty." Dad took some work as a free-lance programmer and set about applying for jobs at other companies. We all were certain he'd quickly find another position, but as the months dragged on and family reserves dwindled, my father suddenly began exhibiting new and shocking behaviors none of us had ever seen before. It seemed as though one day he was a normal productive member of society and the next he'd gone completely mad— spending endless hours writing incoherent notes on pads of paper, creating imaginary villains ("Queen Bedaloo"), hearing voices, and talking out loud to himself. Anyone who has seen the movie *A Beautiful Mind* would likely recognize the signs of schizophrenia, but nothing in my life experience had prepared me for this mental affliction that was, at least to me at the time, equivalent to my father dying. The man whom I'd admired, emulated, and loved ceased to exist virtually overnight. My mother sunk into depression and my brother began exhibiting behavioral problems in high school reminiscent of my own during my freshman year—except far worse. Lex dropped out of high school in his freshman year, never to return to school or work or anything productive (Lex still lives in an assisted living community in California under the care of psychiatrists). It was the beginning of a nightmare that has lasted for over forty-five years. My father never worked another day in his life, and we never carried on a meaningful conversation after my freshman year of college (my father died from pneumonia in December 2007, and I remember he didn't recognize me—even after I'd tried to talk to him for an hour—when I visited him in a hospital the month before he passed away. He couldn't appreciate or understand that his oldest son had become a physician-scientist after all. My mother died years later in February 2014 (thankfully, with a sound mind).

Suddenly, my whole world was turned upside down and clearly I needed to stay closer to home to help my mother. I accepted a position in the junior class at California State University at Fullerton, where I could continue to work at Disneyland, and majored in biology, with a minor in chemistry. While dealing emotionally and physically with ongoing family tragedy, I somehow managed to keep my focus in class and maintained a 3.87 grade point average throughout college, with straight A's in science and math, as I began to submit applications to medical schools.

I must sheepishly admit I never really seriously considered the possibility that I wouldn't be accepted to medical school. I did well on the MCAT medical entrance exams and my grades placed me at the top of my college class at CSU Fullerton. Blindly confident, I was certain I'd be accepted—so confident that I applied only to California medical schools. During the second half of my senior year, I received notification that I'd been placed on waiting lists at the University of Southern California and University of California, Irvine, but initial excitement gave way to alarm, and then devastation, as month after month slipped by without an acceptance letter. Finally, I received notice that the entering classes at USC and UC Irvine had been filled. Confused and embittered, I was suddenly faced with what had been unthinkable just a few months earlier: I would not become a physician.

Early in my senior year of college, as a backup I never thought I'd really need, I had also applied for graduate school in molecular biology and biochemistry at the University of California, Irvine. I was offered a position in the PhD program in May of 1974, and suddenly an afterthought was my only opportunity. I accepted the position and resolved, albeit gloomily, to apply myself to a career in molecular biology research.

Resigned to my fate, I arrived at my first day of graduate school in September of 1974 and attended the program orientation with six other new graduate students from all over the U.S.A. Little did I know that the lingering questions I had about why I hadn't been accepted to medical school would be answered that day in a very inauspicious way. As the introduction ended and the other students scattered into the hall, the graduate program director, a rather dour and intimidating professor who studies herpes viruses, took me aside with another new student. "I want you to know," the professor began solemnly once the others had left, "The other faculty members and I feel strongly that, even though the two of you graduated from the California State University system, there's no reason why you shouldn't have a chance to prove yourselves in this program. If you work hard, I believe you can overcome your limitations." There it was—laid out bluntly in no uncertain terms—my classmate and I were considered second class because we had obtained our undergraduate degrees from the "second-tier" university system in California; not the bright and shining University of California, but the rather plain, and at least to my program director, flawed California State University. It was a sobering realization. (I, and many others like me, have long since proven CSU Fullerton worthy, but it's a way of thinking that nonetheless persists to this day among the academic intelligentsia (and all the Titan NCAA baseball championships in the world won't change that).

11

My first year of graduate school was devoted to "basic training" in classes that provided in-depth knowledge of many topics, including protein and nucleic acid structure and function, virology, and physical chemistry. I excelled in this formal coursework and, after easily passing my oral examinations early in my second year, began my bench research in the laboratory of a kindly older professor named Kenneth H. Ibsen, PhD, whose appointment was, of all places, in the UC Irvine School of Medicine. Dr. Ibsen couldn't be characterized as dynamic, but he was a good solid research investigator with a heart of gold. The laboratory was focused on studying enzymes involved in metabolism and, specifically, pyruvate kinase, a key enzyme at the end of the glycolysis pathway. The work was interesting, and I learned important molecular and biochemical techniques like electrophoresis, isoelectric focusing, and ultracentrifugation that at the time I did not appreciate would be critical to my future career. But my heart was just not in the work—in retrospect, likely because I secretly longed to be a physician. My ambition to become a physician remained a closely guarded secret because, as I learned from senior graduate students in my program, the faculty in the graduate school frowned on students, particularly graduate students, who professed or even hinted at an interest in medical school. Some undergraduates who intended to apply to medical school even hid their true goals in the beginning so that they could avail themselves of opportunities to do research rotations in "closed labs" in the Molecular Biology and Biochemistry Program. For graduate students, plain and simple, the thought of application to medical school was anathema.

After nine months in the lab, I came to the decision that a pure research career was just not right for me. I wasn't sure what else I would do, but the thought of a lifetime in the lab working on biological processes with no direct relevance to human health or disease—at least in my mind—just didn't inspire me. I approached Dr. Ibsen and sheepishly admitted my dark secret. Even though I knew I couldn't expect his support, I intended to leave the graduate program because I still wanted to go to medical school. I remember Dr. Ibsen, his brow deeply furrowed, peered at me for a moment and then asked, "What if you could do both?"

"That would be wonderful! How?" I asked eagerly.

He explained that the medical school a U.C. Irvine had been toying with the idea of offering a combined MD, PhD degree and that he was willing to see if there was a way it could work out for me. I readily agreed, completed an application and was interviewed, but once again an acceptance letter never came. I was teaching undergraduate laboratory classes for my stipend, and I remember the humiliation I felt upon overhearing a group of my students discussing the multiple medical school acceptances they'd received and how they were going about narrowing their choices.

Shortly thereafter, I transferred to another lab in my program that was studying DNA and RNA structure and function, and developmental gene regulation. Jerry Manning, PhD, the principal investigator, was a fresh new faculty member from California Institute of Technology (Caltech) whose Southern California good looks and pageboy haircut gave him the aura of a rock star. I joined two other graduate students, two post-docs and a technician in the lab, and set about studying the expression of cuticle protein genes in *Drosophila melanogaster* fruit fly maggots, which we raised by the disgusting millions in specially-designed clear plastic containers.

Fruit flies weren't the only source of experimental tissues used in the lab. I remember one of the other graduate students worked with RNA isolated from blowfly pupa. The dark brownish-black pupa would arrive in sealed cardboard containers every couple of weeks, and my colleague would grind them up and extract RNA from the hideous puree. Then; one of the containers fell off the lab bench and pupa scattered everywhere. Everyone in the lab chipped in and tried to retrieve them all, but unfortunately there were lots of nooks and crannies beneath the benches, some of which disappeared beneath the floor. About a week passed before the lost pupa began hatching and the biggest flies I'd seen in my life were buzzing around the room colliding with the picture windows that lined the outside walls of the laboratory—and terrifying a particularly squeamish graduate student prone to bloodcurdling screams. It was a week before the infestation subsided and the lab returned to normal.

For a time, the change in environment in the new lab reinvigorated my interest in research. It was a heady time in molecular biology. In 1970, Howard Temin of the University of Wisconsin, Madison, and David Baltimore of the Massachusetts Institute of Technology independently isolated the first restriction enzymes that could split DNA molecules at precise sequences of the four building blocks of DNA—adenine, thymine, guanine and cytosine. They, along with Renato Dulbecco, received the Nobel Prize in Physiology and Medicine in 1975. Using these advances, Paul Berg spliced together DNA from two different organisms and created the first recombinant DNA molecules. Then, in 1973, using the recombinant DNA methods of Berg, Stanley Cohen and Herbert Boyer of Stanford University engineered the first recombinant DNA organism. The methodology became known as gene splicing or genetic engineering, and allowed scientists to manipulate the DNA of any organism.

It was shortly after these seminal achievements that a new assistant professor, whose name I've long forgotten, joined the department and was assigned to lecture the graduate students in the department. He lectured for hours on end, in minute detail, about seemingly esoteric pieces of circular DNA called plasmids, found in bacteria, to the point that the students eventually rebelled en masse against what they perceived as a complete waste of precious time. Some of the faculty supported the rebellion and the material was cut short. Within a few years, these "worthless" plasmids became, and still are, the workhorses of DNA cloning. I learned an important lesson from that episode about student perceptions of what topics are important in their education.

As I marked my first year in the new lab, the nagging feelings about not wanting to spend my life in basic research began to resurface. I'm not sure why my interest waned; I guess the research just didn't inspire me. Finally, despite protests from several faculty members in the department, including Jerry Manning (who eventually became chairman of the Department of Molecular Biology and Biochemistry at UC Irvine, where he recently retired), I made the decision to leave UC Irvine with my MS degree. I really wanted to apply once again to medical school, but realized it was futile without the support of my faculty advisors. So I left and accepted a position as Instructor of Biology and Chemistry at Rio Hondo College in Whittier, where I'd obtained my first two years of undergraduate education.

Hired to update the majors biology program at Rio Hondo, I set out to modernize the curriculum and incorporate laboratory exercises that included some of the modern molecular and cellular methods for students who in many ways reminded me of myself. Full of excitement and eager to excel, but unknowingly yoked with a stigma that could potentially limit the opportunities available to them. Only a precious few would make it into the professional world, but I saw no reason to point this out to them. After all, this was America and anything *really was* possible given persistence and hard work.

Instructors at community colleges must be diversified, so I also taught other courses: nursing anatomy and physiology, microbiology, biology for non-majors, environmental biology, field biology, and even inorganic chemistry. This diversity of disciplines was superb preparation for what was to come—although I didn't realize it at the time.

I loved teaching, especially lecturing, and others said I had a talent for it. Relating to my students was fairly easy, I was only twenty-six years old and my students themselves ranged from eighteen to thirty-five, and even older. Although I certainly wasn't wealthy, my salary was more than adequate for a bachelor living in an apartment, first in Fullerton, and then in Whittier. I bought new furniture and a black 280Z, and spent my free time partying with friends and lounging on Southern California beaches.

In 1978, a bright biology major caught my eye. After she completed my major's biology class, we began an on-again off-again romance that lasted for years, culminating in our marriage seven years later—during my medical internship.

It was also during that time that I first began writing. I loved, and still do, rock and roll music. Oh, I enjoy classical, folk, and even some country music, but I definitely grew up a rocker. I especially loved rock ballads written by the likes of Jackson Browne, the Eagles, and Crosby, Stills and Nash. I relished the skill with which these wordsmiths wove just the right words to create a story and a feeling. During those years, I wrote dozens of lyrical pieces, really poetry intended for songs, and submitted several to the American Song Festival in Los Angeles. One song, *Without You*, actually won an honorable mention and was put to music by a local band. It was the beginning of a lifelong love of writing, any kind of writing: medical, scientific, fiction, or non-fiction.

Despite my relative contentment while teaching college, nary a year passed before I began having doubts about my future. As the months went by, a simple question began to pop into my mind more and more frequently: Will I be happy teaching college for the next thirty years? Somehow, I instinctively knew the answer...*no way*.

I decided to try something a little different. I took a course and earned my California real estate license and went to work part-time and summers at an uptown Whittier real estate office owned by a character named Ed Christmas and his wife Mary (really!), while I continued with my main job teaching at Rio Hondo College.

I had a knack for real estate, earning more the first six months than I did from a year's salary from my regular teaching job. It seemed so simple, just treat people respectfully, listen carefully to what they wanted, and don't try to sell them something that's not right. If you showed them what they really wanted, the rest took care of itself. But the off-hour and weekend demands of the job drove me crazy, to say nothing of what it did to my social life. One day, out of the blue, I just gave it up and transferred my customers and listings to another agent.

Then, about halfway through my second year of teaching at Rio Hondo, I realized the longing I had felt to go to medical school still remained deep inside neurons and their connections in my cerebral cortex. I requested an admission packet from the UCLA School of Medicine and made calls to other schools over the next week.

I studied (using the Stanley Kaplan course, no less!) for countless hours, retook the MCAT and scored in the ninetieth percentile or above on nearly every section. I worked as a volunteer in a local medical doctor's office and gathered and completed applications for forty-some medical schools inside and outside of California, even adding a couple in Canada. As I did these things, however, I kept putting off what I realized was the most critical element of my application. If there was to be any chance at all of success, even the faintest hope, I had to have a letter of recommendation from at least one of my professors from graduate school—the same professors who had viewed students who were interested in medical careers with disdain. Finally, I got up the nerve to write a heartfelt plea for support to both of the professors I'd worked with most closely. I never received a response from Dr. Manning, but just over a week later, Dr. Ibsen sent a brief reply. He graciously agreed to provide the precious reference. I'll always be grateful for his compassion. His simple act of kindness was the key to me achieving my dreams. With a newfound spring in my step, I completed the medical school applications and sent them on their way in the fall of 1979.

Over the next month and a half, I was rejected by more than thirty schools, but offered interviews at eight: Vanderbilt, Tulane, Washington University in St. Louis, University of Southern California, Loma Linda University, UC Los Angeles, UC Irvine, and UC San Diego. I accepted them all, of course, and eventually decided that, if I weren't accepted to medical school, I wouldn't return to Rio Hondo College. I resigned my position on the faculty effective the end of the school year in June of 1980. As a backup, and the Lord knows I needed one, I contacted a headhunting firm to begin applying for pharmaceutical sales representative positions (I interviewed for several sales positions, including at Hoffmann-La Roche, where they told the headhunter, "I was a pretty good candidate but not good enough to hire"—Thank God!).

I only remember one of those medical school interviews—one at Washington University in St. Louis where a physician-scientist asked me, "How are organs affected by blood pressure and how do you measure blood pressure?" I began my answer by reversing the question, and first told him the principles of how you measured blood pressure and then how organs were affected by it. At the end of my response, he smiled broadly. "Young man," he said, "I've been asking that question to applicants for twenty years, and you're the first applicant ever who reversed your answer." "Is that good?" I asked. "That's good," he replied, as he wrote a note on the paper in front of him. I left that interview feeling pretty good about my chances at Washington University School of Medicine.

The months dragged by and the only letters I received were notifications that I'd been placed on the waiting lists at Washington University in St. Louis, UC San Diego, University of Southern California, and Loma Linda University.

June came and went without word, and as the weeks passed, I became more and more frustrated—bordering on distraught. I even considered going back to work at Disneyland for the summer, anything to keep my mind off of what was happening with the remaining medical schools. I became resigned to my fate by the end of June and bought a new metallic-blue Toyota Celica to "cheer me up." I just wasn't going to make it into medical school.

Around the first week of July, I got rejection letters from both Vanderbilt and University of Southern California on the same day. "Both entering classes had been filled." I remember mumbling to myself, "Here we go again," when I opened the letters.

Then, on Friday, July 11, 1980, I walked to the outside mailboxes at the condominium I was sharing with a friend who bought it, Jim Grace (who expected me to move out in a few short months before his wedding). There, inside the mailbox, with a pile of junk mail, was a thin, business-sized envelope from Washington University School of Medicine. I'd never gotten a medical school acceptance letter, but I assumed if I ever did, it would be thick—filled with information about the upcoming year, housing, tuition and other important details. This had to be another rejection. I tore the end off the envelope, and dumped out the single sheet of paper. Unfolding the letter, I read down the page and, with unbridled emotion, leapt straight into the air and whooped with joy as I realized I'd been accepted to medical school! "I'm accepted! I'm accepted! I yelled excitedly—scaring half to death a little old lady who was also checking her mailbox.

I ran and phoned just about everyone I knew, starting with my mother. It was a rousing Friday night to remember, filled with friends and revelry at a favorite nightspot—Goodies

Nightclub in Fullerton. It was the happiest day of my life—other than the day I married my wife, Jennifer, and the births of my children, Grey, Hailey, and Contessa.

The following week, I was also accepted to UC San Diego. As a California resident who was more than a little short of funds, there was no doubt where I would go. I would finally live in La Jolla—just eight years later than I'd originally planned. To this day, however, there's a soft spot in my heart for Washington University in St. Louis (of course the softest spot is reserved for UCSD!) and three times in my career I've come close to joining the faculty of that great medical institution—Washington University. But I'm getting ahead of my story.

Chapter 2
A Glorious Time—When Life was Far Simpler

The four years I spent in medical school were among the happiest of my life. Many of the students, especially those who had gone straight through undergraduate and directly into medical school, found the course work arduous, even grueling, depending on their background. Our graduating class of 1984 was surprisingly diverse. Upon entering, many students had limited knowledge in science. For example, some had majored in English or social sciences. A number, like me, even had other careers before returning to medical school, in some cases working at vocations unrelated to science or medicine. There was also a wide range of ages, and I was far from being the oldest in my class. With this diversity, it was to be expected that some would struggle with the challenging medical school curriculum and a few would even fall by the wayside. That's true of all medical schools, regardless of their academic standing.

Unlike the majority of medical schools in the United States, UCSD doesn't start out the first year with gross anatomy. The original intent, for what began as a rather small school in the University of California system, was to train physician–scientists. With this in mind, the original faculty of the school designed a curriculum with didactic classes that focused on molecular biology, biochemistry, pharmacology, physiology, and neurosciences during the first year, along with a smattering of social and behavioral sciences and a brief introduction to clinical medicine. Gross anatomy was introduced in the beginning of the second year. This model was retained even when the class size expanded to over 120 students per year and is still in place at USCD to this day—although it now appears Gross Anatomy has been moved to the end of the first year of medical school. With my background in molecular biology, biochemistry and anatomy and physiology, the first year and most of the second was fairly straightforward. I'm not saying the first two years of medical school were a breeze, but I had much more time to explore other areas of special interest than many of my fellow students. I doubt I would've been disappointed, even if it had been much tougher. I was on cloud nine, elated to know that I was finally on track to achieving my ultimate goal of becoming a physician, if not a physician-scientist. I was not in the Master Scientist Training Program (MSTP) at UCSD—a combined program that ended with an MD, PhD degree—but many of my closest friends were in that program.

La Jolla wasn't a bad a place to live while going to medical school! I leased a condominium less than a mile from school and shared it with other classmates—and eventually an intern in internal medicine. Surrounded by great natural beauty and what, especially for those who love constant sunshine, is the best climate in the United States, the temptation to skip class and rely on the notetaker, and the syllabus and books, was at times irrepressible. Being the type A personality that I am, I didn't skip class too often, but some of my classmates, including one near the top of the class, slipped away most afternoons to the beach or nearby Del Mar Racetrack. As long as they did well on their exams, nobody seemed to care. Poor attendance wasn't the rule, of course, for the small group classes that included our first clinical experiences with normal physical examinations. Everyone was expected to be present for those classes and most of us were excited to be there.

When you spend eight to ten hours a day, for five days a week minimum, the entire first year and most of the second year, with the same 128 people, it's to be expected that you'd develop strong friendships with some of your classmates. That was certainly the case. I've never been as close to anyone, other than family, as I was to twenty or so members of my graduating medical class. Whatever your interest or background, you all had one powerful and overriding shared attribute—you were training to be physicians.

Most, if not all, of the students in my class were completely serious about the opportunity and responsibility inherent in being a doctor-in-training. Those, like me, who found the two years of formal coursework to be less than totally absorbing, usually participated in other activities. Some did charity work and others worked with less gifted students. Many, including myself, became heavily involved in their required research project. I've long forgotten how it happened, but as I was still completely in the dark about my future choice of specialty, I decided to do a bench research project in rheumatology with Harry Bluestein, MD and Nathan J. Zvaifler, MD. My project involved studying B-lymphocytes immortalized with Epstein-Barr virus, a herpes virus responsible for infectious mononucleosis. I spent hundreds of hours on the project, including many weekends and holidays, and learned many new techniques that I would carry with me into my future academic career as a physician-scientist. There was also a hint of my future interests; I became captivated by this research that had more direct clinical relevance.

It seemed like we just blinked our eyes and the first half of medical school was over. Each of us—except those in the combined MD, PhD program who went off to basic science in a lab—began our clinical rotations, a combination of required and elective stints, in the main teaching hospitals of UC San Diego School of Medicine. Each rotation was, in its own way, fascinating and rewarding, and for a time several of them interested me enough to be considered potential career choices. Among the required rotations that I found most intriguing were general surgery, obstetrics and gynecology (high risk OB especially), and internal medicine. I was also, for obvious personal reasons, fascinated by psychiatry, but never considered it as a viable career option—since I'd spent the prior 10 years of my life dealing with enough mental illness in my own family members.

General surgery came very close to being my medical career choice. This can be totally attributed to the greatest teacher I ever had the privilege and honor to learn from and work with, Professor of Surgery, Nicholas A. Halasz, MD, one of the founding fathers of USCD School of Medicine. Dr. Halasz was also the founding Director of the Transplantation Program at UCSD. He developed one of the best human anatomy courses for medical students in the U.S.A., and received numerous awards and prizes, many related to that program that benefitted all medical students at UCSD. He was a Markle Scholar in academic medicine from 1964 to 1969. He holds the record at UCSD for receiving the Kaiser Award for Teaching Excellence four times. He was also awarded the Chancellor's Associate Award for Excellence in Teaching in 1989 and was voted Physician of the Year at UCSD Medical Center in 1994.

My first interaction with Dr. Halasz, a legend at UCSD School of Medicine, was in that *Human Anatomy* 207 class, the unique anatomy course that he founded and directed at the school. Unlike most medical schools, UCSD's anatomy course for medical students is taught by surgeons and radiologists, not anatomists. Dr. Halasz was a towering influence on all the medical students at UCSD due to his intellect and his outstanding teaching skills that included taking a personal interest in every student. Far and away, *Human Anatomy* was my favorite course during medical school. It was also the most difficult! But it was during my time on the third-year surgery rotation, where Dr. Halasz was my attending, that he had his greatest impact on my career.

Dr, Halasz was a shining example of everything a physician should be. Brilliant, inquisitive, honorable, compassionate, gentlemanly, and fun are all words that come to mind. Even though I had never worked harder or longer hours, I relished each day on the service because of the hour or two each morning and afternoon in which I had the opportunity to round on patients with him or to observe him in surgery. One of the fondest memories from my medical training came from my last day on his service. A young patient complaining of abdominal pain was admitted to the hospital in the late afternoon, and as the medical student on the service, it was my responsibility to take the history and perform the initial examination and workup. It was a subtle case, but the differential diagnosis included acute appendicitis. Dr. Halasz came to see the patient and also had the intern and resident examine the patient. Then he asked us, one by one, beginning with me, whether we'd operate on the young man. I answered that I would, because even though it was subtle, I felt he had rebound tenderness. My confidence, however, plummeted when both the intern and resident said they wouldn't operate, that there was no rebound tenderness. "Well then," Dr. Halasz said, his thick brows shooting up, "I guess Dr. Wilson should be the primary surgeon since he's the only one who'd operate on the patient." It was a wonderful honor for a third-year medical student and my first surgical case as primary surgeon, with heavy assistance from the master himself. I still remember his eyes smiling above the surgical mask with a reassuring nod, as I positioned the scalpel on the patient's abdomen to make the opening incision. *Fortunately*, the young man proved to have an inflamed and swollen appendix, and recovered fully after the surgery.

There were other medical school faculty who had a tremendous impact on me because of their teaching and guidance. John B. West, MD, PhD, pulmonologist, and Harry Bluestein, MD, rheumatologist, were highly influential, but it was Dr. Nicholas Halasz who gave me the greatest academic gift one could ever ask for—the steadfast certainty that I had chosen the right profession and the drive to excel in my chosen field—regardless of the ultimate decision I made about specialty. Dr. Halasz seemed genuinely disappointed when I told him I'd decided against a residency in general surgery during my fourth year of medical school. He told me I shouldn't rule it out; there was still time to think it over. Ultimately, I decided I didn't have the right constitution. I spoke with him, however, in 1994, and surprisingly, he remembered me and my first, and only, appendectomy. He seemed pleased that I had at least chosen a surgical field. Sadly, Dr. Halasz died of cancer in July of 1999. It was a great loss to UCSD, and to me personally. There was more than one time after he died when I wished he were still at UCSD so I could call him up and ask for his advice.

Obstetrics and gynecology also captured my interest for a time, especially reproductive endocrinology and high risk OB. I did a rotation at Balboa Naval Regional Medical Center, taking care of female dependents and navy personnel. It was an incredible thrill caring for expectant mothers and delivering babies, so much so that it made the demanding hours almost fly by. But ultimately it was an odd incident that clinched my decision. It was during a routine gynecological exam in the presence of a female attending, when a patient told me, "Doctor, you have the nicest hands," and then laughed. I blushed bright crimson and fumbled my way through the rest of the exam. I've been told by many of my eye surgery patients—men and women alike—that I have "nice" or "comforting" hands, but these compliments never had quite the same impact. The long nights without sleep that occurred frequently that month were also a factor in my eventual decision to not pursue OB/GYN.

Internal medicine had a magnetic effect on me, and in many ways still does (a big thrill for me personally was my publication in the New England Journal of Medicine). Perhaps it was the intellectual demands of the specialty and the many intriguing subspecialties that drew me to the field. Every patient represented a mystery to be explored—and ultimately unraveled. I still remember one intriguing patient from my early training like it was yesterday. During the fall of 1982, on my very first hospital rotation, a homosexual man was admitted to my service with fulminate *Pnemocystis carinii* pneumonia and oral mucosal candidiasis. Despite treatment, the unfortunate young man died very quickly, but not before the residents on our team realized that we were seeing our first case fitting the profile of the series of Los Angeles patients reported in the June 5, 1981 issue of the *Morbidity and Mortality Weekly Report* (*MMWR*) published by the Centers for Disease Control and Prevention. The term "acquired immune deficiency syndrome" or "AIDS" was used for the first time on July 27, 1982, but it would be several months before Luc Montagnier, MD and his colleagues from the Pasteur Institute in Paris in early 1983, and a few months later Robert C. Gallo, MD and his associates at Bethesda Maryland, isolated the causative retrovirus, initially known as Lymphadenopathy-Associated Virus (LAV), and now named the Human Immunodeficiency Virus (HIV). For me personally, this patient was the first of dozens of AIDS patients I cared for during my remaining years of medical school, including elective rotations at UCLA in Los Angeles and at UCSF in San Francisco, and during my internship at Cedars-Sinai Medical Center in Los Angeles (more on that in Chapter 3).

I relished my third-year internal medicine rotation so much that I scheduled a number of elective rotations in the field, including gastrointestinal medicine at Moffitt Hospital at the University of California, San Francisco, infectious disease at County of Los Angeles Harbor-UCLA Medical Center (Harbor-General) and a sub-internship at Veteran's Hospital at UC San Diego. The latter rotation was a one-month stint where, under supervision, a young doctor in training had his or her first chance to serve patients as the admitting physician on the medicine wards. It was a grueling, but rewarding, month where my interest in internal medicine blossomed.

One of my roommates, Rich, was an internal medicine resident at UCSD, and I admired his dedication and noted the satisfaction he got from his patients. I felt the same way. However, Rich told me a story that made me think twice about internal medicine. It seems that the intern working with Rich on the medicine service diagnosed a severely ill patient to have a volvulus (or twisting) of the sigmoid colon and together they prepped the patient for sigmoid colonoscopy, a potentially curative therapeutic procedure in patients with this disorder, to be performed by the intern and the medical student on their service—who was visiting from another medical school. Rich told me that the procedure was long and difficult and, since the patient was in tremendous pain, they were about to give up, when suddenly the volvulus untwisted with an explosive rejoinder. The grateful patient felt immediate relief, but undoubtedly the medical student and intern did not. Legend has it the exam room had to be closed for two days while a hospital maintenance crew cleaned and painted over the perfect side-by-side silhouettes of the crouching medical student and intern imprinted by flying excrement on the wall behind the colonoscopy table. I'm not certain that's a true story, but Rich swore it was, and I've never forgotten it. But even that didn't dissuade me, and internal medicine remained a clear possibility for the specialty of choice throughout my medical school training.

My first experience with ophthalmology was as a second-year medical student when I took a laboratory elective on the eye. I attended the first two classes, but lost interest once I realized the remaining sessions would focus on the dissection of pig eyes. I'd already dissected dozens of eyes in a comparative anatomy course at California State University, Fullerton, and while teaching anatomy and physiology at Rio Hondo College in Whittier. I didn't have the heart to tell the instructor his course was too rudimentary for me, so I told him I needed more time for my research project in rheumatology—which was also true.

I selected ophthalmology as a brief elective surgical rotation during my third year of medical school. It was only a two-week rotation, but enough to get a little exposure to the subspecialty. Now, at that time, UCSD didn't have the strongest ophthalmology department. In fact, it was probably one of the weakest departments in the school. The Shiley Eye Institute that now exists wasn't even part of the long-range plan when I was a medical student, at least to my knowledge. An illustration of this weakness is the fact that I was the only student in my medical school class, out of 128, who even applied to an ophthalmology residency. This is a dismal showing when one considers that at other schools, such as UCLA and the University of Michigan, ten to twenty percent of the graduating medical student class typically applied to ophthalmology. In order to bolster the program, a new chairman, Stuart Brown, MD, a cornea expert from the University of Pittsburgh and specialist on an esoteric and horrific disease called Mooren's corneal ulcer, had just been appointed. Medical students were given a schedule on the first day of the rotation, and much to my surprise, and delight, I was assigned to join Dr. Brown in his clinic. I showed up at the appointed time and waited patiently for the new chairman to arrive. He appeared a few minutes late and I approached to introduce myself and get his instructions. "Let me see that," he said, reaching for my clinic assignment sheet. He studied it for a few moments and, apparently satisfied that I hadn't made a mistake, said, "It's nice to meet you Steven, but my clinic is a little too busy today. I'm going to have you work with Dr. Weinreb in his clinic." With that, he led me to another part of the department where a young faculty member, whose disheveled hair and glasses reminded me of a scientist I'd known in graduate school, was standing outside an exam room feverishly searching through a clinic chart. "Bob," Dr. Brown said, as we approached, "this is Steven Wilson, one of UCSD's finest, and he's going to work with you today in your clinic." Dr. Brown promptly walked away, as Dr. Weinreb—looking a bit perturbed—shook my hand and nodded for me to follow him into the first exam room. I listened and watched intently as Dr. Weinreb took a history and examined the first ophthalmology patient I had ever seen with the foreign-looking slit lamp microscope equipped with a Goldman Tonometer to measure the patient's intraocular pressure (Dr. Weinreb is a glaucoma specialist!). Once he'd finished, we went on to the next patient, and he showed me how to get a good view of the back of the eyes through an ophthalmoscope and, after measuring the intraocular pressure and doing the slit lamp exam, even allowed me to get a look at the cornea and lens myself. I was totally fascinated with my first high-magnification view of the anterior segment of a human eye. Then, as we stepped to the third exam room, he asked, "Are you ready?"

"Am I ready for what?" I replied with uncertainty.

"Go in there and measure the intraocular pressure in Mrs. Johnson's right eye. But be careful; don't give her a corneal abrasion."

Now, a Goldman tonometer is not a simple device to use properly, even for some senior ophthalmology residents. It really would be much easier if you had three hands to push the tonometer tip against the patient's cornea and turn the dial to measure the pressure. Even then, there's no guarantee, without experience, that you'd get a reliable reading. For one thing, you've got to put the perfect amount of fluorescein dye into the eye to get an accurate measurement. Apply too little, and you see nothing; apply too much, and all you see is an unreadable smear. But I dutifully proceeded into the room and, after introducing myself to the patient, did my best to obtain an accurate reading with Dr. Weinreb standing behind me watching my every move. Finally, I got up from the exam stool.

"Twenty-four?" I said, with no confidence whatsoever.

Dr. Weinreb sat down at the slit lamp, stared intently through the ocular and turned the dial. After a moment, he turned, and without even a hint of a smile, said, "Well, Steven, you clearly don't have a future in ophthalmology."

More than twenty years later, having served together on the Association for Research in Vision and Ophthalmology Board of Trustees, Bob Weinreb and I are friends (he's now the Chairman of Ophthalmology at UC San Diego School of Medicine). I told that anecdote from the podium at a medical conference a few years back when Dr. Weinreb was in the audience, and he had no recollection whatsoever of the incident. Knowing Bob the way I do now, I realize that it was a joke; but at the time, it was a humiliating upbraiding to say the least. Somehow it didn't put me off from ophthalmology, perhaps because two days later I visited the private office of a corneal specialist named Perry Binder, MD. Dr. Binder, now among my good friends in ophthalmology, was incredibly gracious. He showed me the first case of herpes simplex virus keratitis I ever saw, along with a host of other interesting maladies, and then encouraged me to think seriously about ophthalmology.

I did think seriously about ophthalmology, but I was also intrigued with internal medicine. What was I going to do? The difficult question faced by thousands of medical students each year, when they are forced to make a career path decision on the basis of precious little information, stood squarely before me. I didn't make a judgment until very late in the decision period—and even then I equivocated. I decided I would apply for a full internal medicine internship, one where I could continue into residency if I found internal medicine to be my own nirvana. But at the same time, with even less information to go on, I would also apply to ophthalmology residencies.

I was surprised how quickly word got around about what I'd decided to do, and equally surprised when one of my classmates—one I didn't know very well—called me a couple of weeks later and asked if I could meet him for lunch the next day at the medical school cafeteria. "I hear you're applying to ophthalmology," he said as we sat down with our trays.

"Yes," I replied. "I decided to apply two weeks ago."

There was an uncomfortable pause while my classmate took a bite of his sandwich, chewed a bit and then swallowed. "I thought maybe we should talk about where we're applying. You know, so we don't flood the country with ophthalmology applications from UCSD."

I was completely taken aback, at first not thinking he was serious, and then realizing he was being earnest. "Are you nuts?" I finally replied with a chuckle. "We should both apply to all the programs we can. Even then, neither one of us will probably match." My colleague apparently didn't value my advice. A few weeks later, I heard he'd decided to apply to psychiatry residencies instead.

If my memory serves me correctly, I applied only to three internal medicine internships: Cedars-Sinai Medical Center, Harbor General Hospital of UCLA, and LA County General Hospital of UCLA, ranked in that order. I narrowed it down to these three because I wanted to stay in the Los Angeles area during my internship. Several of my medical school friends thought I'd lost my mind. "Do you have a death wish?" one of them asked. You see, most medical students who applied to residencies like ophthalmology, radiology, radiation oncology, anesthesiology, emergency medicine, rehabilitation medicine, or dermatology, took much lighter "transitional" internships. Two of the more popular "easy" internships were the transitional internships at Cottage Hospital in Santa Barbara or Mercy Hospital in San Diego. These highly prized internships usually had a couple of months each on internal medicine, surgery, and OB/GYN, with perhaps one month in the intensive care unit and the other months devoted to electives. Each of these rotations, except perhaps the intensive care unit, was every fourth night on-call. They've changed since 1985, but back then these transitional internships were considered ideal for interns who wanted to maintain a reasonable private life while preparing to enter their chosen field of study outside of internal medicine the following year.

In contrast, my internship at Cedars-Sinai Medical Center, where I eventually matched, consisted of the cardiac intensive care unit (one month), the respiratory intensive care unit (two months), the medical intensive care unit (one month), and the diabetes intensive care unit (one month), intermixed with the medicine wards (five months), the emergency room (one month) and an elective in geriatric medicine at the Wadsworth Veteran's Hospital at UCLA (one month). There was also a four-week block of vacation assigned at some point during that year. All of the intensive care unit rotations at Cedars-Sinai involved every third night on-call and the medicine wards and geriatric medicine rotation were every fourth night on-call. But the difference in rotations and call doesn't begin to describe the dissimilarity between transitional internships and those I was considering. I thanked my friend for his concerns about my unorthodox choice of internship, but reassured him that I knew what I was doing. I wanted to keep open the opportunity to continue in a high quality internal medicine residency. I would soon rue the day I made that decision.

I forget exactly how many ophthalmology residencies I applied to, but the total was something over thirty, including more than ten in California alone. I was offered interviews at thirteen programs. As expected, my application was summarily round-filed without an interview at some of the loftiest programs in the country, like Massachusetts Eye and Ear Infirmary and the Wilmer Eye Institute at Johns Hopkins. However, much to my delight, I received interviews at several other highly regarded residencies like Bascom-Palmer Eye Institute at the University of Miami, Iowa University, Jules-Stein Eye Institute at UCLA, UC San Francisco, Doheny Eye Institute at University of Southern California, Wills Eye Hospital in Philadelphia, Mayo Clinic in Rochester and Illinois Eye and Ear Infirmary in Chicago. In addition, I received interviews at several other programs inside and outside California.

Because I had applied, as well, to the ophthalmology residency at UC San Diego, I was afforded my second interaction with Dr. Stuart Brown, the chairman of ophthalmology. A few weeks after applying, I somehow heard there was a rhubarb going on between the student affairs office at UCSD School of Medicine and Dr. Brown. It seems that the esteemed professor was refusing to offer me an interview unless the associate dean for student affairs provided him with my ranking in the graduating class of 1984 at UCSD. But alas, UCSD had a pass-fail-honors system in place and Associate Dean for Student Affairs, Eric Wahrenbrock, told Dr. Brown that it was not possible to give him my exact ranking, although he reassured him I was near the top of my class. That wasn't good enough for Brown, however, and it wasn't long before he and venerated Dean of the UCSD Medical School, Robert G. Petersdorf, MD, editor of *Harrison's Principles of Internal Medicine* (the virtual bible of internal medicine) and subsequently president of the Association of American Medical Colleges, were at loggerheads over my even getting offered an interview for the third-tier UCSD ophthalmology residency. Well, it's not difficult to predict whose point of view prevails when a first-time department chair in his second year at the helm gets into a squabble with his boss, the dean, especially one with the no-nonsense reputation of Dr. Petersdorf. I was offered an interview a short time later. As you might imagine, however, by this time I'd had one interaction too many with Dr. Brown and I respectfully declined.

And so, at the beginning of November 1993, I took my month off from medical school and began visiting the programs where I'd been granted an interview. With my resources being far less than boundless, I purchased a special Trans World Airlines (TWA, yes the airline that no longer exists!) one-month unlimited ticket that allowed me to fly to any city where the airline flew in the U.S.A., Canada, *or* the Caribbean. The itinerary had to be set up ahead of time and you could delete destinations, but you couldn't add cities or change the order once you began the first flight. Having never traveled much beyond California's borders—except to interview for medical school or travel with my parents to Texas and Oklahoma as a child—I took the opportunity to set up my schedule so that weekends were spent in exotic travel venues: the first weekend in San Juan, Puerto Rico, the second in St. Thomas, and the third in St. Croix.

I set off on my adventure on a sunny Monday morning in San Diego and landed on a rainy, wintry afternoon in Chicago—the closest TWA got to my first interview.

After driving four hundred miles, and getting caught in a speed trap in Wisconsin, I spent that night at a small motel just outside the Rochester city limits, and dressed in a new dark blue suit and red tie, set off bright and early the next morning for my interview at the revered Mayo Clinic. I don't remember any specifics about the interviews that day, except that they seemed to go well and doctors were particularly kind and encouraging, especially Robert Waller, MD, the chairman of ophthalmology. I do remember being awed with the jam-packed patient waiting areas and the impressive, wood-trimmed combined exam room/offices where I met my interviewers. I recall that there were eight applicants there that day: one woman and, including me, seven men—five of whom were wearing blue suits and red ties.

My last interview of the day was around five in the afternoon, and once it was over, I shook my evaluator's hand and made my way out of the main Mayo Building that housed the Department of Ophthalmology to begin my drive to Iowa City for my next residency interview the following morning. I remember it was already dark, and even though it was not yet 6 P.M., the streets in downtown Rochester were nearly deserted. I headed back down lonely 2nd Street SW toward Broadway and stopped for a red light at 2nd Ave SW. While I scanned the darkened shops and waited for the signal to change, I remember distinctly clenching the steering wheel. "Well," I mumbled to myself with a long sigh, "I'll never be back here again."

I recall only two events from my interview the next day at the renowned University of Iowa Department of Ophthalmology. The first was going on a tour of the department led by a guide who opened a door into a dedicated treatment room and proudly pointed out a brand new YAG laser, one of the first delivered in the world, used to blow away "after-cataracts" that formed in the capsule of the native lens left behind after the cataract was removed without opening the eye. I remember the enormous instrument was the size of a small car (today's YAG lasers are tiny by comparison—a little larger than a microwave oven). I was awed by this amazing laser's potential, not realizing my future medical career would be dominated by even more remarkable lasers yet to be introduced to ophthalmology. The second event I recall, was a group interview, sort of an inquisition, with six to eight faculty members in a conference room near the remarkable ophthalmology library in the eye department in Iowa. Professor Frederick C. Blodi, MD, chairman of the department and legendary ocular pathologist and surgeon, posed the first question. "Well, Steven," he said with a warm smile, "tell us what's new about the development of the ciliary body." This question was clearly posed in reference to a small project I'd performed for UCSD Professor David Sevel, MD, a surgeon who had brought boxes of slides of staged human embryo eyes with him when he immigrated to America. Over the years, several medical student volunteers at UCSD had been assigned different structures in the eye to photograph at different time points during embryogenesis for what was eventually to become a textbook on the development of the eye. My structure was the ciliary body. After several weeks of work, I finished my project and made appointments to review the photographs with Dr. Sevel, but finally left the binder of photographs with typed descriptions on his desk when a secretary told me for the third time that the meeting had once again been cancelled after Professor Sevel was called to surgery.

"Well, I'm not sure there's anything new about ciliary body development to tell you," I replied to Dr. Blodi and the interview committee, and proceeded to describe my project and lead them into the more formidable bench research I'd completed in rheumatology. (I presume Dr. Blodi and his colleagues didn't find my projects particularly compelling, since I found out a few months later that I was not highly ranked by the program.)

That night after the interview, I drove back to Chicago and spent the night at a rundown motel across the street from the O'Hare Airport. It was pretty quiet there until about an hour after I turned off the lights to get some sleep. Then, just as I was dozing off, a jet suddenly screamed over the top of my room, followed by another, and another, at approximately one-minute intervals. I found out the next morning that a change in wind direction had prompted the airport to move takeoffs to an alternate runway that ended just across the street from my motel. I spent a long and sleepless night listening to the whine of those jet engines. The next morning, I stumbled out of bed and made my way to the terminal to catch a flight to Puerto Rico.

Later that afternoon, drifting in and out of sleep on a poolside lounge chair, with a Mai Tai drink on the stand beside me, the new Lionel Richie hit *All Night Long* blared from outdoor speakers at the El San Juan Hotel (a hotel remodeled long ago). The lyrics to that unforgettable song seemed to have been written just for me at that moment..."*People dancing all in the street; see the rhythm all in their feet; life is good wild and sweet—let the music play on. Feel it in your heart; and feel it in your soul; let the music take control. We're going to party; karamu, fiesta, forever...come on and sing my song! All night long!*" That was the beginning of a three-day weekend to remember, an awakening of sorts, as I spent the days at the pool and the nights at the nearby Condado Beach Holiday Inn (a hotel long ago torn down)—where pretty local women taught me to merengue in the teeming nightclub that reverberated with Latin rhythms. A happy-go-lucky rancher's son from Montana, Chad, was delighted with English-speaking camaraderie after a month by himself at the hotel. He graciously told the bartender to put my drinks on his tab.

Monday came way too soon! Nearly as tired as I had been when I arrived in San Juan, I boarded a jet bound for St. Louis and connected with a flight to San Francisco where I interviewed at Pacific Medical Center and UC San Francisco. I remember few details about those interviews nor the ones later in the week in Los Angeles at UCLA and USC, except that I felt the interviews had gone well. Content with my performance, I boarded a jet at LAX bound for St. Louis and then caught a connecting flight to St. Thomas.

Except I never got there. At that time, all TWA flights to St. Thomas stopped in San Juan, and by the time I arrived, I'd decided to get off the plane again in San Juan. Bags in hand, I took a cab back to the Condado Beach Holiday Inn. My new friend Chad was still there and delighted to see me again. He made arrangements with his contacts and I got a room in the already full hotel. Not just any room—a penthouse suite on the top floor, overlooking the pool and beach far below. That night I won over $3000 at the blackjack tables in the casino (a small fortune for me at the time) and I remember wondering if Chad had somehow arranged that too.

The next three days are a blur and I'm sure I killed more than a few brain cells that weekend as I sunbathed, gambled, danced and generally let my hair down and painted the island red. I was having so much fun by the time Monday night rolled around, when I was scheduled to leave for another interview, I decided to delay my departure another two days. Truthfully, I'd never been interested in living in the city that will remain nameless where my next interview was scheduled anyway. I called the program the next morning and apologetically told the administrator I'd decided not to come. For good measure, I cancelled two additional interviews scheduled for the following week at programs that also graced the bottom of my personal rank list.

Finally, after five days in San Juan, and despite my cowboy friend's protests, I prepared to leave for my interview at the Bascom-Palmer Eye Institute, but not before promising Chad and my other new friends I'd be back the following Saturday. I made my plane with only a few minutes to spare, and with a contented smile on my face, settled in for a well-deserved nap.

My interviews at Bascom-Palmer Eye Institute in Miami went well and I remember my astonishment at the facilities and my awe-inspiring meeting with Edward W. D. Norton, MD, the illustrious retina specialist and founder of the esteemed program. I met two other legendary ophthalmologists during that visit: pioneering neuro-ophthalmologist-evangelist J. Lawton Smith, MD, who asked me during my interview if I loved Jesus, and renowned clinician-scientist Donald M. Gass, MD, widely recognized as the world's greatest expert on diseases of the macula, the most sensitive area of the retina. (The next time I would meet Dr. Gass was twenty years later when I was chair of ophthalmology at University of Washington interviewing for the chairmanship of ophthalmology at Vanderbilt University, where he was then on faculty.) All three men treated me with extraordinary kindness and respect, and I remember praying as the plane lifted off the tarmac on Friday night that somehow I'd be accepted into that program— despite the fact that a helpful resident had told me to be careful when walking the streets around the eye institute because a staff member had been robbed and shot in a parking lot a few weeks earlier.

My airplane returned to St. Louis, where I connected with a flight to St. Croix, but as you might guess by now, I never got there either. Why should I? I knew a good thing when it punched me in the face. I got off the plane when it landed in San Juan, and with renewed excitement about my career prospects, made my way back to the Condado Beach Holiday Inn. Once again my newfound friends welcomed my return and another three days of revelry ensued before I departed Puerto Rico for the last time for my remaining out-of-state interviews at Illinois Eye and Ear Infirmary in Chicago and Wills Eye Hospital in Philadelphia. These interviews also seemed to go well, or at least that was my impression at the time. Three days later, I returned to Orange County in time to spend Thanksgiving with my family, before one last interview at UC Irvine.

I returned to San Diego with high hopes and began another fourth-year medical school rotation. I think it was family medicine. I relished the San Diego sunshine, along with the low humidity, and the normalcy of being back at school. After reflecting on my rank list while spending a few days at home for Christmas with my parents, who had moved to Anaheim, I finally decided to submit my choices: Bascom Palmer Eye Institute at the University of Miami, UCLA, University of Southern California, UC San Francisco, Iowa University, Wills Eye Hospital, Pacific Medical Center, Illinois Eye and Ear Infirmary, Mayo Clinic, and UC Irvine. I recollect my anxious anticipation as I sealed the envelope, knowing that it was now up to God, and the programs, to determine my future. I kept my order a closely-guarded secret, not even telling my roommates how I'd ranked the programs.

The next few weeks seemed to crawl by, as I waited nervously for notification of the match results. Finally, I came home from school in the late afternoon on a Friday and was met in the living room of our condo by my roommate and classmate, Jim Guyer, a lanky Montana native, with a big grin on his face.

"What's going on?" I asked suspiciously, knowing I was due a practical joke.

"Nothing," he replied, handing me an envelope. "This was in the mailbox when I got home."

I don't remember if it was a letter or a telegram, but I recognized the match logo on the front of the envelope. I took the letter, sprawled across the couch with my head propped on the arm, and tore off the end. "Oh, God!" I blurted out, catching my breath, as I stared at the sentences on the page.

"Well?" Jim demanded, as I lay there in stunned disbelief. "Where are you going?"

"Rochester, Minnesota," I whispered, dropping the notification on the floor beside me. "I don't believe it," I muttered in dazed shock.

"Congratulations!" Jim bellowed, patting me on the shoulder, as the front door opened and my roommate, Rich, strolled in wearing his white physician's coat. "Steve's going to Mayo!" Jim called out.

"Alright! Way to go, Steve!" Rich barked. "Let's party."

After a few more minutes of moping, my roommates finally forced me from the couch and down the street to Carlos and Charlie's El Torito across the street from UCSD School of Medicine. I got over my initial dismay after a margarita and a few chips with salsa. "It could have been a lot worse," I finally said, taking a deep breath.

"Of course it could have been worse," Rich retorted, stuffing the last bite of a fajita into his mouth. "You could've done a whole lot worse than the Mayo Clinic. Where'd you rank it?"

"Ninth out of ten," I replied sheepishly.

"Nine out of ten?" he asked disbelievingly. "Why?"

"Because it's colder than hell there!"

We all had a good laugh and that was the last time I ever felt any regrets over my match results. By the next morning, recalling that I'd foolishly cancelled interviews at three other programs, I thanked God that I'd matched into such a fine ophthalmology residency. Today, looking back on my career thirty years later, I wonder what might have happened if I had gone to those three cancelled interviews. Would I have ranked them ahead of Mayo and been accepted at one of them, and if so, would the entire course of my career have been altered? I also now realize that my heading off to the Mayo Clinic was the single most important event in my medical and scientific career, obviously aside from finally being admitted to medical school. My residency in the hallowed halls of that truly great institution set the foundation for everything else that was to follow, for it was there that I discovered what it really meant to be a physician, learned to be a skilled ophthalmologist, and had my love for research rekindled. But once again, I'm getting ahead of the story.

The next few months of medical school rotations, including my stint as a sub-intern on the medicine wards at the San Diego Veteran's Hospital, seemed to pass very quickly. My girlfriend and I became engaged and then, in March, I'd found I'd been matched at Cedars-Sinai Medical Center in Los Angeles for the internship year—my first choice.

A few more weeks, a great 1984 graduating medical school class celebration in the ballroom at Hilton San Diego Resort on Mission Bay, and it was over. All of my classmates, now finally physicians, dispersed across the country to begin their internships or finished up their combined MD, PhD degrees in labs. Sadly, I never saw many of them again. I kept up with a few for several years with occasional phone calls or visits, especially my good friend Richard Rasmussen, MD, PhD, who went into dermatology (the last time I tried to call Richard's private practice in Oregon in 2016, they told me he was retired and sailing to points unknown to them on his yacht!), but the contacts became less and less frequent as we all became more deeply involved in our own careers and families. Still, I'll never forget those years. They were truly magical.

Chapter 3
An Unsuspecting Plunge into the Vortex

I wasn't prepared for my internship in internal medicine at Cedars-Sinai Medical Center, and I never could have been. Was I prepared intellectually to have the knowledge and experience to diagnose and treat patients? Absolutely. But I wasn't prepared for the grueling emotional and physical strains inflicted by twelve months of medical wards and intensive care units, interrupted only by a four-week rotation in the emergency room and a four-week vacation.

It began auspiciously enough with an early Sunday morning meeting of the new house staff and the Chief of Internal Medicine, James R. Klinenberg, MD, on June 24, 1984. The chief resident for internal medicine was also there, along with thirty or so starry-eyed, fresh medical school graduates. Most of the new recruits in internal medicine were beginning residencies in the specialty, but the others intended to go into different medical or surgical subspecialties the following year. Truthfully, I still wasn't sure what I was going to do. A spot in the ophthalmology residency at the Mayo Clinic awaited me, but I was still in a quandary about the draw internal medicine seemed to have on me.

Dr. Klinenberg had arranged a light breakfast where the unsuspecting lambs could meet each other. Then, the chief resident distributed manuals and went over some program and hospital policies before Dr. Klinenberg gave us a concluding pep talk. Finally, it was time to take us to our first service. My first rotation was on one of the eight teams on the internal medicine wards and, as luck—or careful planning—would have it, my team was on-call that very first night.

The medical ward services were on all-night long call every fourth night. Thus, on any particular night, there would be two services on "long call," two services coming off long call—not taking new admissions—and four teams on short call, who were at risk for up to two new admissions per intern before 3 P.M. Two of these short-call teams would be on-call the following night and the other two the night after that. To explain it another way, a particular service proceeded through a schedule of long call, off call, short call, and short call on consecutive nights, and then repeated the sequence over and over again for the full month on the service. Unfortunately, there weren't enough interns to go around and, therefore, one service had only one intern, rather than the usual two. As chance would have it, I was the single-intern service. Thus, when my medical ward service was on-call, I was the only one taking new admissions to our service, in rotation with another two-intern service that followed the same four-day schedule.

As the late afternoon arrived on that first day, three of the other medicine services checked out to each of the two services on long call, reviewing the status, pending critical tests and other issues for all of the patients on their services, which often totaled anywhere from fifty to seventy-five, or even more, patients. I remember the lonely feeling that swept over me when the last short-call intern finished reviewing his patients and I realized my resident and I, along with the other long-call team, were the only physicians left to cover any new admissions—and all of the other patients on the medical wards at Cedars-Sinai Medical Center.

The senior resident on my service, a happy-go-lucky fellow with perpetually mussed hair, had just completed his own internship. I'll call him Sam. Sam and I reviewed the status of the nine patients who were already on our service, and he let me know who would be paging me from the emergency room if we had any new admissions. Then, patting me on the back, he informed me he'd be in the medical library if I needed any help—which he pointedly told me he was not expecting to happen unless I was a "wuss." That was the last time I saw Sam until morning.

I got my first page from the emergency room at around 3:30 that afternoon. The rest of the night is a complete blur, probably suppressed deep within my subconscious for the sake of sanity. I admitted fourteen new patients to the service that night, an average of one patient every hour. For each one, I needed to do an admission history and physical, order tests, formulate a plan, and initiate treatment, all the while being paged for the other fifty or so patients I was covering for three other medical ward services. Most of these admitted patients also had a private attending physician, but we rarely saw these faculty members until rounds the next morning. If one of the other interns had written for a blood transfusion or blood gas analysis or IV chemotherapy, seemingly always at two in the morning, I'd get paged to do that too. If patients took a turn for the worse—"crashed," in-house staff lingo—then I'd rush to stabilize them, all the while triaging calls about other patients and accepting new admissions. Some of the patients who crashed could be stabilized and remained on the wards. Others, however, had to be transferred to one of the intensive care units. It was one of the latter patients, an old man with severe emphysema from another medical service, who went into respiratory distress and finally stopped breathing. He became my first "code." The code alarm brought the "code blue team"—other residents working on services in the intensive care units—rushing to the room with their crash cart to resuscitate the patient, while I provided assistance—drawing blood, performing cardiopulmonary resuscitation, starting new IVs, or whatever else needed to be done. That patient was finally stabilized and transferred to the respiratory intensive care unit, the "RICU." I ran off to take care of the dozen additional pages I'd received during the code and to see my next two admissions.

Feeling near panic after my ninth and tenth new admissions, and realizing I could barely remember the details of the earliest admissions, much less follow up on their tests, I paged my resident for help around three in the morning. "It sounds like you're getting killed," Sam said sympathetically, yawning across the phone line from his cozy on-call bed, as my beeper began chirping once again. "Just hang in there; you're doing a great job and I know you can handle it. I'll meet you in the cafeteria for breakfast at 6:15, before rounds with our attending. Hasta mañana."

That night was one of the longest of my life, but unfortunately only one of eighty-five nights I was on long call that year. Many weren't as bad, but some were even worse. I did manage to rush to the cafeteria just as it was closing to bolt some food, before my evil beeper beckoned me back to the wards. Needless to say, I never saw the bed reserved for me in the resident long-call suite.

I met Sam in the cafeteria that morning and we reviewed the new admissions over a brief breakfast, before rounding on all of the patients on our service—now swollen to twenty-three—with our attending physician. We also interacted with private physicians who happened to be around or sought us out to discuss issues regarding their patients. After rounds, I spent the rest of the day reviewing test results, re-examining patients, and discharging two people who were stable enough to go home. Once again, Sam disappeared for the rest of the day. Most of the other residents I worked with that year pulled their weight on service and helped when things got tough. Unfortunately, I just had the misfortune of being paired with a notorious slacker on my first rotation on the medical wards (a resident who would later that year be dismissed for stealing narcotics meant for patients).

It was nearly nine that evening when I finally checked out my patients to one of the new interns on long call. I remember the time because, numb-headed with my thoughts racing from some thirty-nine hours at the hospital, I stumbled out of the South Tower of the medical center, trudged down the steps between the medical office towers, and wove across Third Street to a Mexican restaurant, only to find it stopped seating at nine. I stumbled to my one-room studio apartment a few steps down a side street, inhaled a baloney and cheese sandwich, showered, and, after setting my alarm clock for five-thirty the next morning, dropped into bed.

It seemed like I'd just closed my eyes when the alarm jolted me awake. I dressed quickly and lumbered back across the street to begin rounding on the twenty-one patients who were still on my service.

It didn't take the bright new interns on the medical wards long to learn some of the survival skills that would stand them in good stead during the grueling year ahead. "Turfing" and "blocking" were at the top of the list, and medical interns and residents who honed these skills to virtual art forms were at once revered and hated, depending on your perspective on a particular patient. *Turfing* was to somehow manage to transfer a patient off of your own service by convincing another service to take him, perhaps one of the intensive care units if the patient could be proven to be too sick for the medical wards or, even better, to one of the surgical services if the problem could be treated with surgery, so the patient wouldn't "bounce back" to your service when he or she got better. *Blocking* was the reverse—preventing another service from turfing a patient to your service, at least until the next day when your service was off call—from one of the intensive care units , a surgical service, or, a real triumph of persuasion, from the emergency room. (For example, proving to emergency room house staff that a patient's intermittent chest pain wasn't a myocardial infarction, but chest wall pain, because it was reproduced by pressing on the sternum, and the EKG and cardiac enzymes were normal, and the patient could be sent home with nonsteroidal anti-inflammatory drugs.) The ultimate goal of all this frantic maneuvering and gamesmanship entered into by all the interns and residents on the medical services was to reduce the size of your own service to the smallest number of patients possible, especially leading up to the next long-call day—when anything could, and often did, happen.

As bad as the medical wards were at Cedars-Sinai Medical Center, the medical intensive care units were far worse. Firstly, you were on long call every *third* night. This seemingly small change from every fourth night to every third night on long call tripled the intensity and stress—often transforming even the most resilient intern, and I counted myself among them, into zombie-like, short-tempered ghouls. Secondly, the patients in the medical intensive care units were gravely ill—many teetering on the brink of death and were kept alive only by ongoing physician and nurse intervention, drugs and respirators. I spent five of my twenty-eight day blocks in the medical intensive care units—two in the RICU (respiratory intensive care unit, covering respiratory failure, including severe AIDS patients, etc., and overflow from the MICU), one in the MICU (medical intensive care unit, covering drug overdoses, sepsis, GI bleeding, hepatic failure, CNS bleeding and stroke, etc.), one in the CICU (cardiac intensive care unit, covering acute myocardial infarction, unstable angina, congestive heart failure, cardiac arrhythmias and heart blocks, etc.), and one we affectionately called the DICK-U (diabetes intensive care unit, covering hyperglycemic crisis, severe hypoglycemia, volatile blood glucose levels, etc.), so called in reference to the abusive attendings working on the diabetes service. These twenty-eight day stretches of every third night on-call were brutal and at times bordered on sadistic. At one point during the year, I had the misfortune of having two of these unit rotations back-to-back—at least I think I did, but it may have just been a nightmare. Month after month of endless patients and chronic sleep deprivation dragged by with seemingly no end in sight.

Cedars-Sinai Medical Center is often referred to as "The Hospital of the Stars." The hospital complex had two huge towers of hospital wards—the south tower where patients are admitted to house staff under the supervision of their personal attending physician with admission privileges at the hospital, and the north tower where the house staff rarely ventured. This north tower is reserved for the "stars" and other patients usually seen only by their private physicians. The only time we would see these north tower patients was if there was an emergency such as a resuscitation, or if the star was admitted to one of the intensive care units—that were all staffed by house staff and hospital attendings. Late one night in September 1984, when I was on long call and a member of the code team, an emergency code blue was issued from the north tower just as I was prepping a patient for an arterial blood gas draw from the femoral artery in her upper leg. I rushed across the long connecting building that joined the two towers to the stricken patient's room and was quickly met by other house staff. We worked feverishly to resuscitate the patient, whose heart had suddenly stopped beating after he suffered a stroke earlier in the day. I pumped the patient's chest between attempts at electro-cardioversion, as another intern intubated the unfortunate man. Meanwhile, the resident administered epinephrine, dopamine, and other drugs intravenously. But it was not to be and, after more than an hour of feverish work, we pronounced the man dead. Only when I began filling out the required paperwork did I realize who the man was: a legendary Hollywood actor who'd long starred in a popular science fiction TV series. It was my first poignant encounter with the famous, but sadly, it would not be my last.

In return for the assistance provided by the young interns and residents, the private physicians who admitted patients to the house staff services were supposed to provide guidance and teaching. Most of them did, and we were grateful for their instruction and empathy, especially those who understood how onerous our existence was during the internship year. Many of these fine physicians admitted only patients who were likely to be educational to the house staff, while caring personally for their other patients in the private north tower. But there were exceptions, and one of them was a nephrologist who was notorious for his abuse of house staff. Every intern cringed whenever he or she was to receive one of his patients as an admission from the emergency room. We knew all too well what would soon follow. The attending's nickname was "Dr. K" because he had the irritating habit of paging the interns night and day, sometimes dozens of times, to find out if we knew what the latest potassium level was on his patient (K is the elemental symbol for potassium). All of Dr. K's patients were "train wrecks"—patients who had countless medical problems, only one of which was renal failure and every single one of the abusive doctor's patients was admitted to the south tower's house staff services. Once you received one of Dr. K's patients as an admission, you knew the patient would likely still be on your service once you rotated off, and that you'd be forced to tolerate the crotchety old doctor's derogatory comments and constant pages for the duration. As far as we house staff members were concerned, Dr. K seemed to have only one endearing quality. He was a diehard Los Angeles Lakers fan with season tickets near courtside at the old Forum. My colleagues and I used this information to exact the ultimate revenge from the ingrate, but not before we'd endured a year of constant abuse. I'll relate that story later.

Each intern in a demanding program like the Cedars-Sinai medicine internship usually hits some point during the year when he or she contemplates abandoning everything and just walking away. Some actually do, further increasing the demands on those who remain behind. My personal nadir came in December of 1984 when I was assigned to the respiratory intensive care unit (RICU) for the first time. Already near my breaking point from five months of rotations on the medical wards and other intensive care units, I joined that every third night on-call service filled with patients overflowing into the adjoining medical intensive care unit (MICU), itself brimming with patients. More than half of the patients in the RICU were terminal AIDS patients being kept alive on ventilators. They needed constant blood draws, intravenous lines, and other invasive procedures. On top of everything else, there was the constant risk of an inadvertent needle stick. I felt so sorry for the patients in the RICU, many of whom were younger than I was. At that time, there were no effective drugs for AIDS, only antibiotics and anti-virals to treat ravaging infections like *Pnemocystis carinii* pneumonia or cytomegalovirus encephalitis that thrived in their bodies lacking immune protection. When one patient would finally succumb to the disease, another would be moved in as soon as the bed was stripped and the area cleaned. It was a never-ending and discouraging revolving door.

About the middle of December, the MICU got a new admission. A world-famous actor and star of countless motion pictures was in terrible condition—unconscious and consumed with cirrhosis of the liver—his body bloated to four times its normal size. It was a hopeless situation, but since there wasn't a do-not-resuscitate (DNR) order on the chart, our on-call team responded and managed to revive him when his heart stopped beating in the middle of the night. It was only a temporary rescue, for he coded again two days later on Christmas Eve, and this time resuscitation efforts were futile.

My rotation that month was brutal. Even on days following long-call nights, I rarely could leave the hospital before nine in the evening. My routine was to grab a bite to eat and collapse into bed at my nearby apartment, waking early in the morning to begin another grueling day. That holiday season meant nothing to me. I took long call on consecutive days of Christmas, my birthday (December 28), and New Year's Eve. My fiancé and I were to be married in the spring of 1985, but we barely saw each other—until that month I had vacation. I remember going out together on the short-call night before my birthday, and I fell asleep near the beginning of the new hit movie *Amadeus*. It was an existence I wouldn't have wished on my worst enemy.

It was also around this time that the new applicants for the internship year starting June 1985, began coming to Cedars-Sinai for interviews. At the end of grand rounds, just before the first group arrived for interviews, the residency program director cautioned us not to tell the new recruits anything disparaging about the program. After all, if any of the positions didn't fill, everyone would have to work harder. I couldn't help but notice that none of the interns moving on to other programs at the end of the year, including me, were included in lunches and other activities where the recruits interacted directly with current house staff. It wasn't hard for me to understand how I hadn't heard anything but a rosy assessment of the internal medicine program at "Cedars" when I'd come through to interview the previous year. The visit had clearly been orchestrated to allow contact only with house staff who had a vested interest in filling the incoming internship class. I felt it was my duty to let the UCSD medical students graduating the year behind me know what they could expect at Cedars-Sinai, so I sent detailed notes to several students at UCSD.

Somehow I managed to make it through the first half of my internship, but not without all the classic symptoms of depression, including loss of interest in friends and pleasurable activities, loss of appetite (dropping over twenty pounds), and difficulty sleeping. My salvation was a January rotation in the emergency room. There was no call for the first time since July and all of my patients either went home or were transferred to my colleagues on the medical or surgical wards or in the intensive care units. I felt guilty every time I had to page one of them with a new admission, having experienced first-hand the pain of countless heavy admission nights. For me, the best part of the ER rotation was that every night I left for home without any patients I would see the next day—with a clean slate, so to speak.

My fiancé and I managed to get reacquainted that month, but not without bearing some of the baggage that I would carry for years to come. For example, I couldn't sit down to a relaxing dinner without bolting my food down, an acquired behavioral flaw reinforced by numerous long-call nights in the hospital when my beeper forced me to abandon breakfast, lunch or dinner, if I had time for them at all.

There were two memorable incidents from that month in the emergency room. The first was an insanely busy day when every one of the examination lanes in the ER was filled and all the house staff and attendings were stacked up on their assigned patients. The admitting desk nurse, a matronly woman who'd taken a liking to me, winked and said, "Dr. Wilson, all the attendings are tied up. I think you better go see the woman in lane twelve right away."

"Martha, I'm already working up three patients. What's wrong with her?"

"She's feeling light-headed."

"Are you kidding me? The guy in nine has severe abdominal pain and I think he's got appendicitis."

"The surgery resident is already in there. Just go see her. Please."

In a huff, I walked to the exam lane, pulled back the curtain and stopped dead in my tracks. Lying back in the bed with her breasts only partially concealed by a loose fitting hospital gown was a stunning young Latin woman with auburn hair.

"Hi," I stammered self-consciously. "I'm Dr. Steven Wilson. What's your name?"

"Ana," she purred with a coy smile. "You look so young. Are you really a doctor?"

"Yes, I'm an intern," I replied, struggling to maintain my composure and force my gaze away from her ample assets. "What brought you to the emergency room?"

"Well," she said with a heavy Spanish accent, "I spent the day with my friends at the beach. When I drive back to my apartment, I almost black out and my friend Sheri bring me here. I've got a bad head hurt."

I took her history, did a hasty examination and sent off a blood sample. "You have warm hands," she said with a playful smile, as I tried to listen to her heart. The test results confirmed my suspicion; the young woman was merely dehydrated. I started an IV and after a liter of fluid she was feeling much better. Just over an hour later, as I busied myself with other patients, the nurse told me the young woman wanted to thank me. I opened the curtain once again and there she was sitting in the chair next to the bed in the tee shirt and bikini bottoms she'd worn into the emergency room.

"Thank you, Dr. Steve," she said with an appreciative smile, as she stood on her tiptoes to kiss me on the cheek. "I'm leaving now."

"It was nice meeting you, Ana," I said, blushing crimson. "I'm glad you're feeling better."

"Bye-bye," she chirped, as she stepped out through the curtain and sashayed down the aisle toward the admission desk. A group of staff members turned to gawk in stunned silence. Shaking my head amusedly, I watched her slip past my awestruck attending and disappear through the door.

"Thank you, Martha," I said later with a sheepish grin when the rush was over.

"Did you get her phone number?" Martha asked me, smiling impishly.

"Of course not," I replied defensively.

"Would you like it? She said you were cute."

"Martha, I'm engaged, thank you."

"Too bad. Do you know who she is?"

"Should I?" I asked, my interest suddenly roused.

"She starred with Bo Derek in the movie *Bolero*."

"I never heard of her," I replied, shaking my head, "and I've never seen the movie."

"You've never seen it? Have you been on Mars?"

"Martha," I said, rolling my eyes. "I've been in this hospital or in my apartment sleeping most of the past seven months, and I fell asleep in the only movie I went to see."

"Well, if I were you, I'd at least ask her out to lunch. What harm can come from that?"

"Sure, and I bet she'll really be impressed with my 1979 Toyota Celica and the $21,000 a year I get paid for this job."

"You're right," Martha said, as she turned to walk away. "You better not call her."

The other amusing incident occurred on an evening late in my ER rotation when three Playboy Playmates from the nearby Century City Playboy Club came in wearing the brightly colored skin-tight suits with bunny ears and tails made famous by Hugh Hefner. One of them, a blonde, was crying and writhing with pain after an ashtray fell off the bar and landed directly on her big toe. It caused a giant blood blister to form beneath her glossy white toenail. As her friends sat holding her hand in the treatment lane, I injected her toe with anesthetic and inserted a red-hot cautery probe through the center of the nail, releasing the blood and immediately relieving the pressure. It was a cure! The grateful Bunny and her friends left laughing, but not before they invited me to bring some of my "young doctor friends" to a party at their house in North Hollywood the following weekend. As chance would have it, I was at the end of my month on the ER rotation and I was required to return to the merciless medicine wards the following day. I was on long-call on the day of the party, and it crossed my mind only fleetingly, as the new admissions came rolling in.

Around March of that year, 1985, I was feeling very comfortable with diagnosis and treatment of patients. It was the last week of my diabetes unit rotation and I was beginning to enjoy being a "real" doctor. The work was grueling, but the grateful patients, especially the ones

I could nurse back to health, gave me a special feeling. It didn't even bother me that the surgical residents called us medical interns and residents "fleas," since "we were the last ones to leave the body." I just felt a sense of self-esteem and contentment knowing I was making a difference in people's lives and that everything, including all the years of struggle to gain admission into medical school, had really been worth it.

I came to the hospital one morning to round on my patients and to meet with the resident on my service, but the chief resident of internal medicine was waiting for me instead. He told me to finish rounding on my patients and report to Dr. Klinenberg, Chief of Internal Medicine, at the conference room in the departmental offices at 10 A.M.

"What have I done?" I remember asking.

"Just be at his office at 10 A.M.," he repeated.

I finished my rounds and made my way to the conference room at the appointed time. Dr. Klinenberg introduced me to four attendings waiting with him, and asked me to take a seat.

"Dr. Wilson," Dr. Klinenberg began. "This committee would like to ask you some serious questions regarding the resident working on your service. We've received allegations that Dr. Carson [a fictitious name] has been stealing drugs intended for patients."

I was completely taken aback. Speechless, I sat back in my chair and took a deep breath.

"Dr. Wilson, have you noticed anything suspicious during the three weeks you've worked with Dr. Carson?"

"No, never," I replied, shaking my head.

"Have you noticed hyperactivity, hypoactivity, or excessive yawning?" one of the other doctors asked sharply.

"Sir, I don't know any house staff at Cedars who *don't* display those symptoms on a daily basis. We're all chronically sleep-deprived. Most of us spend more than a hundred hours a week in this hospital."

"I understand, Dr. Wilson, but several times this month Dr. Carson checked out morphine to take to radiology when patients had CT scans or other procedures. On some of those occasions, he's claimed he "wasted" the morphine that was left over. Are you aware of this?"

"No, sir, I don't know anything about that."

Dr. Klinenberg looked around the table at each of the other attendings and waited for any further questions. Finally, he stood up and offered his hand. "Okay, Dr. Wilson, thank you for your candor. You can return to the wards."

I never heard another word about the incident and I never saw Dr. Carson again. I heard he'd been dismissed from the residency on the basis of overwhelming evidence and eyewitness reports of morphine theft. It was my first, but certainly not my last, awareness of physicians falling into drug abuse and pharmaceutical theft. Today, most hospitals and state medical societies have specific policies in place for careful monitoring and rehabilitation of physicians who lapse into drug addiction. Fortunately, drug addiction of physicians is surprisingly rare, at least in my experience. The Cleveland Clinic, where I have worked for nearly twenty years has random testing of all hospital personnel, including prior to hiring. I know many colleagues have been tested, but I don't know of any who've had illicit drugs detected in their urine, but that would be confidential information leading to a treatment program.

Late in the spring of 1985, I rotated onto the cardiac intensive care unit (CICU) service. It was a storied service that had seen many firsts, including the invention of the Swan-Ganz cardiac catheter developed by Jeremy Swan, MD and William Ganz, MD, of Cedars-Sinai—a device that revolutionized cardiac diagnostics. At the time, this eighteen-bed intensive care unit—with forty-some step down-beds for patients who were less critical—cared for patients with a variety of heart conditions, including acute myocardial infarctions and heart failure. As the four-week rotation seemingly flew by, I found myself wondering if I was really meant to be a cardiologist. The field was fascinating, rewarding, and demanding. Split-second decisions often meant the difference between life and death. Surprisingly, I even found the every-third night long-call schedule on the service at least tolerable—although almost anything could happen at any particular moment—and frequently did.

Two weeks into my rotation, I had my last brush with another famed patient of the "Hospital of the Stars." I was on long call when a nurse in the intensive care unit paged me during a quick dinner break to ask if I could hurry back. "Dr. Wilson, we're having trouble with a new admission. He's demanding to smoke a cigar."

"You're kidding me," I said suspiciously, smelling a prank—for which the staff of the cardiac unit was renowned.

"No, I'm not kidding," she reassured with a harried tone. "We tried to call his private doctor, but we haven't reached him. Please, can you help? He's disrupting the entire CICU."

"Where's Dr. Charles?" I asked, referring to the senior resident on my service.

"He's putting a line in a patient. He told me to ask you to handle it."

"Okay, what's his name?"

"Milton Berle. Can you hear that? He's cussing at the top of his lungs."

My eyes opened wide. "Milton Berle?! You're messing with me."

"No, I'm not," she persisted.

"Okay, I'll be right there." I hung up the house phone and grabbed the last half of my lukewarm hamburger. I was still suspicious—but I heard "screw you!" echo through the door as I approached the unit. Stuffing the last bite of burger into my mouth, I stepped through the door. The shouts were coming from behind drawn curtains.

"Listen, lady, all I want is a fucking cigar," Berle bellowed, as I pushed through the drapes. "Is that too much to ask?" Three nurses were standing well away from the bed, gaping at the red-faced comedian who looked like he was about to strike. "Who the hell are you?" he demanded when he caught sight of me.

"I'm Dr. Wilson, Mr. Berle, the intern on-call here in the cardiac unit."

"An intern? A fucking intern? Who in the fuck is in charge in this place?"

"I am right now, Mr. Berle, and I want you to calm down and stop yelling," I said firmly, rising to my full six foot-three inches of height and stepping to the side of the bed. "You're disturbing the other patients and some of them are very sick."

"I'll make you a deal, Doc, you let me smoke a cigar and I'll stay quiet."

"Sir, this unit is filled with people breathing highly flammable oxygen and smoking is out of the question."

Just then, the curtain opened and the unit desk attendant stepped in. "Doctor, there's a Mr. Jack Peters [I don't recall the real name] outside to see Mr. Berle."

"Finally!" Berle huffed. "Get him the hell in here."

I stepped out with the head nurse, leaving the other two nurses behind. "What's he in here for?" I asked, as I grabbed his chart.

"He was admitted to rule out myocardial infarction after having chest pain this afternoon."

I picked up the phone and called the lab to get the blood work results directly from the technician. All the tests, including the cardiac enzymes that would have been elevated in the event of a heart attack, had just been completed and all of them were normal, as was the chest X-ray. Then I compared Berle's electrocardiogram from the emergency room to another taken a few months earlier. I found the latter EKG in his medical records chart that'd just arrived from medical records. They were identical—confirming he hadn't had a heart attack.

I got up and walked into the hall. There was a fidgety man in a long coat standing alone outside. I wasn't sure who he was and frankly I didn't care. I had real work to do and it was already nearly midnight.

"Mr. Peters?"

"Yes."

"I understand you're a friend of Mr. Berle's."

"Yes, we've known each other for years."

"Well, he's causing a commotion in the cardiac unit because he wants to smoke a cigar and it's against hospital rules."

"Oh, my God, I'm sorry. He can be one stubborn son of a bitch."

"We've noticed. I just checked his labs and EKG, and he's not having a heart attack. I'm going to move him to a private room here in the north tower. He can't smoke there either, but at least it'll get him away from the sick patients in the cardiac intensive care unit. Come inside and help me get him under control."

We stepped through the curtains where the nurses were still holding Mr. Berle at bay.

"Where the hell have you been, Jack?" Berle growled when he spotted Peters.

"I came as soon as Ruth found me, Milt. The good news is you aren't having a heart attack and the doctor says he can move you out of the intensive care unit."

"I'm not having a heart attack? Then, what the hell's causing this pain in my chest?"

Now, some doctors working in the emergency room were called "walls" and no patient who wasn't really sick got admitted to the hospital on their watch. Others were "sieves," and lacking self-confidence and fearing they'd make a mistake, admitted numerous patients who should have been treated in the ER and sent home. I knew the physician referred to by my fellow house staff as "ultimate sieve" was working down in the emergency room that night.

"Mr. Berle," I asked, "could you take a deep breath for me?"

He took a breath and grimaced.

"Does that hurt?"

"Hell, yes, it hurts," he growled.

"Okay, let me check something," I said, as I placed my thumb on his chest and pressed firmly on his sternum.

"Ouch! Damn it! What the hell are you doing?"

"Is that the same pain?" I asked patiently.

"Fuck, yes."

"Well, Mr. Berle, all your tests for a heart attack are normal, and it looks to me like you've got inflammation in your rib joints and I'm going to prescribe you Indocin. That should make you feel better in just a little while. Meanwhile, we'll move you into a private room where you'll be more comfortable."

"You know, Doc, I always said you can lead a man to medical school, but you can't make him think."

"Milt," Mr. Peters said with a chuckle, "I thought you said that about congressmen?"

"Yeah, so what? I should have said it about doctors."

"Nice to meet you, Mr. Berle," I said, biting my tongue. "I've got to see another patient now."

I went about my business in the CICU and a few minutes later I saw the nurse pushing Mr. Berle toward the door in a wheelchair. Defiantly, he was holding an unlit cigar in the corner of his mouth. I nodded, he nodded, and that was the last time I ever saw him—other than on television. My intervention with the legend, however, had cost me precious time and I was now well behind on working up my earlier admissions. I knew another would soon follow.

Toward the middle of May, I was again back on the medicine wards, and along with all the other interns, counting the days until my internship ended on June 24, 1985. I was on-call with three other interns on the two long-call services and already had fourteen patients on my service when I arrived at the hospital that morning. Three of them were sick enough to be in one of the intensive care units, but the beds there were all filled. We interns knew we were in for a long night when both short-call teams had their new admission allocations filled before eleven that morning. Suddenly, before the clock had even struck noon, the ER floodgates opened and all of our beepers began incessant ringing and wouldn't stop for the rest of the night. By ten that evening, all four of the interns on long call already had fifteen new admissions and three of mine were from the infamous Dr. K. In a daze and feeling like I was about to implode, I found one of my fellow interns sitting behind a nurse's desk sobbing uncontrollably.

"What's wrong, Donna?" I asked, sitting down beside her.

"I'm okay," she said with a heavy sigh. "I haven't even seen my ninth admission yet, and I just got paged from the ER with my sixteenth new patient."

My heart sank. That meant I was up for the next call. Sure enough, before I could even give Donna a few words of encouragement, my beeper rang out with that high-pitched tone I'd learned to detest. I looked at the number; it was the ER. "God help us all," I muttered, as I dialed the number and listened to the ER physician relay details about my newest patient, a chemotherapy patient with a high fever and elevated white blood cell count.

"We're buried down here," my colleague said with an apologetic tone. "I'm sorry, but you'll need to draw the blood cultures yourself. She should already be in her room."

I hung up the phone and quickly triaged my own admissions, four of whom I'd seen only for a moment, and headed for the patient's room to draw the blood cultures. I was just about to draw the woman's blood when my beeper went off again. Ignoring the page, I drew her blood and sent it to the lab, and then sat down to call the ER once again.

"Steve, this is Mike again. I'm afraid you're up again. It's another one of Dr. K's patients with hyperkalemia (high potassium). She's in bad shape."

Suddenly, clenching my teeth, I snapped. "Listen, Mike, I'll take it, but this is my last admission tonight. Do you hear me? If you call me again, I'm walking out the door. Do you understand? I've got thirty-one patients on my service now, four of whom I haven't even examined, and three of them should be in the unit. These patients aren't getting proper care. Peter's over in the north tower working a code and Donna's down at the nurse's station crying. God knows what's happening to Claude. Call whomever you need to call, but we're not taking another admission tonight."

There was a long silence on the other end of the phone before Mike finally spoke up. "I'll see what I can do," he said, hanging up.

I took a deep breath, resigned myself to what might happen, and went about taking care of my own patients and the others who had been checked out to me by other medicine services.

About an hour passed before the chief resident, called in by the attending in the emergency room, found me writing up my history and physical on the septic patient.

"How are you doing, Steve?" he asked, sitting in the chair beside me.

"I'm okay, Kevin. But don't ask me to take another admission."

"We've closed admissions to the medicine services for the night. Any other patients who need to be hospitalized will go to the north tower and be admitted by their private physicians. You did the right thing," he said, patting me on the back.

I'll always remember one other event that happened that night. About three in the morning, I rushed through the radiology department to check the chest X-rays of a patient admitted with fever of unknown origin. I stumbled into the silent, dimly lit department, found the films and jammed them into the viewing box. Satisfied that the lungs, heart and mediastinum were normal, I slid the films back in the folder and turned to walk out the door. At that moment, Peter Cornell, MD, an intern from the other medicine team—and the only other intern headed into eye surgery (at Jules Stein Eye Institute of UCLA)—shuffled through the door with his head down. He looked up with glazed eyes and whispered the single word that now seemed so alluring—almost magical: "Ophthalmology," he muttered just loud enough for me to hear, letting the word flow slowly from his lips like honey. I tiredly nodded my head as I passed by to make my way back to the wards. I didn't offer a reply because none was expected, but at that moment I knew, with a clarity heretofore missing, that my career path had been set in stone. Importantly, at that point in my career, I really had no basis for knowing I would come to love ophthalmology and be intellectually fulfilled by it, but I had faith that was based, more than anything else, on my belief that *anything* was better than this.

Somehow, we all made it through that long night and the following day, although none of us got a minute of sleep until the following evening. Dr. K must have called me a dozen times that day to ask me about the latest potassium level on one of his patients. Meanwhile, my colleagues and I worked non-stop through the afternoon and into the evening to tie up loose ends on each of our patients so we could finally check out to the new long-call teams and stumble out of the hospital to our beds. I pushed through the doors and left the hospital after thirty-eight straight hours of work. Downing a TV dinner in my apartment, I collapsed into bed just after nine.

I anticipated repercussions from the mini-revolt I staged on "the long-call night from hell"— as it became known among those of us who survived it—so I wasn't really surprised when the chief medical resident told me Dr. Klinenberg wanted to see me in his office the following week. Dr. Klinenberg was a gentleman, in addition to being a truly great physician, and I had the utmost respect for him. Feeling contrite, I was prepared to apologize when he opened the door to his office and called me inside. I'm sure you can imagine my surprise when he led off our conversation by complimenting my performance during the past year and asking me to consider continuing on in the internal medicine residency. "Steven, my colleagues and I believe you have the knowledge, skills, and leadership qualities to become chief resident and to pursue an academic career in one of the medical subspecialties. I know you have a position in the ophthalmology residency at Mayo next year, but I'd like you to think about it. Don't give me your answer now. Just let me know in the next couple of weeks."

No mention whatsoever was made about the on-call incident. I did consider the offer—for about five minutes—and called the chief back the following week to respectfully decline. I was going to become an ophthalmologist, and I no longer had any doubt whatsoever.

The last few weeks of internship passed quickly, but as fate would have it, several of the medical interns were handed the opportunity for a little payback—courtesy of my childhood basketball heroes, the Los Angeles Lakers. Dr. K, as I mentioned, had courtside tickets at the Forum, and this was perhaps the greatest season of all for dyed-in-the-wool Lakers fans. The Lakers had met the Boston Celtics in the finals eight times before, with the Celtics winning every series. Once again the teams met in the 1985 finals, and after the years of futility, things weren't looking very promising when Boston ran Los Angeles off the court in game one 148-114. The Lakers rebounded in the second and third games, before the Celtics eked out a victory in the fourth contest (107-105) to even the series at two apiece. Game five was scheduled at the Forum in Los Angeles on June 7 and several of the interns came up with a plan for revenge, even enlisting a few of the nurses in our devious plot. In order to truly appreciate the brilliance of the plan, one must remember that cell phones weren't the primary mode of communication for physicians in 1985; the pager was still king. I happened to be off that night, since I'd been on long call the prior night, and I met several of the other interns to watch the game at a colleague's apartment. At a critical point in the first quarter, after the lead had changed hands several times, we had one of the nurse co-conspirators page Dr. K and continue paging until he answered. "Hi, Doctor, this is the nurse for your patient Katie Smith," she said when he finally got through. "Mrs. Smith's labs came back and her potassium levels are high (her potassium level really was high), and the intern is off on a code. What would you like me to do?" Dr. K, barely holding his temper, gave his orders, hung up without so much as saying goodbye, and hurried back to courtside. The exciting seesaw battle continued into the second quarter until—with the Celtics ahead by a few points—another nurse repeatedly paged Dr. K until he answered. After dutifully reporting another patient's low oxygen level on a blood gas, she tolerated a berating from Dr. K and his admonition not to page him again that night unless there was an emergency and she couldn't find the house staff—"Which should never happen, damn it!" Near the end of the second quarter the Lakers began a run. This time we paged Dr. K ourselves—to a phone number we knew was in the empty on-call sleeping quarters at the hospital—followed by the 9999 code we used to indicate an emergency. We toasted our deviousness as the Lakers lit up the basket to take a double-digit lead at the half. We left Dr. K alone for most of the second half, until the Lakers went cold and Boston closed to within a few points with only a few minutes left in the game. That's when we struck again. One of my colleagues paged Dr. K to a number he would recognize and respect—the medical intensive care unit, again with the 9999 emergency code— and followed it up with a repeat page a few moments later. No one in the MICU was privy to our escapade and, therefore, when the good Dr. K returned the page, it took several minutes to figure out there was no known reason for the page. By now hysterical with laughter, we watched the intense exchange of baskets over the next few minutes until the Lakers finally put the game away.

The following day, I happened to be writing a note in a patient's chart when Dr. K arrived on the wards to round on his patients. I couldn't suppress a snicker when another attending asked Dr. K about the game the night before and he detailed how it had been ruined by a series of emergency pages that seemed to be timed to coincide with key moments in the game. Honestly, I had nothing to do with the onslaught of pages Dr. K got a few nights later when the Lakers finally ended the dark years by defeating the Celtics on the parquet floor in Boston to take the finals. But I suspect most of the house staff felt it wasn't nearly enough payback for the hell he put us through for the entire year I was at Cedars-Sinai or for the countless years he'd been a tyrant to other interns and residents who devotedly served his patients.

The worst year of my life, at least to that point, would be over less than three weeks later—on June 24th. Most of my colleagues would go into their second year of internal medicine residency at Cedars-Sinai, but the rest of us, seven or eight in all, would leave for training in fields outside of internal medicine. The only fellow intern I've seen since is Peter Cornell, who's now a successful ophthalmologist in Los Angeles. The last time I saw Peter, I was a visiting professor at Cedars-Sinai speaking on refractive surgery. I reminded him of that long-call night when we crossed paths in the radiology department. He didn't remember uttering "ophthalmology" to me as we passed, both drunk with fatigue. I think that explains why none of the rest of us contacted each other over the years. We simply didn't want to relive the memories of that year when we often worked 120 to 140 hours in a week, and never less than 85 to 100 hours, except when we were on the emergency room rotation.

I don't want to foster the impression that patients admitted to the house staff services at Cedars-Sinai didn't receive excellent medical treatment. They most certainly did. The interns and residents, along with the hospital attending staff and private physicians, did their utmost to see that each and every patient was provided exceptional care. But this care often came at an appalling emotional and physical price for young physicians just beginning their careers. I also don't want to leave the mistaken impression that what I experienced that internship year was somehow unique to Cedars-Sinai Medical Center; it was not. Many rigorous medical and surgical programs were just as demanding—or even worse. For example, at that time, some internships and residencies had every-third-night long call the entire year, some even every other night for at least a portion of the year. A few had every-other-night call for the entire year. Many esteemed academicians saw this as a test of a young physician's mettle—a rite of passage—as it were. Some trainees fell by the wayside, some leaving medicine forever. A few interns and residents even commit suicide each year in the U.S.A., unable to cope with the intense pressure and expectations. Were there mistakes made due to fatigue and diminished judgment brought on by extreme hours, intense pressure, poor sleep patterns, inadequate diet and other shortcomings? Undoubtedly. On a personal level, I guess it "made a man out of me," but it also left me with other baggage—like impatience, indifference, callousness, and other detrimental traits that have no place in medicine. It took years to rid myself of the worst of these scars, yet some aspects of these characteristics were burned into my psyche forever. (For more on this subject, and steps that have been taken in the U.S.A. to prevent excessively long hours for interns, residents and fellows, see Appendix 1.)

Finally, my last day of internship at Cedars-Sinai Medical Center arrived on June 24, 1985. I turned my service over to a new intern, offering a few words of advice and encouragement, and said goodbye to the fellow interns, residents, and the attendings I'd come to deeply admire. I recall, as though it were yesterday, the feeling of elation that overcame me as I walked out of the south tower of the hospital for the last time and headed down the steps toward Third Street. The only way I can convey this grand feeling is to ask the reader to recall the elation you personally felt the last day of class in high school and multiply it by one hundred. I took the stairs two at a time and joyfully loaded my belongings into a U-Hall truck to begin the long journey to Rochester, Minnesota, to begin my residency in ophthalmology blasting REO Speedwagon's song "Roll with the Changes"—that I've always relished at each breakpoint in my career.

Chapter 4
A Bright, Shining Star

Somehow, at the beginning of July, with the trees heavy with leaves and the bright hot sun beaming down, Rochester didn't seem quite as uninviting as it had been that November evening I drove out of the quiet city, feeling certain I'd seen my last of the tall, gray, marble Mayo Building. Everywhere I looked, there was a softball diamond or playground teeming with kids and adults enjoying the long hot days of summer.

After a brief search of the newspaper and several real estate offices, we were fortunate to find a cozy duplex at the end of a residential circle that backed up to an open field. The friendly and helpful landlord lived in the adjoining unit with his wife and kids. Even in the dead of winter, when the snow crunched beneath snow boots with the characteristic crackle of subzero temperatures, my front door was less than a three-minute walk from the bus stop. From there it was a ten-minute bus ride to downtown Rochester and the Mayo Clinic.

I began my ophthalmology residency on the seventh floor of the Mayo Building a few days later. There were six new residents in the entering group—several of whom had availed themselves of the more civilized internship at the Mayo Clinic. At lunch the first day, I could only shake my head with a sardonic smile as one of my compatriots told me about the months he'd spent rotating through ophthalmology while I was struggling to survive the drudgery of the medicine wards and intensive care units at Cedars-Sinai. I could've had one of those internship positions myself, but instead I'd chosen to go to Cedars-Sinai in California. The four first-year residents who had availed themselves of the Mayo internship were already competent in most of the skills required to perform a meaningful eye examination—refraction, tonometry, slit lamp examination and indirect ophthalmoscopy. I felt light years behind the others in my chosen field and the knowledge that I could rapidly pass a Swan-Ganz catheter into a patient's heart was little consolation.

My first rotation was on the "refraction corridor," and with the help of other residents and attendings, I'd soon mastered refraction and could at least provide a patient with a prescription that had a greater than ninety percent chance of yielding an acceptable pair of glasses. Proficiency with the slit lamp, direct ophthalmoscope, indirect ophthalmoscope, and a variety of other ophthalmology-specific instruments soon followed. Within a few months, I could perform a decent eye exam and recognize when something wasn't normal. I might not recognize some

43

anomaly I'd never seen before, but I knew when the patient needed to go to retina rather than cornea or neuro-ophthalmology.

My entire first year of ophthalmology residency at Mayo was spent examining patients under the watchful eye of the attendings on the various services, including cornea and external disease, glaucoma, retina and neuro-ophthalmology. There was no surgery, much to the chagrin of some of my eager fellow residents, until late in the first year or the beginning of the second year. There was an overnight call schedule for residents that began sometime late in the first year—as I recall, it was an every-sixth night rotation of call from home—a virtual picnic compared to what I'd been through the prior year. I doubt I got called into the hospital more than a dozen times during my first and second year, and when I did, it was rarely for anything serious, although I did suture my share of eyelids lacerated by dog bites or fist fights. I remember being called in about five in the morning on a weekday to see a patient who "had a foreign body in her eye." When I arrived at the exam room, I found a young woman sitting comfortably in the exam chair with one eye closed and an embarrassed smile. She sheepishly told me that she was a flight attendant whose plane was leaving in a little over thirty minutes. After an overnight stay in the hotel, she'd arisen half-asleep to get ready to leave for the airport and accidentally grabbed a vial of Crazy Glue out of her purse rather than contact lens wetting solution, and applied a couple of drops into her eye before realizing her mistake. Trying hard to suppress a grin, I pulled the slit lamp in front of her. Sure enough, her eyelids were glued shut from one corner to the other. It took me two hours to meticulously peel the rock hard glue from her eyelids with a pair of fine forceps. Needless to say, she missed her flight, but nonetheless gave me a big hug once she could finally open her eye.

The rotation schedule was set up so that each resident rotated through ophthalmic pathology just prior to beginning his or her first surgical rotation. During that two-month rotation, time was set aside for practice surgery under the tutelage of one of the attending physicians using a surgical setup complete with an operating microscope, forceps and surgical scissors identical to those we'd soon be using in actual surgery. Within a short time, I'd learned to tie a variety of surgical knots, perform cataract surgery, and even do a decent corneal transplant on cadaver eyes.

Ophthalmology is a microcosm of all of medicine. It has many subspecialties, including surgical retina and vitreous, medical retina, cornea/external disease, refractive surgery, cataract surgery, uveitis, neuro-ophthalmology, ophthalmic plastic surgery and orbit, ocular oncology, pediatric ophthalmology, and ophthalmic pathology. As I proceeded through the first year, I felt drawn toward both ophthalmic plastic surgery and cornea/external disease. As often occurs in medicine, admired mentors created the attraction. On the one hand there was Robert Waller, MD, chairman of ophthalmology and a master ophthalmic plastic surgeon—who eventually became CEO of the entire Mayo Clinic. I didn't get an enormous amount of time with Dr. Waller because he was an incredibly busy physician and administrator. But in the time I spent with him, I felt his interest in me as a person, along with my concerns and ambitions. He taught me about the eyelids and how they function, but the most important thing I learned from Dr. Waller was what it really meant to be a physician when it came to communicating with patients. Never before had I seen a master communicator-physician like him at work. Dr. Waller had a knack for making a five-minute conversation with a patient count more than an hour with another doctor. He remembered their names and details about their personal lives, and showed a real interest in their problems. That meant more to them than the certainty that he was one of the elite surgeons in his chosen field. I remember many of Dr. Waller's patient-doctor interactions, and I strive to apply what I learned from him to my own medical practice on a daily basis.

The other major influence on my early career in ophthalmology was William Bourne, MD, an exceptional cornea and external disease specialist with a profound interest in research. Although my first research project in ophthalmology was a study on the resistance of different types of intraocular lenses (lenses inserted into the eye during cataract surgery) to the YAG laser used to remove "after cataracts," I soon found myself engaged in a number of projects related to different aspects of the cornea (the outermost clear wall of the eye—where contact lenses sit and refractive surgical procedures like LASIK and PRK are performed), including methods for preservation of donor corneas for transplantation and studying the causes of corneal diseases like Fuchs' dystrophy (a disorder of the innermost later of the cornea called the endothelium that, based on histopathological investigations, begins shortly after birth and frequently leads to swelling and opacification of the cornea requiring transplantation to restore vision in the later decades of a patient's life). Within a few months of beginning my research projects, I became utterly engrossed with the beauty, complexity, and importance of the cornea to vision, and with Dr. Bourne's guidance and encouragement, began to be drawn toward that subspecialty.

I involved myself in other projects, too, including a variety of clinical research studies which led to one of my most memorable experiences at Mayo. One afternoon, when I was the resident on-call, I got a page from a resident on the medicine ward in the hospital—I'll call him Dr. Avarice. He told me that one of the patients on the service—a woman who'd recently undergone liver transplantation—was complaining she'd suddenly gone completely blind. "She says she can't even see light," he said.

"Does she have any other neurological symptoms or signs?" I asked skeptically.

"Absolutely none," he responded.

"I'll be right over," I replied.

The first thing that came to mind, as I gathered my instruments to head over to the hospital, was that this might be a case of "functional blindness." For a variety of reasons, usually psychiatric, but sometimes for secondary gain, rare patients become convinced that they are blind and nothing will convince them otherwise. Sometimes it's difficult to distinguish this from malingering, where a patient feigns vision loss for some type of secondary gain, such as to obtain sympathy from loved ones, get out of working (I've seen this several times in prisoners), or to support a lawsuit. With this in mind, I grabbed an optokinetic drum from one of the neuro-ophthalmology examination rooms. An optokinetic drum is a hollow cylinder about ten inches in diameter and a foot long that rotates circumferentially on a handle. The outside of the drum is painted with alternating black and white stripes approximately an inch thick that run the length of the drum. If you rotate the drum in front of the eyes of a seeing person, it elicits an irrepressible reflex that causes the eyes to beat involuntarily in one direction or the other, depending on which way the drum is spinning. All vertebrates, even more primitive animals such as zebra fish, have this fascinating reflex.

I made it to the hospital about ten minutes later and quickly examined the patient. She claimed the blindness had come on suddenly less than thirty minutes earlier. Otherwise, the woman said she felt fine. She denied being able to see even the brightest light from my ophthalmoscope in either eye, even though her pupil responses to light were completely normal, and there were no other neurological abnormalities, such as disorders of eye alignment or movement controlled by several cranial nerves that originate in the brainstem. I dilated her pupils and found everything was normal in both eyes. Finally, I held the optokinetic drum in front of her eyes and gave it a spin. There was absolutely no response, regardless of which way I spun the drum.

I quickly found the resident who had called me and, based on the physical findings, told him I was concerned the patient had suffered a stroke in the occipital lobes in the back of the brain where the pathways to see end, leading to "cortical blindness." I requested that he get an emergency CT scan of the brain and urgent neurology and neurosurgery consultations. I tried to ask some other questions, but the fellow seemed strangely evasive and basically told me he'd handle the situation from there.

I went back to the ophthalmology department to continue seeing other patients, but I just couldn't get the woman out of my mind. A couple of hours later, I called to the nursing station in the hospital to find out how she was doing. Much to my surprise, the head nurse told me that less than an hour after I left, the patient had gone into a rapid neurological decline and was now on life support in the intensive care unit. I practically ran back to the hospital, and just as the nurse had said, found the patient comatose and on a respirator. The resident, Dr. Avarice, was sitting at the nursing station in the intensive care unit writing a note and again he was evasive when I began asking questions about the CT scan and what had transpired since I'd last seen the patient. Finally, realizing I wasn't going anywhere, he told me that he suspected that the patient had a new syndrome that a couple of other patients on intravenous cyclosporine had encountered after liver transplantation in the past few months. In each case, despite normal blood levels of the drug, the patients had developed early neurological signs, followed shortly by total central neurological collapse. My patient had been the first with blindness as the presenting sign. He also told me that, unbelievably, each of the patients had fully recovered after a week or two in a coma once the cyclosporine dose was reduced. I was fascinated and volunteered to do repeat eye and neuro-ophthalmological examinations on the patient if she did recover—explaining that ophthalmologists would likely be enthralled with this new syndrome. My colleague told me repeat exam wouldn't be necessary and that he was planning to write up "his cases" in the near future. I finally left, but I kept tabs on the patient and within two to three weeks she'd returned completely to normal and was discharged from the hospital.

Amazingly, the patient presented to the eye department for a normal eye exam nearly a year later, and by chance, I happened to be the assigned resident. Even more surprising, she remembered me and the "soothing words I had spoken to her" when she'd been gripped with fear about her sudden blindness. Needless to say, I did an exhaustive eye examination, including careful refraction, color vision testing, visual fields and every other test imaginable. She was indeed completely normal, with 20/20 vision in both eyes and no signs whatsoever of the neurological disorders she'd had the last time I saw her.

I presented the woman's case at an ophthalmology grand rounds and a few months later was shocked to find out from one of the ophthalmology attendings that the sweet woman had suddenly died of liver failure. We discovered that an autopsy had been performed, and I contacted the pathologist to find out what the findings had been in the central nervous system and eyes. A couple of days later, Dr. Avarice called me in a huff and ordered me to "stay away from his cases." Surprised by his demeanor, I explained that I only wanted to write a paper for the ophthalmology literature about this individual patient based on my examinations on the day she became blind and my detailed examination nearly a year later showing that her visual system had returned completely to normal. I even offered to include him as a co-author, along with his other colleagues involved in the series of patients. But he didn't want anything to do with a paper for the ophthalmology literature and again told me to "keep my nose out of his business."

The ophthalmology attending on the case, Dr. James Garrity, pointed out that there wouldn't even have been any eye examination follow-up data if I hadn't taken it upon myself to perform the color vision testing, visual fields, and other tests when the patient returned for a normal eye examination. He encouraged me to write the case up for an ophthalmology journal, so once again I requested histopathological slides of the brain from the autopsy. About a week passed, before I got a memo from a standing committee at Mayo Clinic that investigated and arbitrated disputes between physicians about clinical research. I didn't even know there was such a committee, but I appeared at the appointed time and related my story about the patient to the committee members made up of faculty physicians from several departments. The members of the committee listened to both sides and then issued their decision. Since no visual testing would have been performed if I hadn't taken the initiative to do it, I could write up the patient's ophthalmological and neuro-ophthalmological findings, with access to the neuro-pathological findings, in any way I saw fit for the ophthalmology literature, and I could decide who would be co-authors on the paper.

I did just that, and submitted an abstract to the annual meeting for the American Academy of Ophthalmology (AAO). The abstract was accepted for oral presentation, and I presented the paper, the first of my career, to several hundred ophthalmologists at the AAO annual meeting in 1987. Neil Miller, MD, a legendary neuro-ophthalmologist from the Wilmer Eye Institute at Johns Hopkins, was asked to provide a brief discussion of the case following my presentation. It was an exhilarating honor for a third-year resident, nourishing my zeal to pursue academic ophthalmology.

In an attempt to be magnanimous, I contacted Dr. Avarice once I completed the written manuscript and offered to include him as a co-author on the paper with Dr. Garrity and me. Despite the review committee's clear decision, another brawl ensued, with him and several others in his department arguing they should be second, third, and fourth authors, ahead of Dr. Garrity. We could only shake our heads with amused annoyance at their impudence. In the end, Dr. Garrity decided that it all wasn't worth the hassle to continue fighting and the paper was finally published in 1998.

Wilson, S.E. and coauthors, "Cyclosporine-induced Reversible Cortical Blindness," *The Journal of Clinical Neuro-ophthalmology*, vol. 8, pgs. 215–220.

What impressed me most about the entire incident was the grace with which the institution handled the situation and resolved the dispute. Somehow, I doubt Dr. Avarice felt the same way.

Residency in ophthalmology at the Mayo Clinic wasn't all work. We had a lot of good times outside the hospital. Rochester is a small town with somewhat limited activities, unless one was willing to make the two-hour drive to Minneapolis, as we occasionally did, so most outings tended to revolve around other physicians and coworkers at the Mayo Clinic. For whatever reason, at least for the ophthalmology department, a lot of this recreation tended to include sports—softball, basketball, jogging, and just about anything else where there was an element of competition. The driving force behind most of this recreational activity was the chairman who took over the department once Dr. Waller became the CEO of the Mayo Clinic, Richard

Brubaker, MD, known to his friends as Bru. Brubaker wasn't a big man, but his competitive spirit was legendary. It didn't matter what game we were playing—basketball, softball, or ping-pong—once the game was underway, Bru was out to win. I always suspected I was somewhat of a disappointment to him in that regard. Oh, I was competent and competitive at softball, basketball, and even Ping-Pong, but I hated jogging, and that was one of his favorite activities. I remember he and his wife invited us over to run a couple of times. My wife loved to run, but I insisted on following on a bike on the two- to five-mile jaunt. That annoyed Bru, so he searched out trails where no ordinary bike was ever meant to go, at least with me riding it, but I followed nonetheless. One of my favorite Brubaker stories comes from my third and final year at Mayo. One day, out of the blue, Bru decided he was taking up ice hockey. As he did with just about everything, he threw himself into the new sport with fervent passion and was soon scrapping with other players with years of experience at a local hockey rink, including a couple of the ophthalmology residents. It wasn't long before he showed up in the department with a twisted and bruised nose and face. I wasn't there to see it, but apparently he went airborne after a particularly hard check from an opponent and his nose was the first body part to hit the ice. That didn't stop him though. He was back on the ice a short time later.

By the beginning of my third year of residency, I'd become firmly committed to a fellowship in cornea and external diseases of the eye. A new fellowship match was introduced for the first time that year, and I submitted my application for several of the top fellowships in the country. I was already heavily involved in many cornea projects at Mayo, so I also approached Dr. Bourne about staying in Rochester for my fellowship. Dr. Bourne, however, had been instrumental in formulating the new cornea fellowship match and he was honorably unwilling to undermine the process. Thus, he wouldn't commit to me outside the match. About all he would say was that I would "be very competitive in the match for the position at Mayo."

In addition to the several dozen match programs, there were a few cornea fellowships that remained independent of the match. One of these was the two-year fellowship with Herbert E. Kaufman, MD, Marguerite B. McDonald, MD, Stephen D Klyce, PhD, and the many other talented physicians and scientists at the LSU Eye Center in New Orleans. Dr. Kaufman was a legend in ophthalmology and cornea. Well known to all, he had supporters and detractors throughout the ophthalmologic world and the cornea subspecialty, with few people taking a neutral position about the well-known, enigmatic chairman. Virtually nobody questioned the importance of his many contributions to the field, including the first treatment for herpes simplex infection of the cornea. Many, however, had reservations about his hard-edged, pretentious style. Both Dr. Bourne and the second cornea faculty member at Mayo Clinic, Leo Maguire, MD, had been "Kaufman fellows." In addition, many of the top academic corneal specialists in the United States had trained in his programs at Gainesville, Florida, from 1962 to 1977 or LSU Eye Center from 1977 onward. It didn't surprise anyone when I applied there too.

Early in the fall of 1987, I ventured to New Orleans to interview for the two-year cornea fellowship that included one year of clinical training and one year of research. Dr. Kaufman interviewed that year's crop of candidates at least a month earlier than the programs in the match—I'm sure by design. I toured the outstanding facilities in the impressive gray and red three-story institute and interviewed with several of the faculty members. My last interview of the day was with Herbert Kaufman himself. We sat at a conference room table together, and I waited patiently while he thumbed through my application and letters of recommendations. By that time, I was a co-author on eleven medical and scientific papers that were published, or soon to be published, in peer-reviewed journals—ten of these as first author. I noticed Dr. Kaufman spent the longest time looking at that list of articles. Finally, he looked up and smiled. "Well, Steven, is there anything else I can tell you about the fellowship program here at LSU?"

"No, Dr. Kaufman," I replied confidently. "Dr. Bourne and Dr. Maguire were both fellows with you, so I already know a lot about the program."

"Good," he replied with a nod. "I'd like to offer you a position in the fellowship. Let me know by next week whether or not you accept."

I was shocked, never anticipating such an abrupt offer, since my first interview for fellowship programs in the match was still two weeks away. "By next week?" I stammered.

"Yes," he replied with a twinkle in his eye. "We have a number of excellent candidates, and I'd like to have the entering fellowship class finalized by the end of next week." I would come to know that look of amused confidence all too well. He enjoyed having me right where he wanted me. "Give my secretary a call by Friday," he said, as he began to stand up, signaling the interview was over. He offered his hand. "It was nice to meet you, Steven. Give Bill and Leo my regards."

"Thank you, Dr. Kaufman," I replied, regaining my composure. "I'll be in touch with you next week."

I related my experience to Dr. Bourne when I got back to Rochester. "By next week, huh?" he responded with an amused chuckle. "Well, Steve, I guess you'll have to make a decision sooner than you thought."

It was indeed a classic dilemma—a bird in the hand versus two in the bush. But it really wasn't a hard decision to make. By lunch that day, after discussing it with my wife, I'd decided to go to New Orleans. I called LSU the following day to commit and dropped my applications for the match programs.

The match results came out several months later and the Mayo Clinic didn't fill its position, which was not an uncommon occurrence for programs that limited offers to just the best candidates. At that point, Dr. Bourne was free to offer me the corneal fellowship position at Mayo. I smiled and thanked him for his offer, but declined, pointing out that crossing Herbert Kaufman so early in my cornea career was probably not a good idea. Dr. Bourne offered to discuss it with Dr. Kaufman and he didn't think it would be a major issue. "Kaufman will have at least ten fellows running around LSU," he noted. But I appreciatively declined his offer nonetheless. By this time, I was looking forward to going to New Orleans to see how I fared in the larger, high-profile program. It was probably the most important career decision I ever made, and one that, for better or worse, would set the course of my future career.

The medical and surgical residency training I received in ophthalmology at the Mayo Clinic was truly exceptional. In large part, this was due to the amazing group of dedicated faculty members in the ophthalmology department—like William Bourne, Robert Waller, Richard Brubaker, Brian Younge, Thomas Kearns, Thomas Liesegang, Dennis Robertson, Helmut Buettner, just to name a few. All of these faculty members, and many others who have risen to prominence in the department since, were great physicians and wonderful people. I owe them a lot.

Chapter 5
Awakening in the Big Easy–
A Matter of Being There at Both the Right and Wrong Times

I arrived in New Orleans driving a U-Haul truck packed full of furniture and other belongings the first week of July 1998, with my wife following in our Pontiac Sunbird. It didn't take us long to rent a shotgun apartment on State Street Drive in the Uptown area of the Crescent City. My wife found a job at the Ochsner Clinic, and I showed up for the first day of my fellowship eager to go. It took me about an hour to find out things worked a little differently at LSU Eye Center compared to what I'd been accustomed to at the Mayo Clinic.

During my last few months in Rochester, I'd been in communication with Dr. Kaufman's administrators at the LSU Eye Center. They told me to plan on doing my research year first, followed by my clinical year. I'd prepared myself mentally for the research year and was intending to rotate through a couple of the research labs to find the area where I wanted to concentrate my efforts. I showed up early that first morning and was directed to the fellows' office by one of the staff members. It was a large room lined on both sides with desks. Setting my things down on an empty desk, I began introducing myself to half a dozen new and continuing cornea fellows who happened to be in the room. We'd just begun getting acquainted when my name was paged over the PA system: "Dr. Steven Wilson, please call Dr. Kaufman's office." I grabbed a phone, dialed the number and Dr. Kaufman's secretary, Val, answered. She asked me to come to Kaufman's office right away.

I hurried down the hall and Val greeted me with a cheerful smile, before telling me there'd been a change in plans. "Dr. Kaufman decided you'll be starting with the clinical year first, rather than the research year, as originally planned."

Stunned, I began explaining to her that I'd planned to get several research projects underway. She stopped me by raising her hand.

"There's no sense arguing," she said with an amused smile that let me know there would be no debating the issue. "Dr. Kaufman's made up his mind."

"But why?" I queried.

"He's decided you're less likely to take off after your clinical training without completing your research than one of the other new fellows. Consider it a compliment."

"Really?" I asked, surprised by her response.

"That's what he told me. Now, you better hurry down to clinic. Several of Dr. Kaufman's patients have already checked in."

I took the elevator down to the second floor and made my way to the check-in desk, where a jovial black woman named Greta was sitting behind the counter. She welcomed me to clinic and informed me I'd be taking patients who'd been cared for by the prior year's fellow Dr. Rootman. She pointed to one of the niches above the counter already labelled with my name—where a pair of two inch-thick charts with dog-eared covers had been placed.

I grabbed the chart on top and was flipping through it, when a young man wearing a doctor's coat walked up to the desk. "You must be Steve Wilson," he said, grinning. "I'm Jonathan Frantz, one of the other clinical cornea fellows this year. Nice to meet you."

"Nice to meet you too," I said, shaking his hand. "So, what do I do now?"

"Just call the patient and I'll show you to the cornea exam rooms."

I called the seventy-year-old patient and the three of us wandered down the hall to a series of rooms near the back corner of the clinical floor.

"You should've just asked me," the old man joked—with a grin. "I must have been here fifty times over the past five years and had three corneal transplants during that time. Let's see," he said, cupping his chin in his fingers. "You must be my sixth fellow doctor here at LSU Eye Center."

Dr. Frantz shook his head and laughed. "Use whichever room is open. Then, when you're done with your exam, take the chart back to the conference room and present him to Kaufman."

That was the first patient of the hundreds I saw that year. New patients were typically referred from outside of New Orleans or self-referred based on the reputation of the eye center. Almost all of the patients who came from other doctors had serious problems such as chemical burns, multiple prior failed transplants, or were "train wrecks" with a slew of issues, such as an eye with a failed cornea, cataract, severe glaucoma, and an irregular pupil. We saw only a smattering of straightforward cases—such as just-diagnosed keratoconus or Fuchs' dystrophy—in need of a first corneal transplant. Thus, the patients we cared for tended to be challenging, but that enhanced the training and made the uncomplicated cases relatively simple.

I was blessed to have three outstanding clinical cornea fellows grouped with me that year. David Lin, MD, an athletic tennis guru with an easy laugh, had already completed one year of clinical corneal fellowship at Pacific Medical Center in San Francisco and had a faculty position waiting at the University of British Columbia. Subsequently, after a few years back at the University of British Columbia, he established the most successful refractive surgery, cornea, and cataract practice in Vancouver. James Reidy, MD, was a tall, lanky, academic type with a heart of gold. He's was an outstanding faculty member in the Department of Ophthalmology at the State University of New York in Buffalo for many years before he became vice-chair at the University of Chicago. Jonathan Frantz, MD, completed his ophthalmology residency at LSU Eye Center and had already finished his research year in the cornea fellowship. He went on to establish a highly successful refractive and corneal surgery practice in Ft. Myers, Florida. We were all knowledgeable, hard-working, and dependable, sticking up for each other when things got tough, which they often did at the LSU Eye Center. Frantz and Lin were at each other's throats a few times during the year, in my estimation because each gauged the other to be his major competitor for "superstar" clinical cornea fellow that year, but somehow the team worked with only a few relatively minor eruptions.

Besides Herbert Kaufman, there were three other clinical cornea faculty members at the LSU Eye Center. Marguerite McDonald, MD, already a megastar in ophthalmology, was destined to become one of the most influential and respected ophthalmologists—male or female—in the world, especially in the exploding field of refractive surgery. She performed the first excimer laser vision correction procedure in the world on normally-sighted eyes of patients with myopia at LSU Eye Center in 1988. Michael Insler, MD, a respected cornea specialist, had moved his practice from nearby Tulane—perceived as the enemy at LSU—a few years earlier. Bruce Barron, MD, was an excellent corneal surgeon who always seemed to get the work nobody else wanted, like putting in a synthetic keratoprosthesis in a cornea in which a human donor corneal transplant was no longer an option due to repeated rejections or severe vascularization. All four of the clinical fellows were assigned to work in clinics and surgery with Dr. Kaufman the entire year. Each of us rotated with the other three faculty members for differing periods, with more total time being spent with McDonald than with Insler or Barron. Thus, during a typical week we'd each spend three half-days in clinic and at least one day in surgery with Kaufman. The remaining half of the week would be some combination of clinic (almost always two to three more half-days) and surgery with McDonald, Insler, and Barron. The variety of cases and approaches made for a strong clinical training experience.

It follows from our schedule that the majority of the fellows' corneal surgical training was provided by Herbert Kaufman, MD, primarily because he had the biggest practice. All four of the cornea fellows would show up at the operating rooms at Hotel Dieu Hospital every Wednesday just before seven in the morning, and with Dr. Kaufman's direction and assistance, we'd simultaneously operate on two patients in adjacent rooms, completing anywhere from four to twenty cases on a particular surgery day. At the beginning of the year, Dr. Kaufman would perform the majority of each case, turning over portions of the surgery to individual fellows as the skills of each allowed. Two-thirds of the cases were anterior segment reconstructions where, in addition to transplantation of the cornea, it was also necessary to perform other procedures, such as remove an old intraocular lens, suture in a new intraocular lens, and repair a distorted iris. With such intensive experience, any of the four of us could excel in any cornea case by six months into the fellowship.

Conversely, Marguerite McDonald provided the majority of our refractive surgery training. At that time, the excimer laser was still an investigational device used in research patients enrolled in clinical trials to gain FDA approval for photorefractive keratectomy (PRK). LASIK hadn't been invented yet. Thus, the refractive cases the fellows performed were restricted to epikeratophakia (a procedure in which a layer of donor corneal tissue with an appropriate shape was sutured into position on the corneal surface) to treat nearsightedness, aphakia (eyes that had cataract surgery without insertion of an intraocular lens), or keratoconus. We also performed a few radial keratotomy (RK) procedures. RK is the procedure in which radial, nearly full-thickness, corneal incisions are used to correct low to moderate nearsightedness, and it was the dominant refractive surgery procedure throughout the world at that point in time.

Epikeratophakia was first performed at LSU Eye Center, but there's long been disagreement about who actually invented it. Dr. Kaufman first presented a lecture describing the procedure at the American Academy of Ophthalmology annual meeting in 1979 (The Jackson Memorial Lecture). Ted Werblin, MD, a former Kaufman fellow who stayed on the faculty at LSU Eye Center for a couple of years after completing training, argues he was the first one to conceive of epikeratophakia. Werblin claims he was driving into work one day and the characteristic above-ground tombs in a cemetery in New Orleans gave him the idea of putting the new tissue on top of the patient's cornea rather than inside.

The surgical procedure developed prior to that time to correct high-nearsightedness or any level of farsightedness was "keratomileusis." Keratomileusis was developed in Bogota, Colombia, by Jose Barraquer, MD, the father of refractive surgery. Keratomileusis was demanding: a procedure in which a disc of the patient's own central cornea was excised, frozen, lathed to a precise curvature to correct the refractive error of the eye, and then returned to the cornea—a surgery far too complex for ordinary mortals. It really doesn't matter at this point who originally thought of epikeratophakia, since the procedure, like radial keratotomy, has been abandoned. Laser vision correction, in the form of PRK or LASIK, has proven to be more accurate and reproducible, and within a few years became the dominant refractive surgical procedure in the world.

Within a month or two of the beginning of the academic year, the clinical cornea fellows had settled into the weekly routine of clinic and surgery. It was a wonderfully exciting time to be at LSU Eye Center. The faculty members were on the cutting edge in virtually every area of cornea and refractive surgery, corneal imaging, corneal disease, and corneal physiology. Each of the fellows found clinical research projects to work on and it was my great fortune to become involved in studies of corneal shape or contour (called corneal topography) with Stephen D. Klyce, PhD. A few years earlier, Dr. Klyce, who up to that point was best known as a corneal physiologist, had been challenged by Dr. Kaufman to develop a better way of evaluating the shape of the corneal surface and the effect of the surgeries on that shape. In response, Dr. Klyce invented the world's first corneal topography instrument. With the help of two fellows who preceded me, Leo Maguire, MD, and Stephen A. Dingeldein, MD, Dr. Klyce began using his instrument that transformed images of concentric rings or mires reflected from a patient's cornea (with a device called a photokeratoscope) into color-coded contour maps of the anterior corneal surface, which is the most important light-focusing surface of the eye. The only problem was that the original device required painstaking point-by-point electronic entry of the mire locations for each patient's cornea before the topographer's computer and plotter would provide the corresponding map. Thus, it took several "fellow hours" for each map to be generated—a very inefficient instrument for a clinic where dozens of patients needed analysis on a typical day. Luckily, Dr. Klyce had been working with a New York start-up company, Computed Anatomy, to develop the first fully-automated corneal topographer. This new device, the Corneal Modeling System, or CMS, arrived with considerable fanfare at LSU at the beginning of my fellowship. The CMS was about the size of a large oven and occupied its own room. The raw data from each eye was stored on one or more floppy discs that were filed in dozens of file cabinets in the same room. This instrument allowed topographic maps for both eyes of a patient to be generated in just a few minutes. The information derived from these maps forever changed corneal and refractive surgery. Dr. Klyce and I began gathering topographic maps from the corneas of hundreds of patients and research subjects, and published a steady stream of medical and scientific papers about normal corneal shape, the effects of contact lenses and surgery on corneal shape, and improvements in the technology, such as mathematical descriptors that provided useful quantitative information about the shape of the cornea. The surface regularity index, or SRI, one of those quantitative descriptors, is still in use today and was the precursor to many other indices provided by other models of corneal topographers used by cornea and refractive surgeons throughout the world. Steve Klyce and I teamed up to publish more than twenty articles and book chapters from those two years of work, including the first paper on the effects of excimer laser PRK on corneal topography, published with Dr. McDonald. Steve, Margeurite and I remain great friends. During that two years, I also wrote papers on topics such as corneal transplant rejection and suturing methods for corneal transplants with other fellows and faculty members. It was truly an amazing opportunity to be at LSU Eye Center when the institution was at the forefront of the fields of cornea and refractive surgery.

Nineteen eighty-eight to 1990 were incredibly exciting years to be at the LSU Eye Center. In addition to the major advances occurring in corneal topography already mentioned, it was also during this time, after several years of research, that Marguerite McDonald, MD, led the first phase II and phase III clinical trials of excimer laser photorefractive keratectomy for correction of myopia with the VISX excimer laser to gain FDA approval. Beginning first with non-seeing eyes of volunteers, the first being a patient named Alberta Cassady who had a melanoma of her conjunctiva and orbit that mandated that her eye be removed for treatment. Mrs. Cassady had a normal cornea and asked if anyone could use it for research. Her eye became the first normally-sighted eye to have PRK. I watched Dr. McDonald do one of the first groups of seeing eyes and I was in the clinic the next morning with the rest of the fellows and about twenty visitors, including several VISX employees and VIP ophthalmologists from all over the country, when the first patients had their one-day follow-up visits. Even though it was a Saturday morning, the clinic was buzzing with excitement. I took my turn examining each patient and overheard a local corneal specialist as he leaned over to another visiting colleague and whispered, "This crap will never work." But work it did! Over the next few months, dozens of sighted volunteers were enrolled in the study. The results weren't perfect—this was a work in progress—but anyone who saw the patients realized we were witnessing a revolution in the laser surgical treatment of nearsightedness—with related procedures for astigmatism and farsightedness clearly in sight.

That clinical year seemed to pass by in a flash. It wasn't all hard work though, and we definitely had more than our share of fun. There were parties, festivals, and, of course, Mardi Gras, where formal balls and King cakes reigned supreme. Some of my fondest memories are from days when Dr. Kaufman and Dr. McDonald were both out of town giving lectures, which occurred very frequently since both professors were in demand all over the world. We fellows used this time for research projects, but always looked forward to a leisurely lunch at one of New Orleans' finest restaurants, like Commander's Palace, Paul Prudhomme's K-Paul's, or Mr. B's...of course, as our limited budgets allowed. Those were wonderful days that still come to mind often and bring a smile to my face. Not surprisingly, I still consider the restaurants of New Orleans my favorites in the world.

Numerous gags and shenanigans that the staff, residents, and fellows at LSU Eye Center played on each other spiced up the 1988–1989 academic year. One particular prank tops my list of fond memories. Excimer laser surgery was still experimental during that year. Thus, the fellows couldn't participate in the clinical trials with the excimer laser and, therefore, epikeratophakia and radial keratotomy were the only refractive surgical procedures we could perform on patients. As we approached the second half of the year, it was traditional for the cornea fellows to begin doing radial keratotomy cases with Dr. McDonald. But, as the time grew near, I made the decision that I wasn't going to perform radial keratotomy (I never believed in this procedure that flattened the central cornea with anywhere from two to more than sixteen nearly full thickness incisions), and so I told the other three cornea fellows I'd decided to turn my RK cases over to them. Not surprisingly, this began an immediate competition between Dr.

Lin and Dr. Frantz over who'd get the lion's share of my spoils—to the point that the friction between the two, seemingly always just below the surface, began to boil over. Always a bit of a schemer, I hatched a plan for a memorable year-end prank. But which one of my colleagues would bear the brunt of my devious plotting? Surely not Dr. Lin, the one who'd arguably saved my life a year earlier when he'd rushed me to the hospital after I suffered a severe gastrointestinal hemorrhage brought on by Feldene. Jonathan Frantz it had to be. Besides, I knew my compatriots well enough to know the plan taking shape in my mind would work only with good Dr. Frantz because the scheme depended on one important factor: if there were anyone in the eye center Dr. Frantz had less rapport with than Dr. Lin, it was Stuart Shoffner, MD, a cornea fellow in his research year who rotated into Dr. Frantz's prior position as Marguerite McDonald's dedicated excimer laser research fellow. I suspect the enmity was attributable to it being hard for Jonathan to accept another in his place at this seminal moment in the history of refractive surgery when excimer laser PRK was becoming a worldwide sensation.

Anyway, I convinced Dr. McDonald to take a starring role in a grand hoax involving Dr. Shoffner. We picked a day when there was no afternoon clinic and set up the prank while Dr. Frantz was out of the building for lunch. Once things were in place, I waited impatiently in the clinic for nearly a half hour for Dr. Frantz to reappear. Just when it seemed he wouldn't show and the scheme would fail, he walked through the door. I headed straight toward him shaking my head with mock exasperation.

"What's going on?" Dr. Frantz queried.

"I'm sick of this place. McDonald is letting Shoffner do an RK in the procedure room."

"What?" he gasped, his eyes bulging in disbelief. "That's nonsense!"

"They're back there right now."

Dr. Frantz made a beeline for the back of the clinic. This was totally unacceptable: one of the *research* fellows was doing refractive surgery, and even worse, it was Stuart Shoffner. I followed close behind, as Frantz pushed through the outer door and peered through the porthole window into the procedure room. Sure enough, there they were—Dr. McDonald, Dr. Shoffner and the scrub nurse wearing blue gowns and masks with a patient covered and draped on the bed. Shoffner was sitting in the "captain's" chair at the top of the patient's head. I felt Jonathan tense, as we watched Shoffner place the lid speculum into the eye to hold it open. Finally, unable to watch from a distance any longer, he pushed through the inner door with me right behind him. Dr. Frantz took up a position just behind Shoffner and watched with growing exasperation as Dr. McDonald talked him through the corneal thickness measurements and then told the nurse to set the diamond blade. The tension in the room was palpable as Shoffner delineated the intended incision lines with an inked marker pressed against the eye. With all the commotion going on, Dr. Frantz didn't notice the other two clinical fellows—Dr. Lin and Dr. Reidy—standing quietly in the corner of the room, fighting to suppress their laughter.

"Diamond knife," Dr. Shoffner called to the nurse, holding out his hand.

The nurse pressed the instrument into his hand and Dr. Shoffner, peering through the scope, slowly brought the knife down toward the eye. Dr. Frantz leaned forward to watch, as Dr. McDonald called out one last instruction.

Suddenly, without warning, the patient sat up on the table beneath the surgical drapes. With a primal growl, he ripped off the drapes and turned to face the surgeons. It took a moment for this bizarre turn of events to register with Dr. Frantz. Suddenly, as boisterous laughter erupted around the room, he realized that the "patient" wasn't really a patient after all, but one of the third-year ophthalmology residents.

"I doff my *chapeau*," Dr. Frantz offered, as he bowed and swept his hand in an arc from the top of his head, before turning and walking unceremoniously from the procedure room.

There were still two weeks left before the academic year ended. As word spread through the eye center about my prodigious prank, I fully expected some sort of retaliation. But the retribution never came; I guess because Jonathan knew it was born of playful fondness, rather than an attempt to humiliate him. Besides, it would've been a hard con to top!

As the clinical year ended and my research year finally arrived, Dr. Lin and Dr. Frantz headed off for their new jobs outside of New Orleans, Dr. Reidy migrated to the research labs, and another new group of corneal fellows showed up at the eye center. Two new recruits joined two of the prior year's research fellows to form the new clinical foursome. Other newly arrived cornea fellows headed into research, as the revolving door spun and a new year began.

I'd been rethinking plans for my research year during the last few months of my clinical year. Of course, I wanted to continue the corneal topography projects I'd begun with Stephen Klyce. But, with more experience, I'd come to realize there was an obvious area where I could apply skills I'd already mastered to develop a niche in corneal research for my own program—my prior training and experience in molecular biology and biochemistry. I decided to use those skills to investigate communication between cells within the cornea that were mediated by proteins called growth factors, like epidermal growth factor (EGF) and its receptor. The entire field was wide open and I saw an opportunity to make a significant contribution. First, however, and with apprehension, I went to Dr. Klyce and told him what I wanted to do. I've always appreciated his support at that moment when another scientist might have felt betrayed by my desire to focus a significant proportion of my energies elsewhere. But we continued working together, as I began interacting with a cornea fellow from England named Stuart Cooke, MD. Dr. Cooke was experimenting with a new molecular biology technique called the polymerase chain reaction (PCR). I soon learned the basics of the methodology. With the guidance of a knowledgeable technician, I was soon applying PCR to explore the expression of growth factors in the rabbit lacrimal (tear) gland. I didn't realize at the time the impact this return to my roots would have on my career in corneal research, but within a few months, I'd learned several new methods that had emerged since I finished graduate school over a decade earlier. It all came flooding back and almost everything I'd learned from 1974 to 1977 was still relevant—gel electrophoresis for resolving hundreds of proteins or nucleic acid fragments in complex mixtures and centrifugation for isolating cells and their organelles. Many other techniques and methods had been improved, but were still familiar. Soon I felt right at home, almost as though it'd been predetermined.

The second year passed so quickly, with many memorable events. Stephen Klyce and Marguerite McDonald were married in a grand wedding attended by hundreds of guests from all over the world that included a glorious reception at the New Orleans Museum of Art. My wife and I brought a little one into our lives . . . no, not a baby, a feisty Dalmatian puppy named *Excimer*—after the laser. Rambunctious and smart as a whip, he became famous throughout the ophthalmology world. I made the mistake of bringing him to the LSU Eye Center when he was only twelve weeks old. He promptly made a deposit—first in the clinic conference room beneath Dr. Kaufman's feet and then in Dr. McDonald's office. Luckily for me, they're both dog lovers!

My research went well, and I demonstrated conclusively that epidermal growth factor was produced in the rabbit lacrimal gland, where it likely became a component of tears to modulate corneal epithelial cell proliferation and differentiation, and corneal healing after injury. Interestingly, that paper was never published. It languished somewhere in an enormous cluttered pile on the desk of the professor who ran the lab where Stuart Cooke and I worked until long after I'd left for my first position at another university. I finally repeated the experiments using human autopsy tissues and published the work. But once again, I'm getting ahead of the story.

Suddenly, it was time to begin looking for my first faculty appointment. There weren't many academic positions that offered a combination of clinical and basic research opportunities available at that time in cornea and refractive surgery. In fact, there were only three. The Mayo Clinic had opened the Scottsdale, Arizona satellite, but the research program was not well developed. I decided to look at opportunities at universities with strong reputations in basic research. The two good fits were in the departments of ophthalmology at UT Southwestern Medical Center in Dallas and Washington University in St. Louis, where I'd first been accepted to medical school. I visited both programs and quickly decided on UT Southwestern because the research support and salary offered was much higher. I agreed to begin my new position as assistant professor of ophthalmology at UT Southwestern, with associated Parkland Memorial Hospital, on July 1, 1990.

Looking back at what has transpired at the LSU Eye Center since I left in 1990, I realize how fortunate I was to be there at its zenith. Within two years of my leaving, the program began a precipitous decline greased by the departure of Marguerite McDonald, MD, and several other faculty members, including renowned retinal surgeon Gholam A. Peyman, MD. The split between Dr. Kaufman and Dr. McDonald was especially acrimonious—in my opinion brought on by Dr. McDonald's rise to prominence in refractive surgery. Try as I may to stay out of the feuding, it became more and more difficult as the years went by and the bad blood boiled. It seemed so sad and so unnecessary, and unquestionably took away much of the luster of Dr. Kaufman's last years as Director and Chairman of Ophthalmology at LSU Eye Center. Years later, in 2003, when the eye center was searching for a new director and chairman, I was a short-list candidate for the position. During my interviews, I discovered the dean and chancellor of LSU School of Medicine had no intention of supporting further eye center growth—despite the fact that the program continued to be the top department in the medical school in total research funding from NIH, even exceeding internal medicine and other much larger departments. It was a bit surprising when I received no support from Dr. Kaufman to become the next chairman. To the contrary, he actively opposed my candidacy. This was likely attributable to his disapproval of my continued friendship with Stephen Klyce and Marguerite McDonald and concerns about what I might do about the commercial discount LASIK center ($299 an eye!) where he and another faculty member worked part time. He had good reason to be concerned about the latter: I wouldn't have tolerated members in the department being involved in this type of nonsense. In the end, the dean named an internal candidate with little research background as the new chairman and director, signaling that LSU Eye Center's days as a force to be reckoned with in ophthalmology and vision research were over forever. That new chairman didn't last long either.

However, I remain eternally grateful for the opportunities that my fellowship at LSU Eye Center opened up for me. Both the clinical and research components of my career were enhanced by the time I spent with the outstanding faculty and cornea fellows at that institution. There were also many intangibles I took away from my experiences. Probably the most important was that my eyes were opened to what was really happening in the medical world. I learned that when it came to new technologies, surgical procedures, and approaches, a healthy dose of skepticism was a good thing. I learned that all too often the perceptions of companies producing new technologies and drugs were tainted by the concern for the bottom line and the demand for profits. "Advances" were often touted prematurely and efforts were made to suppress negative perceptions or data. I've often wondered if I would have developed this same level of skepticism if I'd stayed at Mayo Clinic to do my cornea and refractive surgery fellowship. There, I wouldn't have been exposed to the countless new approaches and technologies that often came first to LSU for testing—and frequently failed miserably. Somehow I doubt it, and this cynicism and the search for "evidence" to support or refute claims and dogma has served me—and my patients—well over the past three decades as I've practiced refractive and cornea surgery.

Chapter 6
Trial by Fire

After four years of college, three years of graduate school, four years in medical school, a year of internship, three years of residency and two years of fellowship, I began my first faculty appointment at UT Southwestern Medical Center in July of 1990, with twenty-five percent of my time devoted to clinical care of private patients and seventy-five percent focused on my fledgling research program. In a typical week, I'd have two half-days of clinic and spend the rest of my time in the lab. Surgery was scheduled at Zale Lipshy University Hospital every two to three weeks for a half day, depending on the needs of my patients. I also took emergency call in rotation with the other faculty members in the department. My clinical practice was restricted to external disease, cornea and cataract surgery, since the FDA had still not approved the excimer laser and we weren't involved in clinical trials to gain FDA approval for any of the lasers being developed. Thus, my typical surgical cases were cataracts and corneal transplants. There was no necessity for me to be more active in the clinic since the chairman of ophthalmology, James McCulley, MD, along with another faculty member, was also a specialist in external disease, cornea, and cataract surgery.

My first laboratory was a 15-foot by 25-foot room on the seventh floor of the building that housed the ophthalmology department at the medical school. I used the start-up funds provided from my recruitment offer to hire a research technician and purchase equipment and supplies to explore communication between cells in the cornea and lacrimal tear glands. Within weeks of my arrival in Dallas, we were using PCR, northern blotting, immunohistochemistry and other cell and molecular biology techniques to identify specific growth factors produced in corneal cells and determine their functions in corneal physiology. Initially, most of our work focused on corneal endothelial cells on the back surface of the cornea that play a major role in maintaining proper hydration of the cornea needed for good vision. If these cells are lost, the cornea swells, resulting in decreased vision and, eventually, painful corneal erosions. Many people who need corneal transplants, for example with diseases like Fuchs' dystrophy or pseudophakic bullous keratopathy (PBK), must have the endothelial cells on their corneas replaced since human corneal endothelial cells have minimal capacity to divide and replenish themselves. At that time, little was known about the elements that regulated division of these cells or the likely related growth factors, cytokines, or receptors produced by corneal endothelial cells. That became an early focus of my research.

One of the major factors that drew me to UT Southwestern was the research program of two scientists working in the cell biology department at the medical school—Jerry W. Shay, PhD and Woodring "Woody" Wright, MD, PhD. Shay and Wright were collaborators who, among other things, worked on the molecular and cellular events involved in cells becoming immortal—an important step in the development of cancer. Most cells in a human or animal have the capacity for only limited cell division before safety controls block them from further proliferation and they become "senescent." Stem cells that have the capacity for indefinite proliferation are a notable exception to this rule. While reviewing the research interests of faculty at UT Southwestern School of Medicine, I learned that Shay and Wright were studying these safety controls and methods for overcoming the blocks to extend proliferation in different types of cultured cells. One of my goals was to develop methods to generate sufficient human corneal endothelial cells in culture for experiments in my lab and, potentially, to augment the endothelial cells on donor corneas that had insufficient endothelial cells to be used for corneal transplantation. Brimming with enthusiasm, I scheduled an appointment to meet Jerry and Woody shortly after I arrived in Dallas. At the agreed time, I made my way over to the building that housed their labs in the medical school. As I walked down the corridor scanning the room numbers, I noticed two men standing at the end of the hall watching me. As I got closer, I recognized Dr. Shay and Dr. Wright from photos I'd seen in a UT Southwestern research faculty brochure.

"Hi, I'm Steve Wilson," I said with a smile, thrusting out my hand.

"Nice to meet you, Steve," the taller of the two men replied with a grin. "I'm Jerry Shay. Woody and I were just discussing why an ophthalmologist would want to meet us, and the only thing we could figure out was you might have gotten confused about a paper we published on enucleation several years ago. But that was enucleation of cells, not eyes."

"No, I'm not confused—at least about this," I replied with a laugh. "I want to use your SV40 large T antigen and E6/E7 systems to generate cell lines so I can study growth factor and receptor expression, cell senescence and other functions in human corneal cells."

"Really?" Shay asked with surprise, glancing at Woody.

"That's right," I responded amusedly. "I attended graduate school in molecular biology and biochemistry before medical school."

We all shared a good laugh and Jerry showed me into his office. That day Jerry and I began a collaboration that would last for the next seven years and would include a shared NIH grant from the National Cancer Institute on stromal-epithelial interactions in normal and cancerous breast cells. This partnership was probably the single most important event in my early faculty research career.

Within a few months, Shay helped me generate new corneal endothelial cell strains, many of which are still used by cornea researchers throughout the world. Using these cells, along with cells cultured from the discarded remnants of human donor corneas, my technician and I generated exciting new data and published several papers in prestigious eye research journals like *Experimental Eye Research* and *Investigative Ophthalmology and Visual Sciences*. By March of 1991, I'd generated sufficient data to submit my first NIH grant to the National Eye Institute. By that summer, I was notified that my "RO1" proposal *Corneal Endothelial Cell Growth and Senescence* had been ranked in the top ten percent of grants submitted for the visual sciences.

"That's incredible!" one of my young colleagues commented upon hearing about the score. "I've never heard of a score that high on a first submission."

I didn't realize at that moment how fortunate I'd been, but my spirits were dampened just a few months later when, instead of the award notice detailing my funding, I received a gut-wrenching letter from the National Eye Institute notifying me they'd decided to delay funding until at least September of 1992 rather than funding the grant as expected on December 1, 1991. As might be expected, I was outraged by the unexplained decision. I'd worked my tail off for years to get to the point where I could submit an NIH grant ,and after getting a very high score, was then told the grant wouldn't be awarded after all—at least for nearly another year. It was a devastating setback that put my lab in limbo. I couldn't support a research fellow or hire another technician to help with the research, and I didn't have the funds to explore other areas I'd detailed in the new grant. But what could I do about it? In a fit of frustration, I naively decided to do the only thing I could—write my U.S. congressman and senators about the unfairness of the decision made by NIH and the impact it would have on my lab and research program.

I know now that writing a letter to my representatives was a rather stupid thing to do, at least at that stage of my career. If my lab were to become successful, I'd be dependent on the good graces of NEI staff for the balance of my research career (and many of these professionals were so supportive of me over the last 25 years). But at such a critical moment in my development as a researcher, I could think only of the present and what the delay meant to my program. I mailed off the letters and two weeks later, again without explanation, and much to my surprise, I received an award notice funding my grant immediately. To this day, I don't know whether the letters I wrote to my federal representatives had anything to do with the sudden reversal by the National Eye Institute. It's possible they did and in the process I angered NEI staff, but none of them ever mentioned it to me. On the other hand, knowing them as I do now, I wouldn't have expected them to say anything.

As it turned out, this was only the first of many frustrations I had with NIH and its system of grant review and funding during the next twenty-five years. Despite these disappointments, I owe the National Institutes of Health, the National Eye Institute, and really the American people, an enormous debt of gratitude, because without this funding support, I'd never have accomplished anything meaningful in research. I'd be remiss not to thank two wonderful NEI administrators who helped me immensely over the years—Lore Anne McNicol, PhD and George A. McKie, DVM, PhD.

However, dealing with the cold and inflexible review system at the Center for Scientific Review—where grants undergo "peer evaluation" and ranking for funding—was always challenging, and as I will detail later, at times downright demoralizing.

I'd been on the faculty at UT Southwestern only for about a year when the ophthalmology department administrator came to find me in my office late one Friday afternoon.

"Dr. McCulley sent me to let you know," she began after greeting me, "Dwight Cavanagh and Jamie Jester have agreed to move their lab here from Georgetown University. What do you think?"

I stared back with surprise for a moment and then shrugged my shoulders. "It sounds like it's a done deal. I'd say at this point my opinion doesn't matter one way or the other."

"Well, Dr. McCulley just wanted to make sure you heard it from him first. Have a nice weekend."

James Jester, PhD, was a well-respected corneal researcher, and there would be no reason for me to be upset about him coming to the department. I'd have a colleague with overlapping interests and someone to collaborate with on research.

H. Dwight Cavanagh, MD, PhD, had come through the department a couple months earlier and interviewed with many of the faculty members in the department under the guise of "providing an outside evaluation of the department." My colleagues and I hadn't thought much about it at the time since outside departmental evaluations were not that uncommon. None of us, however, had suspected the real purpose of his visit. To be sure, I knew only a few details regarding Cavanagh's background, but what I did know was reason for concern. He'd been a powerful chairman of ophthalmology at Emory University in Atlanta in the 1970s and 1980s and had built a well-respected powerhouse of a program, but had been forced out under dubious circumstances a few years earlier. A book, *Waking up Blind*, authored by an Atlanta adversary of Dr. Cavanagh's, was written about the episode. Whatever the specific details, I've always felt just about everyone deserves a second chance. So, I welcomed Cavanagh when he showed up a few months later. However, I quickly learned something else about the man…when you talked with him, it was almost impossible to get a word in edgewise. There's one brief conversation I remember having with him while waiting for the elevator outside the department offices a few months after he arrived.

"So, you got your NIH grant; that's great," Cavanagh said, nodding his head up and down several times for emphasis. "That's really great. Now just be content with that and hustle your tail off to get your work done. My advice is to not apply for any more NIH grants. You don't want to piss people off."

Taken aback, I quickly changed the subject as we stepped into the elevator. That was one piece of advice I promptly ignored. Even at that early stage in my career, I knew that one of the foremost goals of an academician was to attract as much research support as possible. That was the only way to build a first-class research program and have a major impact on one's chosen field of study.

That same year, in 1992, I was named a "Research to Prevent Blindness William and Mary Greve International Research Scholar" in recognition of the importance of our work. This award also provided critical funds to increase the pace of our early research.

My technician and I worked hard over the next two years. Along with a number of vision research collaborators, we not only completed most of the work outlined in my first NIH grant, but also made a number of other significant contributions to understanding the biology of the cornea. These included characterization of several growth factor and receptor systems through which the cells of the cornea communicate with each other, including the novel discovery of two alternative receptors used by cells to regulate their responses to key growth factors during wound healing. In collaboration with Jerry Shay, we also demonstrated that these growth factors and novel receptors were also expressed in breast tissues. Within two years, we'd published papers in both fields and generated sufficient preliminary data to apply for two more NIH grants: one entitled *Corneal epithelial cell growth factors and receptors,* submitted to the National Eye Institute, and a joint grant with Jerry Shay; *Stromal-Epithelial Interactions in Breast Cancer,* submitted to the National Cancer Institute. Both R01 grants received high scores from the NIH study sections that evaluated them and appeared certain to be funded in late 1994.

But that's when the National Eye Institute threw me another wicked curveball. After grants submitted to NIH are evaluated and ranked by area-specific study sections organized by the Center for Scientific Review (CSR), they then pass to one of the institutes that make up NIH, depending on the area of focus of the proposal. At the National Eye Institute, the National Advisory Eye Council—a group of ten or so scientists and clinician–scientists selected by the institute director—subsequently review the rankings provided by the study section and act upon the grants. The NEI director, and several other NEI and NIH staff members, also serve on the council and attend the meetings. The NEI staffers set the agendas for "the Council" meetings, determining what will be discussed. Most of the time, this step in the funding process is merely a formality and rarely do the members of the Council alter the decisions made by the study sections that evaluate vision-related grants. Thus, grants typically get funded according to their priority scores, depending on the funds available to support extramural research that particular year. Occasionally, the Council decides to boost the priority of a grant that has "high program relevance" to a fundable level or makes some other minor adjustments, but rarely more. But that wasn't the case when my second NEI vision research grant came before the Council. A few weeks after the committee met, an NEI staff member notified me that, "the Council has decided on a new policy." Henceforth, no clinician-scientist could simultaneously be a principal investigator (PI) on more than two NIH grants, if one or more of the grants were funded by the National Eye Institute, even if the investigator spent most of his or her time in research. In my case, however, the Council and NEI staff decided I'd be given the option of combining my *two* NEI grants, my original corneal endothelial grant and the new grant *Corneal epithelial growth factors and receptors,* into *one* grant. If I did so, I'd be awarded half of the additional funding the new grant would have brought to my laboratory. In recognition of the decrease in funding I'd incur by combining the two National Eye Institute grants, I was instructed by NEI staff to decide which of the proposed areas of research in the two grants (called specific aims) I would abandon and which I would pursue.

There was nothing to be gained in arguing the decision based on the new policy; it wouldn't have accomplished anything. I grumbled a bit to the NEI staff member in charge of the extramural cornea research portfolio, but acquiesced to the decision. I guess I could have sent off another batch of letters to my congressman and senators, but I was several years wiser and at that point I appreciated the impact this course of action could have on my future career and my standing with NEI staff, including the director of the National Eye Institute, Carl Kupfer, MD.

Kupfer ruled as the first and only director of NEI from 1970 to 2000, after Congress established the institute in 1968. I'd come to understand that Kupfer wasn't someone to be taken lightly. I've known many staff and scientists at NEI over the years, and I've heard it said many times that Kupfer freely gave professional titles at the institute, but never yielded significant power. He and he alone made all the important decisions—even the mundane ones. For those who don't know the man, the best analogy I can make to Dr. Kupfer's power, influence, and style at NEI was J. Edgar Hoover's dominance of the Federal Bureau of Investigation. Similar to Hoover's tenure at the FBI, Kupfer made many important contributions to vision research as director of NEI, such as demanding that a large portion of the NEI budget go to funding extramural investigator-initiated research grants that promoted the growth of vision research programs at universities throughout the United States. However, many inside and outside the NEI accused him of being petty and closed-minded. I'll never know for sure whether my earlier letters to Congress came to his attention, but if they did, this new policy "established by the National Advisory Eye Council" could have been my payback. One thing is certain: the members of the Council didn't just think up the new policy on their own. At any particular moment in time, almost all the Council members are NEI-funded investigators and as such are beholden to the NEI director. In the case of Kupfer, all understood that what he valued most from his wards was obsequiousness. Thus, I doubt they would have fiddled with NEI funding policy without his knowledge and blessing, if not his direction. Who were these National Advisory Eye Council members in 1994? I've long since forgotten most of the individual's names, but there's one I'll never forget. The representative in the area of cornea research, my field of investigation, was none other than my mentor Herbert E. Kaufman, MD, Director of the LSU Eye Center in New Orleans. As "the chief" himself would frequently say, "Interesting, isn't it?"

The net effect of the "new Council policy" was that my laboratory ended up with less total funding than if I'd just stuck to vision research and gotten the two NEI grants, as Jerry Shay and I split the funding from the smaller cancer grant funded by the National Cancer Institute. Thus, I had $420,000 per year in direct cost funding rather than $550,000—essentially three fewer technician or post-doctoral fellow positions to carry out the labor-intensive work detailed in our grants. The $420,000 probably seems like an enormous amount of funding to the layperson, but it's not for laboratories involved in expensive cell and molecular biology research. Many labs run by PhDs or MDs working in this or similar areas had far more funding—as much as a million dollars of funding per year—and it was difficult to remain a contender in such a highly competitive field when one's lab had less funding than others in the field. I knew several researchers who had three or four NIH grants with twice the total funding I had. Penalizing an investigator for success—what a great way to motivate clinician–scientists and foster collaborative interaction between researchers in different fields! After thinking over my options for a few weeks, I decided to abandon my research devoted to corneal endothelial cells and corneal transplantation. I never worked on corneal endothelial cell biology again (until just recently) and often wondered what contributions I might have made if the Council and NEI hadn't slashed my funding for that area.

Several months after that Council meeting, I showed up for the annual Kaufman Fellow's Dinner—the last I attended because, by that time, only a handful of people came—at the annual meeting of the American Academy of Ophthalmology. That year, the meeting was in San Francisco and about twenty of us dined at a five-star Chinese restaurant at Ghirardelli Square. There was a shortage of cabs following the dinner and, after waiting nearly thirty minutes, four of us, including Dr. Kaufman, piled into a taxi that the doorman had flagged down. The group made small talk until another former fellow, who carried most of the conversation, got out at his hotel. At that point, there was a lull in the conversation.

"A funny thing happened at the National Advisory Eye Council meeting a couple of months back," Kaufman offered awkwardly from the front passenger seat. "Steve Wilson had too many NIH grants."

I glanced at the fellow sitting beside me in the back seat and he stared back in silence with a knowing frown.

"I guess I would have been better off just sticking to eye research," I replied, referring to my shared National Cancer Institute grant.

"Well, I'm proud of what you've accomplished," he continued as the cab pulled up to my hotel. "Keep up the good work."

"Thank you, Dr. Kaufman," I said, knowing that was all he'd have to say about what happened. I fished through my pocket for my wallet.

"Don't worry about it," Dr. Kaufman said, turning in his seat, "I'll get the fare."

"Thank you," I replied, scooting out of the car. "Have a good meeting."

I stood there and watched as the cab pulled away.

***

There were a lot of changes in my personal life during those first couple of years in Dallas. My marriage to my first wife didn't last the first year in "the Big D." My wife longed to return to California, and I wanted to pursue the best opportunities in academic medicine, wherever that happened to be. Our relationship ended in amiable divorce in the summer of 1991.

I began dating again after we split up, but the first girlfriend only lasted a few months. On a fall evening later that year, I showed up early for a meeting of the Dallas Academy of Ophthalmology held in the Faculty Club at UT Southwestern. I was standing with a small group of ophthalmology residents in the middle of the nearly empty room when the entrance door opened and a striking brunette with long curly hair stepped into the room. As all heads turned to admire the petite beauty, the ill-at-ease young woman made a beeline for the opposite side of the club to where another representative of Merck Pharmaceutical Corporation was standing. (Merck was hosting the dinner that night.) The residents and I resumed our conversation, but I wandered over to where the two women were talking a few minutes later.

"Hi, I'm Steve Wilson," I said to the smiling brunette. "I'm here to save you from the residents."

"Nice to meet you, Dr. Wilson," she replied with a chuckle. "I'm Jennifer and this is Martha."

Martha grinned with amusement, but left a moment later as I struck up a bantering conversation with Jennifer, completely oblivious to the growing crowd in the room.

The dinner was served and I joined Jennifer at a table with several other physicians. She had to shush me more than once when the speaker finally began his talk. Halfway through the talk, much to my chagrin, she got up to leave. I followed her out to the foyer and said, "Where are you going?" "Church choir practice," she replied. "Well, can I at least have your phone number?" That was the beginning of a slow-developing romance that culminated in our wedding at the Mansion on Turtle Creek on New Year's Eve 1994, just over four years later. Those who know us well will tell you, there's a lot more to our story—a whole lot more—but that's a tale for another time. For now, let me just say that Jennifer remains my wife and closest friend, and the wonderful mother of my three amazing children.

***

I managed to put the NIH funding disappointment behind me and continued my research on cell interactions in the cornea, and in the normal and cancerous breast tissues. The medical school rewarded me with a new lab with over three times more space, but, unfortunately, it was in another building five minutes away from the ophthalmology department. The labs around us worked in microbiology and other fields unrelated to our area of interest, which made us feel isolated. Nonetheless, we continued to make important contributions to understanding the mechanisms regulating wound healing in the cornea. One of our most important discoveries related to corneal physiology was made in 1993. Over at least the twenty years prior to my lab opening at UT Southwestern, multiple investigators independently discovered, and rediscovered, that the cells called keratocytes in the anterior corneal stroma seemed to disappear when the surface layer of the cornea, called the epithelium, was injured. Different researchers proposed varying explanations for this observation, including artifacts from histological processing of the corneal tissue and swelling of the tissue. The best I can figure, Claes Dohlman, MD, former chairman of ophthalmology, and his colleagues at Harvard School of Medicine, were the first to notice this phenomenon in 1968.

Dohlman CH, Gasset AR, Rose J. "The Effect of the Absence of Corneal Epithelium or Endothelium on Stromal Keratocytes." *Investigative Ophthalmology and Visual Sciences,* 1968;7:520.

I hypothesized this disappearance could represent death of the cells through a planned and highly orchestrated form of "programmed cell death" called apoptosis. I still recall my elation when I looked through a microscope at a histological section of an injured cornea stained with the TUNEL assay that detects fragmented DNA characteristic of apoptosis. Every keratocyte in the anterior third of the stroma of the specimen was darkly stained, indicating they were indeed undergoing apoptosis—a finding we subsequently confirmed with electron microscopy. We went on to demonstrate that the dead cells in the anterior stroma were replenished within a week or two of the injury.

I presented our observations for the first time at the annual meeting of the Association for Research in Vision and Ophthalmology (ARVO) in Sarasota, Florida, in 1994, and published the work two years later—after initial rejection by *Investigative Ophthalmology and Visual Sciences.*

Wilson SE, et al., "Epithelial Injury Induces Keratocyte Apoptosis: Hypothesized Role for the Interleukin-1 System in the Modulation of Corneal Tissue Organization and Wound Healing," *Experimental Eye Research,* 1996; 62:325.

Up until that time, keratocytes were thought of as relatively quiescent cells that spent their time maintaining and repairing the collagen and other matrix materials that made up the corneal stroma. When I finished my ARVO presentation, David Maurice, PhD, a towering pillar of corneal research, stood up and approached the microphone in the aisle, an event sufficient to strike terror in the heart of any young cornea investigator. Dr. Maurice was legendary for posing thorny probing questions.

"Young man," he began in his authoritative, haughty British accent, "are you also suggesting that keratocytes have the capacity to undergo cell division?"

"Yes, Dr. Maurice," I replied confidently, "after twenty to thirty percent of the cells in the stroma die, I don't see how the cell density could otherwise return to normal two weeks later."

"Hmm," he muttered, yielding the microphone to the next inquisitor, much to my relief.

It would be several years before James D. Zieske, PhD, and his colleagues at Schepens Eye Research Institute in Boston, demonstrated conclusively that the remaining keratocytes in the posterior and peripheral stroma did indeed begin to proliferate twelve to twenty-four hours after the original epithelial injury.

Hutcheon SR, Guimaraes SR, and Zieske JD. "Keratocyte Proliferation in Response to Epithelial Debridement," *Investigative Ophthalmology and Visual Sciences,* 1999;40:S622.

But the genie was forever out of the bottle, and my lab, along with several others, continued to unravel the complex cell-cell interactions and cellular changes that are fundamental to understanding wound healing in the cornea. To this day, these cellular changes in the cornea after injury or infection remain the major focus of my laboratory research program.

This keratocyte apoptosis response is immediate—occurring before an excised cornea that has an epithelial scrape can be plunged into fixative. James M. Hill, PhD and Roger Beuerman,

PhD—both also at LSU Eye Center—and I collaborated a few years later to demonstrate that the response likely served as an immediate defense mechanism to prevent the spread of viruses—like smallpox, herpes simplex virus (HSV) and adenoviruses—from the epithelium of the cornea to underlying stromal keratocytes (a cellular firebreak of sorts) prior to mobilization of the immune response.

Wilson SE, Pedroza L, Beuerman R, Hill JM. Herpes simplex virus type-1 infection of corneal epithelial cells induces apoptosis of the underlying keratocytes. *Experimental Eye Research.* 1997;64:775.

It would be over twenty more years before my postdoctoral fellows and I demonstrated that the same apoptosis response occurs in posterior stromal keratocytes when the corneal endothelial cells are gently scraped, initiating a posterior corneal wound healing response, and likely also serving as a cellular firebreak to help retard the extension of viruses like HSV and cytomegalovirus that can infect the corneal endothelium (HSV or CMV endotheliitis) from spreading into the corneal stroma prior to a response by the immune system.

Medeiros CS, Lassance L, Saikia P, Wilson SE. Posterior stromal keratocyte apoptosis triggered by mechanical endothelial injury and nidogen-1 production in the cornea. *Experimental Eye Research.* 2018;172:30.

My group also made a new clinical research discovery in 1993. Will Lee, MD, professor of internal medicine at UT Southwestern, and I, along with several other colleagues, discovered that three patients with a horrible, unrelenting corneal ulcerative disease called Mooren's corneal ulcers had underlying chronic hepatitis C virus (HCV) infections in their livers and that the disease in these patient's corneas responded to interferon alpha injections used to treat the hepatitis C virus-mediated liver disease. We published our findings in perhaps the most prestigious journal in medicine, The New England Journal of Medicine.

Wilson SE, Lee WM, Murakami C, Weng J, Moninger GA, "Mooren's Corneal Ulcers and Hepatitis C Virus Infection: A New Association." *New England Journal of Medicine,* 1993;329:62.

Although further research has shown that only five percent, or so, of Mooren's ulcer patients have underlying HCV infection, the discovery provided treatment for those who do have the HCV-associated disease and a paradigm for the type of underlying disorders that had the potential to lead to Mooren's ulcers.

As my lab grew, I sought involvement in training graduate students in one of the basic science programs at UT Southwestern. I applied to become a graduate advisor and faculty member in the program, but was turned down because "I had too many first author papers on my curriculum vitae, as opposed to senior-author papers written by students." In my opinion, it was a bogus effort to exclude me so there would be more graduate students for professors already in the program, since at that point I'd been out of my fellowship for only four years. I was so disappointed by this decision that it was a major factor in my eventual departure from UT Southwestern.

Another issue was the low level of support for vision research at UT Southwestern. Many of my colleagues inside and outside ophthalmology believed that the all-consuming goal of the president and dean of the medical school was to win Nobel Prizes. UT Southwestern already had four Nobel Prize winners: Michael Brown, MD, and Joseph Goldstein, MD, received the 1985 prize in physiology or medicine for their work in cholesterol metabolism; Johann Deisenhofer, PhD, received the 1988 prize in chemistry for elucidating the three-dimensional structure of a large membrane-bound protein molecule; and Alfred Gillman, MD, PhD, received the 1994 prize in physiology or medicine for his work on G-proteins and intracellular signaling. It's hard to argue with this impressive record at UT Southwestern, but it seemed that a disproportionately enormous share of the available research support at the university went to funding these labs and those viewed as *prospective* Nobel Prize winners, while many of the rest of us received little institutional support. To be sure, vision research wasn't a priority in Dallas like it was at other institutions—like Johns Hopkins, UCLA, Washington University, and the University of Miami—where prominent eye institutes were located.

There was an additional disappointment that convinced me I needed to consider other opportunities. The ophthalmology department became a participant in the clinical trials of a new excimer laser manufactured by a company that was seeking to gain approval from the FDA, and despite my prior training and experience, I was not included as one of the co-investigators in that study. I began to feel I'd always be the "junior" cornea specialist in the department, despite the chairman supporting my promotion to tenured associate professor on the regular, as opposed to clinical, faculty tract.

Near the end of 1993, Henry Kaplan, MD, the chairman of ophthalmology at Washington University in St. Louis (yes, the same university that was the first to accept me to medical school), contacted me to ask if I'd be interested in moving my research program to the growing ophthalmology and vision research program at that preeminent institution. I decided to explore the opportunity, and after making several visits to interview and evaluate the program, I accepted an offer to move to St. Louis. I met with Dr. McCulley, submitted my resignation at UT Southwestern, and began making arrangements to leave Dallas. About two months before I was due to depart for St. Louis, I selected a real estate agent and made an appointment the next weekend to list my home for sale. As the day of our meeting approached, I developed a strange premonition that something wasn't right. To this day I'm not sure what triggered my uneasy feelings, but my angst grew when Dr. Kaplan didn't return my call on a Friday. The next morning, just an hour before my appointment with the real estate agent, I managed to convince the operator at Washington University to put my call through to Dr. Kaplan's home.

"Hello, Dr. Kaplan," I said when he answered the call himself, "this is Steve Wilson. My real estate agent will be here soon and I was just checking to make sure everything's on track."

An uncomfortable silence ensued before Kaplan finally cleared his throat. "Didn't you get my letter?"

"No," I said, my mouth suddenly feeling dry as a bone, "what letter?"

"Well, just last week the department merged with a group here in St. Louis and the faculty feel there'll be too many cornea specialists in the system. I've decided to withdraw my offer."

"But, Dr. Kaplan, I'm seventy-five percent research," I replied incredulously.

"I'm sorry," he responded uncomfortably.

I took a deep breath. "You could have called," I said pointedly, before setting the receiver down on the phone, not waiting for his reply.

I got a two paragraph letter from Kaplan the following Monday notifying me that the offer had been withdrawn. As fate would have it, the next time I ran into Hank Kaplan was four years later when Jennifer and I stepped into an elevator in the Intercontinental Hotel in Paris while attending the International Congress of Eye Research. Kaplan and his wife, the only other passengers on the elevator, looked up with surprise and we all stood staring at each other for a moment. A few months prior to this chance encounter, Kaplan had been unexpectedly dismissed as the chair of ophthalmology at Washington University in St. Louis, for reasons that never became general knowledge. I, on the other hand, had just accepted the chair of ophthalmology at University of Washington in Seattle. The irony of the moment didn't escape either of us.

"Congratulations," Kaplan offered rather sheepishly.

"Thank you, Hank," I replied, as the elevator doors opened and our wives stepped out into the lobby. "I hope you enjoy Paris."

Jennifer and I turned and headed out of the hotel down the *Champs Elysees* toward the *Arc de Triomphe.*

Sometimes, it's the things that don't happen that determine the course of a career and that certainly was true in my case. Jim McCulley graciously took me back into the fold and I picked up with my research and clinical practice at UT Southwestern—as though nothing had happened.

It was about this time that I began to pursue creative writing—a hobby I'd dabbled with since college when I wrote lyrics for songs. I'd also written a couple of short stories, none of which I'd ever attempted to publish. My academic career in medicine and science necessitated loads of writing, but that was a very different style compared to short stories or novels. Jennifer and I were returning from vacation in early 1994, and finishing a novel by one of my favorite authors, I stuffed the paperback into my bag.

"How'd you like it?" Jennifer asked, looking up from her own book.

"The plot was pretty lame," I replied, leaning back into my seat. "I think I could think up a better story."

"Why don't you then?" she muttered amusedly, going back to her book.

That night I sat down at my computer, a Macintosh Plus, and began drafting the outline for a novel that came to be titled *The Price of Privilege*, the tale of ophthalmologist Justin Chase, who's accused, tried, and convicted of murdering his estranged wife on the basis of tainted DNA evidence. I did research for the novel by visiting the famous old building that housed the Dallas Police Department—the same building where Jack Ruby shot Lee Harvey Oswald—and the morgue at the County Coroner's office behind Parkland Memorial Hospital. Much to Jennifer's chagrin, I also dragged her to Huntsville for a three-day holiday stay at the Bluebird Bed and Breakfast so I could study the Texas prison system, including the former Ellis I unit that housed the most lethal death row in the U.S.A. and where my tale reached its climax. The resulting novel has yet to be published, but it began my process of learning to write dialogue and presaged *Winter in Kandahar*, my first work of fiction published in late 2003, followed thereafter by *Ascent from Darkness* and *The Benghazi Affair* that make up the Stone Waverly Trilogy. Along the way, I also wrote *The Ghosts of Anatolia: An Epic Journey to Forgiveness*, a novel that won the Foreword Reviews Book of the Year Gold Award in Fiction in 2010 and the Runner-up Award in General Fiction at the Hollywood Book Festival in 2011.

Nothing had changed, however, with my adequate, but at times frustrating, situation at UT Southwestern, so I was receptive when a colleague called nine months later to tell me about an opportunity at the Cleveland Clinic Foundation in Cleveland, Ohio. Within a few months, I'd agreed with the new chairman, Hilel Lewis, MD, to move my laboratory to Cleveland. My primary appointment was to be in the Department of Ophthalmology, with a secondary appointment in the Department of Cell Biology, where my laboratory would be located. One of the factors that attracted me to the Cleveland Clinic, an institution with an eye program that at that time wouldn't have been considered in the top fifty academic ophthalmology departments in America, was the plan to build a new eye institute. Another factor was the assurance of the chairman that I'd be included in the refractive surgery program—in addition to cornea and external disease.

This time the opportunity didn't evaporate. Jennifer and I sold our home in Plano and headed for Cleveland in the early summer of 1995, just a month after my promotion to tenured associate professor became final at UT Southwestern.

I'm grateful to James McCulley for the opportunities he provided to me at UT Southwestern. Many chairmen of academic departments throughout medicine, not only ophthalmology, pay lip service to research, enthusiastically describing opportunities during the recruitment process, but expecting young faculty members to spend eighty or ninety percent of their time in clinical care while struggling to establish their program in clinical or basic research, and often providing only minimal support to achieve their goals. That was not the case with Dr. McCulley. His support played an important role in my early development. I strived to similarly mentor young faculty when I became chairman of a department, and I believe it is critical for other leaders in academic medicine to do the same.

I queried Dr. McCulley about his job as chairman of ophthalmology during my tenure at UT Southwestern. I recall him saying, "I like the job fine, but I hate the people problems." At the time, his comment didn't mean much to me, but I would come to know exactly what he meant a few years later. I'm sure I made my own contribution to his "people problems" as I lobbied for research support, lab space, clinical opportunities, and even salary. I guess I could have been characterized as a rather challenging faculty member. McCulley and I laugh about it now. I've long since come to realize that the most talented faculty members are also the most challenging. Learning to keep these gifted, but demanding, people happy and productive is one of the most important duties of any department chairman.

Chapter 7
An All Too Brief Sojourn at the Cleveland Clinic

I received a call from the chairman at the Cleveland Clinic, Hilel Lewis, MD, just about ten days before Jennifer and I departed from Dallas. After exchanging pleasantries, he cut to the chase. The current medical director of refractive surgery at the Cleveland Clinic had just announced his departure to start a private refractive surgery practice just across town. Dr. Lewis asked if I'd be willing to assume this position directing refractive surgery once I arrived in Cleveland. Stunned by the news, I considered his proposal for a few moments, before accepting the position—as long as he agreed to recruit someone else if the responsibilities interfered with my research program. He agreed, and in a heartbeat the course of my medical career changed forever.

I began my appointment a few weeks later and found the refractive program to be in turmoil. The departing medical director and I were scheduled to overlap a month. All of the employees of the program, save one, had agreed to leave with him to the new facility a few miles east of the Cleveland Clinic. It turned out that the lone holdout, a refractive surgery technician, was also leaving, but stayed behind for a couple of months to report on my activities. It was my first and only experience with academic espionage! As it turned out, the circumstances couldn't have been better for me. The mass departure of the existing refractive personnel provided me the opportunity to hand pick new staff and mold the center as I saw fit. Within a few days of my arrival, one of the best ophthalmology operating room nurses at the Cleveland Clinic approached me about heading up the staff in the reorganized section. I hired her immediately. An excellent technician soon followed, along with a new refractive surgery fellow from Brazil, Marco Helena, MD, who decided to stay at the Cleveland Clinic rather than follow the defectors. Marco was the second of more than a dozen excellent research and clinical fellows from Brazil I trained. My new position was off to an auspicious, albeit unexpected, start.

There remained one major predicament: the FDA had still not approved the excimer laser and the departing refractive group was heavily involved in performing radial keratotomy (RK) and automated lamellar keratoplasty (ALK)—procedures I felt uncomfortable about due to lingering concerns about patient safety and clinical outcomes. There were two patients scheduled for RK before I arrived who had already had the procedure in one eye, and after taking a refresher course, I performed their surgeries. The results were reasonably good, but my experience with the imprecision of the procedure only reinforced my bias and I decided against doing any more RK procedures. I never did perform ALK on patients, especially after we evaluated and published the results of the cases that had already been done in the journal Ophthalmology.

Helena MC, Robin JB, & Wilson SE. "Analysis of Corneal Topography after Automated Lamellar Keratoplasty (ALK)." *Ophthalmology,* 1997; 104:950.

We concluded that ALK was inaccurate and associated with far too many complications—many potentially serious. The departing group was performing some excimer laser PRK procedures with a Chiron excimer laser that was in clinical trials, but that instrument left with the departing faculty member (fortuitously, because that particular model of excimer laser was never approved for use in the U.S.A.).

As fate would have it, the FDA approved the Summit Apex excimer laser for correction of low to moderate myopia a few weeks later on October 25, 1995. The Cleveland Clinic purchased the new laser and I took the FDA-mandated courses while it was installed. Soon, we were busy beyond our wildest expectations. So busy, that refractive surgery occupied all of my clinical time. I made the decision to stop performing cataract surgery and corneal transplants, except for emergency situations when I was on-call. Shortly thereafter, I became a certified instructor for the Summit Apex excimer laser.

It didn't take me long to discover that refractive surgery was a perfect complement to my basic research program. First, there were very few emergencies in refractive surgery. Thus, for the most part, when I was in my laboratory, I didn't have to worry about being called to clinic to care for patients referred with corneal ulcers, transplant rejections, or other urgent corneal problems. There were several other clinical faculty members at the Cleveland Clinic who specialized in caring for these patients. Thus, my research time was just that—dedicated to research. In addition, the surgical outcomes and many of the potential complications of refractive surgery are associated with corneal wound healing and, therefore, my clinical and research activities were a perfect match.

My research laboratory was also up and running quickly. I purchased new equipment before I arrived and hired a PhD postdoctoral fellow shortly after my arrival. Several additional researchers joined our team during the first couple of years in Cleveland, and the laboratory continued to make important contributions related to cell-cell communications and wound healing in the cornea. I was invited to serve on several editorial boards, including *Investigative Ophthalmology and Visual Sciences* and *Experimental Eye Research,* two of the premiere vision research journals, in addition to being elected by my peers to serve on the Program Planning Committee for the cornea section of the Association for Research in Vision and Ophthalmology and being appointed to the Long-range Planning Committee for that organization. I was also appointed Professor of Cell Biology, Neurobiology, and Anatomy at the Cleveland Clinic Foundation Health Sciences Center of the Ohio State University. These activities, in addition to my clinical and research responsibilities at the Cleveland Clinic, kept me extremely busy.

The most rewarding aspect of our brief sojourn at the Cleveland Clinic Foundation was the opportunity to interact and collaborate with several outstanding scientists inside and outside of vision research. Joe Hollyfield, PhD, joined the Department of Ophthalmology at the Cleveland Clinic as the Director of Ophthalmic Research just before I arrived and became a wonderful colleague and friend. George R. Stark, PhD, a member of the prestigious National Academy of

Sciences, was the director of research at the Cleveland Clinic Foundation. George and I collaborated on several projects related to Jak-Stat and other pathways involved in communication within individual cells. I found the research environment at the Cleveland Clinic to be superb, and this was a wonderful period during my career.

About the only troubling aspect of those three years was lingering angst among my fellow faculty members in the Department of Ophthalmology—related to ongoing changes the chairman made to enhance the quality and national standing of the department. There were some decisions I didn't agree with at the time, but I would come to understand all too well that change was necessary, and inevitable, when a new chairman came to a department. Status quo and comfort do not necessarily lend themselves to excellence, and change is always painful for faculty and staff who've found a cozy niche under the prior department leadership.

One of my most exciting responsibilities in Cleveland was the opportunity to participate in planning and designing the new eye institute building at the Cleveland Clinic. Ground breaking occurred during my second year, and a beautiful new building designed by renowned architect Cesar Pelli began to rise at the corner of Euclid and East 105th. My contributions were in the design of the refractive surgery center and, to a lesser extent, the research facilities. I had no clue at the time I would depart Cleveland before the building even opened and that I would not have an opportunity to work there for many years.

My personal life also underwent enormous change in Cleveland. Jennifer and I had grown up in modest newer homes in Texas and California, but on a lark we moved into a grand, three-story historic home in Shaker Heights—that cost a fraction of what we would have spent in Texas and California. We were only the third owners of the 1910 vintage French Colonial graced with English gardens overflowing with daffodils, tulips, daylilies, golden rods, azaleas, rhododendrons, roses, and Black-eyed Susans, surrounded by towering maples and oaks. The feature of the home we relished the most was the four-room basement the original owner assembled from an English pub that was forced out of business by prohibition in the 1920s. Fitted with a buzzer at the top of the stairs and three-inch thick carved wooden doors—along with hardwood floors, ceilings, and walls, an ornately carved bar that seated six, and an antique slate pool table—it had undoubtedly served as a speakeasy during the prohibition years. We entertained many new friends from the Cleveland Clinic and throughout the Cleveland area in that wonderful home that forever changed our perceptions of architectural beauty.

Jennifer and I settled into an idyllic existence, even learning to love the beauty of winter in Shaker Heights. We decided to start a family shortly after our arrival in Cleveland. Getting pregnant turned out to be quite a struggle, but finally in the early fall of 1998, tests confirmed that Jennifer was carrying *twins*, with a due date in March of 1998. What an incredible and fulfilling time that was for both of us.

•••

One morning in the fall of 1998, when Jennifer was a few months pregnant with the twins, I was editing a manuscript in my office, when my secretary popped her head through the door to tell me a Dr. Winn was calling from the University of Washington in Seattle. It turned out to be the Chair of Neurosurgery at the University of Washington School of Medicine, H. Richard Winn, MD. Dr. Winn told me he was leading the search committee for the position of chair of ophthalmology at the medical school in Seattle and that my name had been submitted as a potential candidate.

"Would you be interested in considering the position, Dr. Wilson?"

"Really?" I queried. "I thought that position was open a couple of years ago."

"Well, it was," he replied, "but the former dean died in a storm in the Himalayas and a new dean had to be selected before we could continue the search. I think it's an excellent opportunity for someone with your background and experience."

I knew little about the ophthalmology program at the University of Washington, but I did know that the university had an outstanding reputation in vision sciences, internal medicine, and neurosurgery. Becoming chairman of a department had been a long-term goal for me, but I hadn't anticipated an opportunity arriving this soon. My mind raced through a litany of pros and cons as Dr. Winn described details regarding the position. Finally, I decided there was no harm in considering the post.

"I'm interested," I finally replied. "How about if I speak with Jennifer tonight and give you a call tomorrow?"

"That'll be fine. Tell Jennifer all those things she's heard about the rain in Seattle were just rumors we spread to keep too many people from moving to the Pacific Northwest."

I called home and asked Jennifer out to dinner. "Great," she said, "I haven't had a chance to pick up anything." Jennifer had continued working for Merck and now was responsible for a large territory east of Cleveland. I made a reservation at our favorite restaurant—Tutto a' Pesto, a quaint little Italian café in Shaker Heights.

"Honey, how would you feel about moving to Seattle?" I asked after the waiter brought our drinks and took our order.

"Seattle?" she said, setting her bread back on her plate. "Why?"

"The chairman of the search committee for chair of ophthalmology at University of Washington called today to ask if I'd be interested in the job."

Jennifer's expression melted into a forlorn frown. "Steven," she said with a sigh, "you're settled in your lab and the new refractive program is going great, we have wonderful new friends, we just finished remodeling our house, we both love living in Shaker Heights, and I'm three months pregnant. Do you really think this is the right time?"

"Probably not, but why don't we at least look? They'll ask me to come alone for a first interview and then the dean probably won't offer me the job anyway. The worst that can happen is we'll end up spending a few days visiting Seattle. I've always wanted to see the Pike Place Market…you know, where those guys throw fish around."

"Okay," she replied, taking my hand with an understanding smile, "I'd like to see Seattle too, and I think you'd make a great chairman."

The next day I told my chairman, Hilel Lewis, about my decision to look at the position in Seattle and called Dick Winn. He made the arrangements for my first visit and I took a trip to Seattle a few weeks later.

Academic ophthalmology is a relatively small group. Two of my friends called in the weeks leading up to my first visit to tell me that they'd heard I'd be interviewing in Seattle and to let me know there were rumors going around it was a done deal. They'd both been told the position would be offered to the interim chair in the department, Richard Mills, MD, former president of the American Academy of Ophthalmology. According to the rumors, the university was merely going through the motions before it made an internal offer. I thanked my colleagues for their calls and began to wonder just what I was getting myself into. I decided to go ahead with my visit to Seattle anyway. After all, it might be the only chance I had to see white-capped Mount Rainier—at least if the sun were out!

Dick Winn, an unassuming-looking character with a perpetual grin and a certain panache, picked me up at the airport in Seattle. "I suppose you've heard this search is a done deal," he said straight away with his characteristic raspy tone, as we pulled away from the terminal.

"Actually, I have heard that," I replied, returning his smile.

"Well, Steve, I want to reassure you that nothing could be further from the truth. This is a real search and Paul Ramsey himself will tell you that when you see him. You can bank on it."

"I'm glad to hear it," I replied, glancing through the rain on the windshield at the long line of traffic trying to merge onto the freeway ahead of us.

We went on to talk about details regarding the history of the Department of Ophthalmology at UW (Carl Kupfer, MD had been the first chair for a brief period before becoming the first Director of the National Eye Institute), some of the faculty issues, and Dick's sense of the opportunity and problems I'd face if I came to Seattle. In retrospect, it was an honest and accurate assessment. I'd come to learn that Dick Winn said what he meant and meant what he said, and that I could rely on anything he told me.

My interviews were limited to the ten or so members of the search committee, in addition to the Executive Director of University of Washington Medical Center, Robert Muilenburg, and the Vice President for Medical Affairs and Dean of the School of Medicine, Paul G. Ramsey, M.D., in addition to a couple of other administrators from the medical school. I saw an ophthalmology department in desperate need of new blood and energy, complete remodeling of its labs and offices and additional space. There was one old laboratory area in the department that was little more than a 2200-square-foot storage closet. On the plus side, the department had newly remodeled clinics at University of Washington Medical Center and Harborview Medical Center. I met two faculty members from the department—Bryan Sires, MD, PhD, and Kris Palczewski, PhD, and both were enthusiastic about my coming to Seattle. Dick Winn hosted a dinner with several of the members of the search committee, many of whom were chairs of other departments at UW School of Medicine, at wonderful Canlis Restaurant overlooking the shimmering lights of Union Bay. It was a magical evening and I enjoyed everyone I met—all, that is, except one buffoon retina surgeon from the Department of Ophthalmology who repeatedly asked me how old I was in conversations with other members of the search committee, as if to emphasize my relative youth. This fellow went on to make it perfectly clear I was not his choice for the position in front of several other apologetic committee members. He was apparently assuming that the rumors about the position being reserved for the internal candidate were accurate. I dismissed him for what he was and didn't let his rudeness affect my perception of the others. It even snowed while I was there for that first visit to Seattle. At the time, I remember considering the snow a good omen.

I thought my first interview with Dean Paul Ramsey went well, although I sensed he might feel somewhat uncomfortable speaking one-on-one. We discussed faculty and space issues in the department, but talked only superficially about financial issues such as clinical and research revenues, endowments, and reserves. That, he said, would be included in a second interview—if one were scheduled. We also talked about my clinical specialty in refractive surgery and my vision for the future of the ophthalmology department and the vision research program at UW. After all, with over forty NEI-funded principal investigators in nine departments, UW clearly had one of the largest vision research programs in the world. All in all, I left feeling better about the opportunity at University of Washington than when I arrived. Jennifer, however, listened with trepidation to the details of my visit.

I went back to work at the Cleveland Clinic and a couple of weeks passed before I heard from Paul Ramsey. He was planning on traveling east in the next few weeks to watch his daughter participate in a sporting event, and he wanted to know if he could stop in Cleveland to see the Refractive Surgery Center at the Cleveland Clinic, and take Jennifer and me out to dinner. I told him we'd be delighted to see him and the visit was arranged.

Dr. Ramsey's visit to Cleveland was a short one. I gave him a tour of the ophthalmology department in the Crile Building of the Cleveland Clinic, including the excimer laser suite, and pointed out the new eye institute that was under construction on an adjacent parcel of land. Jennifer joined us for dinner at a restaurant downtown. I had the impression that Dr. Ramsey was just as interested in meeting my wife as he was seeing the refractive surgery facility, and I thought this was a wise approach since, in my experience, most chairman's spouses have a major impact on the important social affairs of academic departments. Jennifer was at her bright and beautiful best and I remember being so proud she was my wife. I'm sure she made a great impression.

Two weeks later, in early December, Dr. Ramsey's assistant called to schedule a second visit to the University of Washington. Jennifer had fallen on the stairs at home and broken her foot and was now six months pregnant on crutches. We made the trip together in mid-December. UW put us up for four nights at the Four Seasons Hotel in downtown Seattle. Jennifer and I enjoyed dinner alone the first evening at a five-star restaurant in downtown Seattle, followed by a performance by Cirque du Soleil. The next day, I had a series of meetings with individual faculty members from the Department of Ophthalmology, including the interim chair and internal candidate, Richard Mills, MD. Under the circumstances, Dr. Mills was remarkably gracious. I remembered wondering if I could have been as gracious if I were in his position. One thing he said at that first meeting, surprisingly our first ever despite the relatively small size of the ophthalmology field, stuck with me, "I've been surprised how easy this job is." I'm not certain, but I suspect he might not have agreed with his statement a few years later. I know I wouldn't have. The other department faculty members varied in attitude from extremely amiable to patently hostile. The latter applied to only a couple of long-term faculty members who clearly viewed me as an unwanted and unneeded intruder. I also had an opportunity to meet the former chair of the Department of Ophthalmology—for twenty-seven years—Robert Kalina, MD. Bob couldn't possibly have been more accepting or more gentlemanly and remained supportive, without being intrusive, during my entire tenure in Seattle. Looking back twenty years later, the mind-sets of the existing faculty of the department really didn't change much over the five years I held the position of chair at the University of Washington. Most supported the changes I brought to the department, but a few didn't and were hostile from the very beginning—either blatantly or in a passive-aggressive manner. Not surprisingly, the unreceptive faculty tended to be longstanding clinicians who'd grown comfortable in cushy tenured positions in the department and feared the changes I'd bring would rattle their tranquil existence. That, I believe, is a situation faced by every new chairman of an academic department—regardless of the field or institution. It is quite simply a fact of life one must be prepared to face when venturing into the position of a departmental chairman.

I also met with the ophthalmology department administrator who'd been in her position for more than a decade. She seemed pleasant enough, but even before meeting her, I'd already decided a change would be needed based on my discussions with several ophthalmology departmental faculty members. I'd need to learn details about medical school policies and departmental finances first, but I made a mental note to include an option to make that change in my agreement letter—assuming my candidacy progressed.

I had lunch that day with as many medical school department chairs as could attend, followed by a meeting with Brian McKenna, the head of the faculty practice plan UW Physicians, David E. Jaffe, the executive director of Harborview Medical Center, and several other administrators from throughout the medical school. I remember being skeptical about Brian McKenna within five minutes of beginning to speak with him. At the time, I didn't realize the importance his obvious limitations would take on for the medical school and me in the years to come.

Finally, after a very long day, I made my way to the dean's office for my last appointment with Paul Ramsey. He offered me coffee and then commenced our meeting with an unexpected declaration, "Steve, I want to begin the process of offering you the chair of ophthalmology here at UW."

"Okay," I replied, taken completely by surprise.

"The members of the search committee and I, along with the key leaders in the administration who've met you, have been impressed with your vision for the department and we'd like you to join us at UW. We're willing to provide the resources you need to augment the quality and reputation of the Department of Ophthalmology, including reasonable new space for departmental laboratories and offices. I'd also see you having a key role in enhancing the overall vision research program here at UW."

"Thank you," I replied, feeling a tad uneasy, because there was still so much more information I needed to even begin to make a decision.

"I think you're scheduled to meet with Bob Gust downtown tomorrow," he said, glancing at a copy of my schedule,

"Yes, tomorrow morning," I replied.

"Good. Bob will go over the department space and finances and provide you with a summary of the departmental accounts. Then, when you get home, I'd like you to write a letter detailing what you'd need to come to the University of Washington as the new chair of ophthalmology and to establish a refractive surgery program at University of Washington Medical Center. Can you get a letter to me in the next two weeks?"

"Yes, I'm sure I can."

"Good. Well, you've had a long day. Enjoy the rest of your trip and please let me know if you have any more questions or concerns."

After Paul Ramsey and I shook hands, and said our goodbyes, I walked out to find my car in the parking lot and felt more than a little anxious about the important decision I now had to make. Not only was it important for my career, but also for Jennifer and our soon-to-be-born twins. That night at dinner in the Hunt Club at the Sorrento Hotel with Jennifer, Dick Winn, and a few of the other search committee members, I felt distracted and frankly overwhelmed. Dick sensed my angst. As the three of us walked out to the parking lot later that night he said, "Steve and Jennifer, I predict you're never going to be totally comfortable with this decision, but this is the logical next step in Steve's career, and Seattle is a wonderful place to live and raise your children."

"Thank you, Dick," I replied. "We're grateful to have the opportunity to consider the position and I appreciate you and the committee making me your first choice."

"You're a perfect fit. Please let me know if there's anything I can help you with as you continue your discussions with the dean."

We said our goodbyes, and Jennifer and I made our way back to the Four Seasons Hotel. Even though I was dog-tired, I laid awake for hours that night, long after Jennifer had fallen asleep, mulling over what I knew could be the most important decision I'd make to this point in my life. I recalled that only ten years earlier I'd been a third-year resident at the Mayo Clinic. Still, I was confident in my abilities, realizing I'd probably become the top candidate based on two factors: first, I was an experienced refractive surgeon who'd already built one academic refractive laser center, and second, I was a NIH-funded vision scientist who had the tools to communicate with the vision science community at UW. But it all seemed so sudden, almost surreal. I tossed and turned into the early hours of morning before I managed to fall into a restless sleep.

Early the next morning, I walked around the corner from the hotel and took an elevator to Robert Gust's office on the twentieth floor of the Puget Sound Plaza Building. A part of the eleven-acre *Metropolitan Tract* owned by the University of Washington in downtown Seattle, the exceptionally valuable land is also occupied by the Financial Center, the Cobb Building, the IBM Building, Rainier Square, the Skinner Building, the Four Seasons Olympic Hotel, and the Olympic Garage. The top floors of the Puget Sound Plaza offered an imposing view of the waterfront, the Puget Sound, and the Cascade Mountains. The *Metropolitan Tract* had been the original site of the University of Washington before it moved to its current Montlake site on the shore of Lake Washington. The long-term leases for this prime downtown Seattle real estate remain an important source of revenue for the University.

Gust met me in the waiting area, led the way to his office overlooking the Puget Sound, and sat across from me at his meeting table. A thickset, middle-aged man of medium height with a full head of brown hair and a prominent mustache, Gust was the Associate Dean of Management and Administration at UW Medical School. His reputation preceded him during my meetings with several medical school chairs: I'd already learned the axiom: "Medical School Deans come and go, but Bob Gust is always here."

Gust was hired away from Executive Consulting Group (ECG) when he was in his 20s by Robert Van Citters, M.D, the dean of UW School of Medicine during the late 1960s and throughout the 1970s. Gust had been *here* when David C. Dale, MD, became dean in the 1980s and was fired after three years without explanation by UW president William P. Gerberding. He was *here* when the subsequent dean, Michael Whitcomb, was forced to step down after getting caught in a drunken tryst beneath a freeway overpass in Seattle in 1990. He was *here* when Philip J. Fialkow, the dean proceeding Paul Ramsey, and his wife died in an accident in Nepal in 1996, shortly after hiking up 17,500-foot Se La.

Article, Associated Press, Bodies of Seattle Couple Uncovered in Nepal, , Nov. 4, 1996

My first impression was that Gust seemed rather gruff and arrogant. He barely cracked a smile the entire meeting and made a point of telling me he, "never socialized with medical school chairs or faculty members."

After we exchanged pleasantries, he passed me a dossier that contained several pages detailing Department of Ophthalmology working, reserve, and endowed accounts, in addition to scaled maps of departmental office and laboratory spaces. There were also maps of the clinical spaces in UW Medical Center and Harborview Medical Center.

"You'll notice that the department has substantial reserves," he began. "Dr. Kalina was a rather austere chair and that puts you in a good position to address some of the space and faculty issues in the department. A portion of those funds must be retained in reserves, but there's around $1.5 million you can use to help accomplish your goals. You'll also notice that there are currently three state-line positions in the department. If you accept the chair, you'll receive two more from the dean's office, one for yourself and one to recruit a new faculty member to the department. Dr. Kinyoun occupies one of the existing state-line positions, Dr. Kalina another, and the third is open after Dr. Lindquist's departure several years ago. You'd be free to use the later position as you see fit, but Dr. Kalina's state-line position will revert back to the dean's office when he retires. The department also enjoys the support of the Bishop Foundation in the form of annual funding of one hundred percent of the Bishop Professor's salary. That position is currently open and can be filled with approval of the Bishop board. Review this later at your leisure and let me know if you have any questions."

I poured over several pages of details about the accounts as Gust sat waiting. Finally, I looked up from the documents. "I expect that funds would also be provided by the medical school for remodeling the departmental offices and labs, and for remodeling new space that would be included in the offer."

"That would be up to Dr. Ramsey, but let's assume he's expecting you to ask for at least partial coverage of those expenses."

"I also plan on including several new positions that aren't covered by the current state-line positions," I continued, feeling him out for insight to use in preparing my written proposal.

"You should detail what you think you need in your letter to Dr. Ramsey. You'll notice the last few pages include a map of the departmental offices and labs, as well as adjoining space currently occupied by members of the neuropathology department. The dean will likely entertain requests for transferring at least a part of this adjoining space into the ophthalmology department to accomplish your goals and to accommodate your own lab. There are also maps of the department's clinical space in UW Medical Center and Harborview Medical Center."

"Good," I said as I glanced over the departmental floor plan, "this will be very helpful."

Gust and I spent a few more minutes talking about the medical school and the Department of Ophthalmology before I took my leave and headed back to the Four Seasons Hotel. The next time I saw Bob Gust was at a status meeting I had with him a few months after my arrival in Seattle. When I sat down with him, I politely asked how things were going and he replied, "A lot better since you agreed to come here." I chuckled, realizing that as a relatively minor department compared to internal medicine, surgery, or pediatrics, ophthalmology was really a very small part of Mr. Gust's concerns. Looking back on all that transpired after that meeting, it would be the last amiable encounter I'd have with him.

Jennifer and I enjoyed a leisurely lunch at a seafood grill a short distance from the hotel and then met a real estate agent that UW had arranged to show us around Seattle neighborhoods during the next two days. We concentrated on communities near Lake Washington, Lake Sammamish, or the Puget Sound because it seemed absurd to move to Seattle and not have at least a view of the water. We didn't find any houses we'd be interested in buying because, after living in Shaker Heights for three years, we were infatuated with older homes and the homes that fit our preferences in Madison Park, Capitol Hill, or Queen Anne were completely out of our price range. To say we suffered from severe sticker shock would be an understatement. The prices for similar properties in the Seattle area were four to six times more than what they were in the most prestigious neighborhoods in Shaker Heights and Cleveland Heights. I don't remember this setting off alarms about difficulties that would arise in hiring faculty if I were to take the position at UW, but it should have. The cost of living in Seattle would prove to be a huge issue when I began recruiting to rebuild the department.

Jennifer and I left Seattle after our five-day visit with a lot more information about the department, medical school, and Seattle, but still harboring doubts about whether it was the right time and place for us. We mulled over the decision for a couple of weeks, while I prepared my letter for Paul Ramsey. Finally, we decided we'd take the plunge if the negotiations went well. I ultimately decided I wanted to accept the new challenge.

As I prepared my letter, I reviewed the floor plans Bob Gust had given me and decided I would ask for all of the space occupied by the neuropathology section adjacent to the Department of Ophthalmology. That approximately six thousand square feet represented only a small fraction of the space in the pathology department, and I was told neuropathology would "soon" be moving to Harborview Hospital anyway. It was also necessary to estimate the funds needed to remodel the existing department offices and labs and the new space that would be incorporated into ophthalmology. I found this to be very difficult because some space just needed painting and re-carpeting, while several areas needed anything from additional cabinets to having a laboratory constructed from the ground up. I asked officials in the construction office at UW for estimates on construction costs per square foot for the different types of remodeling needed and did my best to come up with reasonable numbers. I also had to estimate the seed money necessary for new faculty recruits, in other words, what would be needed for each new faculty member to support him or her until grant funding and, in the case of physicians', clinical collections could support his or her salary and research program. This, of course, varied depending on whether the recruit was a pure scientist, clinician-scientist, or pure clinician, and also whether he or she was an established faculty member with existing grants or a candidate right out of training. I based the funds requested on my own career needs at different stages and aimed for a balance between newly-trained and established faculty. Coming up with estimates to launch a refractive surgery program was fairly straightforward. After all, I'd already done this once before. I finalized my letter just over three weeks after my visit and sent it to Dr. Ramsey by overnight express mail.

Bob Gust called me just over a week later to review my proposal. Ramsey wanted to divide my requests into personal recruitment needs—salary, startup resources for my research lab, and funds needed to establish a refractive surgery program at UW Medical Center—and those directed to the department—new faculty positions, space, and remodeling costs. There was agreement on my personal requests, other than the pending development of a business plan for establishing the refractive surgery center. It was the request for the department we needed to negotiate. Gust told me the dean could agree only to a portion of my new space request. He told me that the neuropathology section of pathology would need to retain approximately thirty percent of its space that I'd earmarked for the Department of Ophthalmology. Beyond that, the dean offered funding for new faculty positions and remodeling that came to approximately fifty percent of what I'd requested. That would mean not having resources to recruit as many new clinical and research faculty members as I'd planned and not receiving sufficient funds from the dean to totally remodel the existing departmental office and lab spaces, which was desperately needed after more than thirty years of occupancy with little more than an occasional paint job.

I asked Mr. Gust if the dean would provide a written counterproposal, including the specific room numbers of spaces that would be transferred to ophthalmology and other details such as the amounts for new state-line positions, funds for recruitment, remodeling, and establishing my lab at UW. Gust agreed to ask Dr. Ramsey to prepare a letter. I told him I'd let the dean know about my decision within a week of receiving this final offer.

So there it was! My decision basically came down to my willingness to accept an offer that would undoubtedly improve the lot of the ophthalmology department at UW—including more space, limited remodeling, a few new faculty positions, and a refractive surgery program—but would not allow me to achieve all the goals I had set for the program. It was a dilemma faced by most academics when considering the chairmanship of a medical department, regardless of their field. Rarely did an offer include everything a candidate wished for, especially in this era of declining reimbursement for medical care.

Paul Ramsey's letter arrived just over a week later, the same week our twins, Remington Grey and Hailey Loraine, were born. I went over the counterproposal with a fine-toothed comb, reconfirming all the room numbers and the funds dedicated to each category. Jennifer and I discussed the offer, my position at the Cleveland Clinic, and the advantages and disadvantages of living in Seattle, leaning first one direction and then the other on our decision. I queried a few close friends about specific aspects of my offer and considered Dick Winn's comment about the chairmanship being the next logical step in my career.

Finally, around the end of February, I decided to accept the position at UW. The first person I told, even before conveying my decision to the dean at UW, was my chairman at the Cleveland Clinic Foundation. Then, I called Paul Ramsey's office. He seemed rather surprised, but pleased, when I told him I'd decided to accept the position at UW. Ramsey and I exchanged pleasantries, and he told me he'd inform the faculty in ophthalmology at UW of my decision later that day.

"When would you plan on starting here in Seattle?" he asked.

"How about sometime in June or July?" I responded.

"That sounds fine. Let my assistant know when you want to visit to search for a home. I'd like you to review the UW Medical Center business plan for refractive surgery to make sure you think it's reasonable. I'd also like you to meet with Bob Gust to get his help in coordinating your lab space and other immediate needs."

"Great," I replied, "Jennifer and I plan to visit again within a month."

"That's perfect. Please send me a letter indicating your acceptance of the offer and let me know if you have any other concerns. We're delighted you're coming, Steve."

"Thank you, Paul. I'm excited about the opportunity. I'll see you soon."

I called Dick Winn, chair of the ophthalmology search committee at UW, a few minutes later and let him know I'd accepted the position. His enthusiasm upon hearing of my decision remains one of my fondest memories. The little remaining apprehension I had about UW and my new position melted away as he told me—for probably the tenth time—how wonderful Seattle and the UW were, and how Jennifer and I were going to absolutely love the Northwest. I'd sadly recollect Dick's enthusiasm for the University of Washington a few years later when unforeseen events transpired that made his life a living hell.

I received several energizing welcome notes from UW ophthalmology faculty by e-mail later that day, including a gracious note from Dick Mills, MD, the interim chair, signaling that Dr. Ramsey had informed faculty members in ophthalmology of my acceptance. I heard nothing at all from several other senior faculty members in the ophthalmology department. I learned later that faculty members were taken completely by surprise by the announcement. Apparently, there'd been yet another rumor circulating within the ophthalmology department in Seattle that "my negotiations with the dean had gone sour during his visit to Cleveland." God knows how anyone there even knew about Paul Ramsey's visit. One of the younger faculty members told me that the ophthalmology clinic at UW Medical Center had been "like a wake" after the notification, with even those who welcomed the announcement being hesitant to reveal their true feelings.

I was completely in the dark about the feelings of the few faculty members who opposed my appointment as the new chair at UW—with the notable exception of the pompous surgeon who served on the search committee. Certainly, none of the others expressed their concerns to me during my interviews. My first clue about what I'd face from some in the department came when Jennifer and I made our second home searching visit to Seattle in June of 1998. That trip happened to coincide with the Resident-Alumni Day gala dinner held to honor the residents and fellows who were completing their training in the Department of Ophthalmology. The function, held at the Columbia Tower Club on top of the Bank of America Building, was attended by most of the residents, fellows, and faculty from the department. It was customary for the graduating senior residents to prepare a video highlighting their experiences at UW and to include segments roasting some of the faculty who'd taught them ophthalmology. I was featured prominently in that video—as Darth Vader, Dark Lord of the Sith and Master of the Dark Side. The context of the film left no doubt I was most certainly viewed as such by some of the senior faculty members in the department. I chalked it up as a warning shot of what was to come and set out to change the perceptions of those who opposed me through fairness, hard work, and leadership.

Jennifer enjoyed a humorous moment at that dinner. She wandered into the bathroom and was speaking to Jan Kalina—the former permanent chair's wife.

"Are you one of the new resident's wives?" another young woman in the lounge asked Jennifer, who at thirty-three years old looked like she was twenty-three.

"No," Mrs. Kalina answered, with a chuckle. "This is Jennifer Wilson, the new chairman's wife."

"Oh, I'm sorry," the young woman gasped, clearly mortified. "I mean—I'm not sorry you're Dr. Wilson's wife, I meant—I'm sorry, I didn't know who you were. I'm Peggy Smith. My husband Frank is one of the second-year residents."

"That's quite all right," Jennifer replied, "it's nice to meet you, Peggy."

Our last few months in Shaker Heights passed very quickly. The Cleveland Clinic made a counter offer to keep me in Cleveland. But I'd given my word to Paul Ramsey, and I can honestly say I've never used an offer from one institution to improve my lot at another. Once I've made up my mind to leave a position, I've always negotiated what I thought was a fair offer, and if I accepted, merely informed my current employer. Some consider it almost sport to collect offers from multiple institutions or to use an offer from one institution to improve one's situation with another. I guess there's nothing unethical about that, but it was never my style and I didn't appreciate it once I became chair—and few chairs do. I left the Cleveland Clinic on good terms, even helping the department identify a new medical director to fill my refractive surgery position. Two of my PhD postdoctoral fellows decided to move with me to University of Washington, and I made arrangements for them to start early and organize my research lab. Jennifer and I said our goodbyes to colleagues and friends in Cleveland, sold our home in Shaker Heights, and prepared to leave.

The only problem we encountered was finding a new home in Seattle. We made several trips without finding anything appealing we could afford. We didn't even consider making an offer on any homes we saw. Prices were through the roof and anything desirable sold overnight in those pre-9/11 years. We wanted to live somewhere near the water, but couldn't afford houses around the university, so we began looking across the floating bridges north and east of Lake Washington. Finally, our real estate agent called us a couple of days before our fourth trip to tell us she'd found the perfect home in a gated community on a hillside overlooking Lake Washington's Juanita Bay—a part of the city of Kirkland. She asked us to come two days sooner, "before it disappears from the market," but I couldn't depart early because I had patients scheduled in clinic. Sure enough, by the time we arrived on Friday night, there had already been an offer on the home. But the sellers hadn't accepted because the offer was contingent on a spouse seeing the house on Sunday.

We made arrangements to see the home early the next morning and within ten minutes we'd decided we wanted to make an offer—and we weren't messing around—full price, with a 60-day closing. We drew up the papers and our agent presented the offer early that afternoon. By dinner the sellers had accepted and we had our new home. It was early July and things seemed to be coming together nicely.

The timing was such that we needed to be out of our house in Shaker Heights a month before the closing of the new house in Kirkland. I stayed with our good friends, the Hollyfields, in Shaker Heights while Jennifer took the twins to San Antonio to visit her family. Jennifer left the kids with her parents and we flew to Paris for the International Congress of Eye Research (where my elevator encounter with Hank Kaplan occurred). Then, Jennifer and I returned to Cleveland, loaded up our Suburban with two dogs, along with other items we didn't want to entrust to the movers, and headed east on I-90 bound for Seattle. Five days later, after passing hundreds of bikers heading in the opposite direction to the annual motorcycle rally in Sturgis, South Dakota, we arrived in Kirkland and picked up the keys to our new home. The movers weren't due to arrive until the following day, so we laid out sleeping bags on the floor in the master bedroom and, leaving our Dalmatian, Excimer, and Labrador Retriever, Brittney, in the house, headed off to downtown Kirkland for dinner.

We picked a restaurant with a view of Lake Washington and struck up a conversation with our waitress. Once she found out we were just moving into the area, the woman recommended her sister for interior design. Jennifer jokingly told her we didn't need an interior designer, but we could sure use a nanny. A few minutes later, the waitress returned to tell us the chef's new fiancée was moving to Seattle and that she'd been working as a nanny in California for the past few years. Jennifer scribbled our new address on a piece of paper (we didn't have a phone yet), and the young woman contacted us a few weeks later. Maria would be our nanny for the next five years. Everything seemed really to be coming up roses!

Chapter 8
Arrival in the Emerald City—Seattle

I began my tenure as chair of ophthalmology at the University of Washington in September of 1998. To say the least, it was humbling to have been chosen from among many excellent candidates for this position at a medical school with annual revenues of $1.4 billion, ranked third in the United States in total NIH research funding, graduating 175 doctors a year, and with over fifteen hundred faculty and one thousand medical residents.

Within a week of my arrival, I received a call from Belding Scribner, MD, emeritus professor at UW, inventor of the arterio-venous shunt that made long-term kidney dialysis possible, and a legend in Seattle. His invention saved millions of lives worldwide. Dr. Scribner and his wife Ethel invited us for a delightful lunch on his charming houseboat on Portage Bay—just a short row across the narrow bay to the medical school. Having had one of the first corneal transplants many years earlier, Dr. Scribner was interested in the latest developments in corneal transplantation, even though his original transplant was still functioning just fine after more than twenty years. Dr. Scribner was seventy-seven years old in 1998, and he told us several endearing stories about his years on the faculty at UW. On a later visit, he proudly showed me galleys of his correspondence that had just been accepted by the *New England Journal of Medicine*.

Schribner BH, Blagg CR. Effect of dialysis dose and membrane flux in maintenance hemodialysis. N. Eng. J. Med. 2003;348:1491-4.

He also gleefully told us about all the years he'd rowed a one-man boat across the bay to work at UW. His experiences set me to thinking, and soon I was traveling to UW across Lake Washington in a 21-foot powerboat from our home on Juanita Bay to a slip I rented on Portage Bay directly adjacent to the medical school—at least during the warmer months. This cut my travel time by at least half and eliminated the agitation of fighting traffic on the congested 520 floating bridge. Dr. Scribner and I spoke from time to time during my five years at UW and Jennifer worked with Ethel in the UW Faculty Spouse's Auxiliary, but sadly he drowned in June of 2003, after apparently falling into the water surrounding his houseboat on Portage Bay, a place he truly loved. I'm grateful that my career path provided me the opportunity to get to know him.

Per UW code, the senior faculty of the Department of Ophthalmology, the full professors, voted in favor of my appointment as tenured professor. The actual vote wasn't disclosed to me, but by now I harbored no delusions that it was unanimous. I'd heard ongoing chatter about the angst and discontentment of some faculty—even from a distance of over two thousand miles. Clinical fellows had to be appointed to the faculty at a rank of clinical instructor. When I put forward my new fellow Mark Walker, MD for a vote, so he could accompany me to Seattle, a cadre of faculty members, led by the surgeon who served on my search committee, tried to block his appointment. The purported reason for this clear personal challenge was "concern about the impact the new refractive and corneal surgery fellow would have on resident education in the department." This was patently absurd. There wasn't even a rudimentary refractive surgery program at UW before my arrival. Also, the department had employed two retina fellows—the subspecialty of two of the dissenters—for decades, and in my mind it was indisputable that fellows actually contributed to the education and experience of residents, if care were taken to integrate the clinical and surgical experiences. Other faculty members, however, supported my fellow's appointment and the final vote was something like eight to two. The margin on similar votes requiring faculty concurrence would grow in future years as I recruited new faculty members to the department, but I could nearly always bank on two opposition votes on virtually any issue that came before the faculty. I hoped eventually these holdouts would come to accept my appointment as chair and the new direction the department was headed, but they never did.

I tried to be tolerant of the faculty who chafed at my presence, but after withstanding the petty backbiting for over a year, I'd had enough. I doubt any of the chairmen I worked under would have tolerated it for a week, much less a year. What I found particularly hard to stomach was the fact that the malcontents, although senior faculty, were the least accomplished faculty members in the department. Their medical skills were outdated—to the point that I received ongoing complaints from other physicians inside and outside the department. One community doctor approached me at my first Washington Academy of Eye Physicians and Surgeons dinner meeting and asked, "When is UW going to get a real retina service?" These faculty members also published precious little and what research they did tended to be in clinical trials they had no role in initiating. Therefore, they served only as conduits to test other people's ideas. They prided themselves on their teaching, but some of the resident ophthalmologists, and even their own fellows, blatantly mocked them.

One of these faculty members subsequently had the audacity to inform me that, as fellowship director in the department, he couldn't in good conscience support the appointment of any more clinical fellows—*after* the faculty had adopted new guidelines to preserve resident experience if glaucoma or ophthalmic plastics faculty decided to train clinical fellows. First, I pointed out the ridiculousness of his position considering that there had been clinical fellows in his subspecialty for many years. Then, I informed him, as was my prerogative as chair, that he was no longer fellowship director, but allowed him to remain residency program director. But he still didn't get my not-so-subtle hint. He continued to resist my efforts to incorporate refractive surgery in the residents' clinical experience and opposed other changes the majority of faculty members supported to enhance resident training and experience. Finally, I decided to relieve him of the residency directorship and assume the position myself for a period of time—eventually recruiting one of the younger faculty members to take the position. Ultimately, I believe the residents benefited immensely from this change and others—such as the recruitment of new faculty—that occurred in the department. The residents told us this directly in their annual reviews of the program.

I don't want to give the impression that my early experience as chair of ophthalmology at University of Washington was dominated by these negative undertones. To the contrary, my first two years at UW were overflowing with contentment and happiness, primarily due to the many hardworking and supportive faculty members who accepted and even fostered change in the department. I'd be remiss not to mention individuals like Bryan Sires, MD, PhD, Krystoff Palczewski, PhD, Jack Saari, PhD, Phil Chen, MD, Devin Harrison, MD, Avery Weiss, MD, as well as faculty whom I recruited to the department later, including David Saperstein, MD, Anuja Bhandari, MD, Raghu Mudumbai, MD, Mark Greenwald, MD, and Francoise Haeseleer, PhD. I strove to support the careers of these individuals with all the effort, resources, and connections at my disposal, and it was my relationship with these outstanding clinicians and scientists that sustained me through the difficult years to follow. I also want to once again mention Robert Kalina, MD, and his wife Jan. As my predecessor, Bob couldn't have been more helpful and supportive. Jennifer and I became very fond of them.

In recognition of Dr. Kalina's twenty-seven years of service to the department, I sought an appropriate acknowledgement of his many contributions to the residents and faculty. I decided to name the newly remodeled departmental conference room and library the "Robert E. Kalina, MD, Conference Room." Dean Paul Ramsey, MD, supported me in this, but a few months after submitting the proposal, I got a response back from the university committee that governed the naming of facilities at UW. "Dr. Kalina will have to *die* first." I was appalled by this decision, as was Dr. Ramsey, and perseverance led eventually to a reconsideration of this ridiculous decision.

I also enjoyed tremendous support from emeritus faculty of the department, including Roger Johnson, MD, and Melvin Rubin, MD, and UW vision research faculty who had primary appointments in other departments such as John Clarke, PhD, Anita Hendrickson, PhD, Thomas Reh, PhD, Fred Rieke, PhD, and Tony Pham, MD, PhD. Members of the Bishop Foundation Board of Trustees were also very strong supporters of the research program in the department of ophthalmology.

No one understood the difficulties of being the new chair of ophthalmology at UW better than the chairs of other departments in the medical school. I remain eternally grateful for the extraordinary wisdom, insight and friendship of the chairs I served with on the Medical School Executive Committee, Clinical Chairs Committee, UW Physicians Board of Trustees, and many other leadership groups in the medical school. I can honestly say I never worked with a more talented group than the nearly thirty department chairs at UW School of Medicine, and I could depend on most of them for help and guidance when difficult problems arose. Some deserve special recognition—Richard Winn, MD, Chair of the Department of Neurosurgery and chair of the search committee that brought me to UW, Bruce R. Ransom, MD, Chair of the Department of Neurology, F. Bruder Stapleton, MD, Chair of the Department of Pediatrics, Frederick A. Matsen, III, MD, Chair of the Department of Orthopedic Surgery and Sports Medicine, Ernest A. Weymuller, Jr., MD, Chair of the Department of Otolaryngology, George E. Laramore, MD, PhD, Chair of the Department of Radiation Oncology, Richard C. Veith, MD, Chair of the Department of Psychiatry and Behavioral Sciences, Walter V. Stolov, MD, former Chair of the Department of Rehabilitation Medicine, and John Clark, PhD, eventual chair of the Department of Structural Biology.

I mentioned Richard Mills, MD, and his remarkably gracious demeanor during my second interview for the chair. For the most part, that continued after my arrival in Seattle, although we had a few rather strained meetings the first few months. One in particular related to the new *Ray and Grace Hill Endowed Chair in Ophthalmology* that came to the department shortly after my arrival. Bob Kalina had cultivated a relationship with the Hills for many years, and when Mr. Hill died, Mrs. Hill endowed the chair with a $1.5 million contribution. Dr. Kalina opined that I should be named to the endowed chair so I could "spread the money around" (the interest revenue derived from investing the principal) each year to different faculty members in the department. I, however, saw the gift as an opportunity to attract an outstanding new clinician-scientist to the department. I explained my position to Dr. Mills when he came to me in early 1999 to make the case that he should be named to the endowed chair. It was difficult to argue with Dr. Mills' logic. He'd been a pillar in the department in both glaucoma and neuro-ophthalmology for many years, was an exceptional clinician and teacher, published many important medical articles, and had served as President of the American Academy of Ophthalmology, as well as in many other academic leadership positions. But as much as I wanted to give a chair to Dr. Mills, I stuck to my decision. Dr. Mills left to become the Chairman of Ophthalmology at the University of Louisville in Kentucky less than a year later. Just a year after leaving Seattle, Dr. Mills made a surprise announcement that he was resigning his chairmanship because of unfulfilled recruitment promises. Dick returned to a private practice in Seattle and shortly thereafter I nominated him for appointment as Clinical Professor of Ophthalmology at UW, and I had to change the rules to accomplish it. Up to that time, clinical faculty had to devote a half day a week of their time to teaching at one of the medical school hospitals or clinics, a service burden that few active physicians could bear in an era of declining reimbursement. Several other potential clinical faculty candidates also had issues with this time requirement. I drafted a new policy with more reasonable time obligations, and with the agreement of the faculty and the dean, was able to enhance resident education by increasing the clinical faculty in the department. Dick Mills and I see each other from time to time at meetings, including the American Ophthalmological Society. It's always a pleasant encounter that frequently includes a chuckle about the job both of us sought and neither ended up wanting.

I used the *Ray and Grace Hill Chair in Ophthalmology* endowment to recruit David Saperstein, MD, a retina and vitreous surgeon-scientist from Emory University and overnight UW "had a real retina service." Dr. Saperstein is a world-class surgeon and an active clinical and basic science investigator. Within two years of his arrival, he became the top revenue generator in the department of ophthalmology. Patients were clamoring to get into his clinics for advanced retina and vitreous surgery and laser therapies for diseases like age-related macular degeneration, retinal detachment and diabetic retinal disease. I was precluded from naming Dr. Saperstein to the Hill chair until he was promoted to associate professor, but the funds from the endowment supported his salary and laboratory efforts. Unfortunately, I'd already tendered my resignation from the medical school once Dr. Saperstein was promoted to associate professor in 2003 and he could not be named to the endowed chair until the new permanent ophthalmology chair was named and concurred with the decision. Following at least two failed searches for a new permanent department chair, Dr. Saperstein left the department of ophthalmology for private practice in the summer of 2006, and never did receive the Hill chair promised to him at the time of his recruitment.

I knew upon arrival that my laboratory would have to be "temporarily" placed in the basement of a hospital building that was near the building that housed the rest of the Department of Ophthalmology laboratories. The space was good, but we were as isolated from other investigators with similar interests, as we'd been at UT Southwestern. Within a few months, however, Bob Gust told me there would be an even longer delay before the dean could transfer the new space adjacent to the department offices and labs promised in my recruitment agreement. There were three reasons given and I doubt any of them were new revelations. The first excuse was that two of the promised rooms were labs involved in litigation by a former faculty member in the Department of Neuropathology at the university—who had not received tenure. Second, some of the space was being used as a microscopy room by an older neuropathology professor who had the potential to make a major donation to the medical school. Third, a clinical lab in the promised space couldn't be moved until the new Research and Training Building was completed at Harborview Medical Center. None of these issues was discussed with me during my recruitment to UW.

William J. Bremner, MD, PhD, Vice Chair since 1987, became Chair of the Department of Medicine in December of 1998. Suddenly, in the early summer of 1999, since the lab space I currently occupied was earmarked for the department of medicine, it became a priority to move my lab into part of the space promised to me on the eighth floor of the RR building. We were given two weeks' notice of the complex move involving dozens of delicate instruments, heavy freezers, refrigerators, glassware, supplies, and chemicals, as were the occupants of the clinical lab where we'd be moving. On the Friday prior to our planned move, which was to occur the following Monday, I went to inspect our new lab space and got hopping mad. The floor was still cluttered with debris and discarded chemicals the prior occupants had left behind. Worse still, the departing group had literally ripped the permanent cabinets and lab benches out of the wall in one section of the one thousand-square-foot room, exposing unpainted drywall. One wall had a gaping hole. In addition, the tile floor had been destroyed in several places—with multiple areas ripped up to expose bare concrete. Many ceiling panels were also missing or damaged and there was a water leak in one corner of the room. In short, it looked as if a bomb had been set off in the lab. Appalled, I sent a terse hand-carried memo to the dean's office describing the atrocity and asserting that I had no intention of using my remodeling resources to repair the damage in the lab. I also refused to move until the repairs were completed. The dean sent Bob Gust to assuage my fury. Mr. Gust delayed the move for two weeks, rallied university construction crews to repair the ceiling, floors, and walls, agreed that the missing cabinets and lab benches would be replaced at the dean's expense, and added $50,000 to my laboratory recruitment package. We still had to cram into two thirds of the lab while ongoing construction continued in the other third——a situation that lasted for several months—but at least some attempt was made by the dean's office to right the wrong. Despite these efforts, the department had received only about twenty percent of the new space promised during my recruitment, and nearly a year after my arrival at UW, there was no timetable for the rest of the space being transferred. It would be another year before half of the remaining space was transferred and a year after that before the rest, still needing major construction to build labs, would be delivered. Is this space tango an unusual event for new chairs at a medical school? Sadly, it is not. Indeed, I've come to realize that these sorts of delays on promised space are the rule rather than the exception, not only at UW, but at most medical schools. Hopefully, an effort is made to give a realistic timetable, but I've found this is rarely the case in speaking with department chairs at other institutions.

The flood that occurred in the chair of obstetrics and gynecology's office at UW was another incident I remember from that time. This happened around Christmas time when a pipe ruptured in the ceiling in Steven G. Gabbe, MD's departmental office. Several inches of water ruined many of his papers and files. Steve told me no one from the medical school administration went to see what happened or what needed to be done to fix the problem. Maintenance put up a plastic tarp beneath the ceiling in his office, in case the leak recurred. When he left UW six months later in March of 2001, to become dean at Vanderbilt School of Medicine, repairs still hadn't been made. Dr. Gabbe went on to become CEO of Ohio State University Wexner Medical Center from 2008 to 2014.

Dr. Gabbe's interest in burnout began when he was a chair at UW. He found that this was a common problem among academic chairs in obstetrics and gynecology in the U.S.A., and he and his collaborators ended up publishing pioneering studies on burnout in OB-GYN chairs. I believe any former medical school chairs can relate to the findings of these studies.

Gabbe SG, et al. Burnout in chairs of obstetrics and gynecology: Diagnosis, treatment, and prevention. American Journal Obstetrics Gynecology 2002;186:601.
Gabbe SG, et al. Changes in the burnout profile of chairs of departments of obstetrics and gynecology over the past 15 years. American Journal Obstetrics Gynecology 2018;219:303. e1-6.

Later, he and his coworkers did a study of medical school deans in the U.S.A. and Canada. Surprisingly, the latter study found that only 2% of these deans exhibited high levels of burnout.

Gabbe SG, et al. Burnout in medical school deans: an uncommon problem. Acad. Med. 2008;83:476.

My foremost priority during the first year after I became chair of ophthalmology was to gain a solid understanding of the financial situation in the department. Clinical departments in major medical schools are complex enterprises with many, often competing, activities related to three principal goals: excelling in clinical care, teaching, and research. In 2005, the UW Medicine Board of Trustees added another goal to this list—compliance. The yearly budget for a unit the size of the department of ophthalmology at UW with significant basic research efforts would be somewhere between $7 and $15 million, including the budgets for the clinical efforts at our four major hospitals—UW Medical Center, Harborview Medical Center, Children's Hospital and Regional Medical Center, and the VA Puget Sound Medical Center. This was peanuts compared to the budget of the Departments of Medicine or Surgery, but keeping the books balanced while funding new and ongoing initiatives was a constant struggle.

Adding to this complexity were ongoing budgetary issues at each of the individual hospitals, each with separate leadership and often-competing goals, that made up UW Medicine. For example, enhancements of ophthalmology services at Harborview Hospital were looked on unfavorably by administrators at UW Medical Center—who feared a decrease in their own revenues due to competition. In addition, the medical school had its own expenses and initiatives that were paid for in large part from a "dean's tax" of twelve percent on clinical collections. Also, there was a nine percent charge for the clinical billing activities of the UW Physicians practice plan, salaries for UW Physician staff (including Brian McKenna), and malpractice insurance for UW physicians and limited advertising for the overall UW practices. The clinical revenue that remained covered the departmental budget to pay for administration, secretaries, supplies, and other expenses in ophthalmology. Whatever was left after these other costs were paid was available for faculty salaries. With this scenario in mind, it's not difficult to understand there would be heavy pressure on faculty salaries as clinical reimbursement from Medicare, Medicaid, and insurance companies progressively declined for both clinic visits and surgery.

It's important to point out that only a very small proportion of our budget was derived from state support, despite the University of Washington School of Medicine being a state institution. The actual amount averaged about nine percent of the departmental budget in the interval 1998 to 2003—a paltry sum compared to peer institutions such as the University of Texas. Other states also made contributions to the UW School of Medicine budget, since UW is the primary medical school for the five states that comprised the WWAMI region—Washington, Wyoming, Alaska, Montana and Idaho. These resources were directed to the medical school, however, and were intended to pay for the training of medical students from these states. A subspecialty department like ophthalmology played only a small role in this activity. Therefore, in terms of direct support for the department of ophthalmology from the State of Washington, the aforementioned five "state-line" positions providing partial support for faculty positions were the only tangible resources derived from the state to support our programs. The amount of yearly funding provided by a state-line position varied from approximately $50,000 to $100,000 per year, depending on the rank (assistant, associate, full professor, or chair) of the supported faculty member.

One of the peculiar idiosyncrasies of the UW system is an archaic incentive program that has been in place for many years. Only regular clinical faculty can participate in the program (i.e.: not acting assistant professors, research faculty, or clinical faculty in private practice) and individuals are typically eligible for incentive only if the portion of the collections available for income from their clinical activities—clinic and surgery—covers their base salary. To put this more concretely, if a faculty member's annual salary were $150,000 and she had clinical activities that yielded $175,000 toward income after the dean's tax, UW Physicians billing charges, and departmental expenses were subtracted, then the $25,000 excess would be placed into a departmental incentive pool. The faculty who enjoyed state-line salary support had the capacity to more quickly cover his or her base salary and contribute earlier to the incentive pool. For example, if this same faculty member with a $150,000 salary also had a $50,000 state-line position, then only $100,000 of the base needed to be covered by clinical activities before contributions were made to the incentive pool. It sounds like a reasonable system, and it would be if everyone were pulling his or her weight, but in practice there were several problems with the system. If one or more faculty members weren't sufficiently active in clinic or surgery to cover their base salary, then the deficit had to be paid out of the incentive pool, reducing the amount available for distribution to those who energetically contributed to the pool. In ophthalmology, those with less clinical revenue than needed fell into three groups. Group one was new faculty members who needed a few years to build a busy clinical practice. As chair of the department, I planned for the shortfall for new faculty members when hiring and covered the deficit from reserves for a period of two to three years to protect the incentives earned by established hardworking colleagues. The second group that didn't generate sufficient clinical revenue to cover their salaries were those in subspecialties of ophthalmology that were critical to patient care and teaching, but which were labor intensive or without surgical procedures (or both) and, therefore, yielded lower revenue from billings for patient services. These faculty members, for example in neuro-ophthalmology or ocular pathology, usually had lower salaries than surgeons, but still there could be shortfalls in covering salaries that would pull funds from the incentive pool. A strategy I used to avoid this was hiring faculty members with more than one area of specialty, for example, both glaucoma and neuro-ophthalmology, to combine coverage in a needed non-surgical area with the potential to cover salary in the second area of expertise. Chairs in all clinical departments, inside and outside of UW, must constantly strive for the proper balance in their faculty members to provide needed medical coverage without upsetting the financial applecart.

Unfortunately, there is a third group of faculty who are the bane of department chairmen everywhere. These are the faculty who, for a variety of reasons, never generate sufficient clinical revenue to cover their salary, and therefore, are constantly a drain on departmental budgets and incentive plans. In some cases, these faculty members just don't have the interpersonal skills and bedside manner to build a busy practice. These are certainly qualities that a chair and other faculty consider during the recruitment process, but they are qualities that are intangible and can be difficult or impossible to evaluate, especially in a candidate who's beginning his or her first clinical practice. Occasionally, limitations such as these, usually combined with clinical, research, or teaching deficiencies, contribute to a young faculty member not being recommended for tenure by his or her fellow faculty members and having to leave the university. In my experience, however, it's faculty members who were once active, but decline in productivity over time—especially after receiving tenure—who are the real problems. Most chairs in tenure-based academic systems are strapped with one or more of these "deadwood" faculty members who seem content to just hang around and do as little as possible. Dick Winn, MD, Chair of Neurosurgery at UW, told me many times about similar burdens he'd supervised in his department since the day he arrived in Seattle. These unproductive faculty members would never be tolerated in a system such as the Cleveland Clinic or Mayo Clinic—where there's no tenure. They'd be given their walking papers within a year. However, once tenured, it can be nearly impossible to motivate or terminate faculty members who are not self-motivated and who, therefore, weigh heavily on the morale of the other faculty. It's very difficult to be working your tail off to excel in clinical care, teaching, and research, while colleagues around you are dawdling through the day, seeing a few patients, doing a little surgery now and then, and possibly publishing a case report on a patient they see every year or so—especially when you discover you're losing a portion of your own pay to cover the salary of these loafers. I inherited a couple of these difficult individuals at UW, including a tenured professor with a very modest salary in one of the highest revenue-generating subspecialties of ophthalmology. This fellow also enjoyed one of the department's state-line positions and still was a financial burden to the other faculty members. I'm fairly certain that the loss of one of the most productive faculty members in the department—to a major competitor in Seattle—two years prior to my arrival—could be traced to this hard-working surgeon finally getting enough of contributing his sweat and toil to paying the salaries of these academic parasites. As a result of these faculty members, who didn't pull their weight, in addition to unavoidable increases in department expenses, incentive payments for each six-month period amounted only to a few thousand dollars for even the most productive faculty members.

Almost all chairs have such faculty—hopefully very few—and once they become tenured it is a nightmare to deal with them. The chair can cajole and try to use peer-pressure or other motivational tools to alter behavior, but my experience, and that of many other chairs I've talked with, has been futility since these faculty members have typically lost all scruples about the effects they're having on others. Commonly, they possess some false sense of entitlement, because "I'm a good teacher and I paid my dues in the past" or some other justification. At UW, with its tenure-based system, I had few alternatives in dealing with these slackers. I limited their annual salary increases to the bare minimum. The dean's office wouldn't let me give any faculty member a zero percent increase, or I certainly would have done so. Even a one percent increase for two years in a row was enough to trigger an inquiry by the faculty senate and that, according to medical school administration, was to be avoided at all costs. So, I had to resort to giving the bare minimum that wouldn't trigger faculty senate scrutiny. I also whittled away at the perks of these faculty members, slowly taking away desirable administrative positions, secretarial support, roomy offices, prized clinic or surgical times, or even nearby parking spaces—trying somehow to motivate them to do their share. It never worked, but at least I could give these trappings to faculty members who were busting their behinds contributing to the academic and financial well-being of the department. Regardless of how much was taken away, these individuals refused to be motivated, typically looking for ways of being even more of an irritant to the chair and other faculty. If anything, the more they were marginalized, the less effort they expended and the more of an embittered burden they became to other faculty members and me. They never quit either. The sad truth is they had nowhere else to go, since they were unprepared or unwilling to venture out into the unprotected, real world and often hadn't kept up with innovations in their subspecialty.

Even seemingly trivial changes I made to departmental spaces, in the interest of fairness or optimal use of resources for an expanding faculty, were met with scorn and angst. Right next door to my office was a bright and sunny (for Seattle) room that had been used for years as a conference room/faculty lunchroom/library. A couple of the senior faculty seemed to have time to hang out there for hours each day just shooting the breeze. For nearly a year and a half, I heard the boisterous laughter of one of our idle *prima donnas* reverberating through the walls. Meanwhile, several junior faculty members didn't even have offices. Finally, I moved the journals and books to the remodeled conference room and converted the lunchroom to an office that eventually held two office-less assistant professors, along with a secretary. The outcry was unbelievable, and even three years later there was ongoing petulance about the change. Such was the sense of entitlement that had crystallized over the years.

Some of our new programs helped ease the financial challenges in the department during the first few years. With guidance from Robert H. Muilenburg, executive director at UW Medical Center, and his administrative staff, the new refractive surgery program got off to a rapid start. A satellite of the ophthalmology clinical space in UW Medical Center was remodeled prior to my arrival. Excellent nurses and technicians were hired, and internal and external marketing was begun. Despite heavy competition within the Seattle and Vancouver regions, the program grew rapidly. Since my recruitment package included a large chunk of my salary being covered by the dean's office for the first two years, the departmental share of the revenues from refractive surgery helped to balance the precarious budget.

Chapter 9
Here a Crisis, There a Crisis . . . Everywhere a Crisis

Ongoing budget challenges are not UW-specific problems; all chairs of clinical departments deal with them constantly. I spent hours of time poring over spreadsheets and speaking to other clinical chairmen inside and outside UW about dealing with these issues during the five years I was chair. An important part of my job was to limit these problems as much as possible. It was natural I would immediately turn my gaze to our biggest source of departmental income—clinical revenue—and to the organizations responsible for ensuring we received what we were due—the University of Washington Physicians (UW Physicians) and Children's University Medical Group (CUMG) faculty practice plans—non-profit organizations that report to the dean of the School of Medicine, his assistants, and the UW Board of Regents. UW Physicians and CUMG were created to allow UW physician faculty to bill for services provided to their private patients. Similar faculty practice plans are in place in most university-based medical systems in the United States.

Brian McKenna had been executive director of UW Physicians and CUMG for over fifteen years, and I previously highlighted my inauspicious first meeting with him during my recruitment interviews at UW. I met with Mr. McKenna several times during my first year at UW, with and without the ophthalmology department administrator, trying to get a handle on the department's clinical collections. My last meeting with him was on August 30, 2001. These meetings were without a doubt the most frustrating and unproductive of my career, irrespective of the subject matter. Each time we met, I came prepared with spreadsheets and pointed questions about uncollected bills and after every meeting I left feeling even more befuddled and discouraged about the state of affairs, and the lack of direction at UW Physicians. For example, it took me over a year to drag out of McKenna the crucial piece of information that UW Physicians-disseminated professional fee collection rates were based not on what we were actually due from a particular group—typically Medicare, Medicaid, Blue Cross, or some other third party payer—based on law or negotiated agreements, but on the charges that a full fee cash-paying patient would be charged. Thus, when we receive spreadsheets and charts showing that collections were thirty-five percent, for example, it was not based on the true collectable amount, but some phantom number that would have been accurate if every patient was charged the full-fee for their services, which rarely was the case. This nonsensical information would drive hardworking faculty members to distraction, and rightfully so. I remember as though it were yesterday, when I finally realized how UW Physicians was generating these statistics at the umpteenth meeting I'd had with McKenna. (By this time, I couldn't help viewing him as a personification of the annoying wimp of a character named Poindexter from the *Felix the Cat* cartoon.)

"Brian, this is an absurd way to report collection efficiency," I gasped, sitting back in my chair in dumbfounded disbelief. "Why do you do it this way?"

"This is the way we've always done it," he replied with a clueless deer-in-the-headlights look on his face.

"Do you realize the impact your reporting in this manner has on my faculty?" I asked, appalled that it had taken me so long to get to the bottom of something so fundamental. "It saps the drive right out of them. I must have had half a dozen faculty members point to these numbers and ask me why they should see more patients when UW Physicians doesn't collect the fees anyway."

"Well," McKenna replied contritely, "I guess we could report it both ways."

But it never happened, not on that fall day in 1999, nor before McKenna was forced to step down as UW Physicians Executive Director in November 2001, when a whistle blower-generated scandal and federal investigation shook UW School of Medicine to its very core.

Sadly, my belated discovery—the same one every chair of a UW clinical department had probably made for themselves at some point in their tenure—did not sweep away a veil to reveal a shining model of efficiency. To the contrary, the deeper I looked, the more alarmed I became at the ineptness of UW Physicians. I grated at the rosy picture McKenna painted during his regular presentations at the Medical School Executive Committee (MSEC) despite the many unanswered queries my colleagues and I posed to him and his staff. I stewed when faculty members brought egregious examples of incompetence to my attention, such as when a cataract surgeon happened to discover that one of the patients he was preparing for cataract surgery in the second eye still hadn't paid for the surgery on his first eye performed two years earlier. I went through the roof when a UW Physicians administrator offhandedly mentioned that "UW Physicians simply doesn't have the resources to follow-up on denied claims that are less than $100," which was the case for almost all of our physician fees for clinic visits, a critical part of ophthalmology reimbursement. Apparently, I wasn't the only chair who was upset about what was happening at UWP. Someone generated a fictitious dialogue between a junior executive at a medical insurance company and his boss and e-mailed it anonymously to all the clinical chairs, the dean, and Brian McKenna. As I recall, it went something like this:

"Mr. Baxter, do you have a minute, sir? I think I've discovered something that should finally earn me that promotion I've been denied the last two years."

"I pretty busy, Hastings. What is it?"

"Well, sir, I've discovered that the UW Physicians practice plan at the University of Washington never appeals denied claims that are less than $100. We can save millions by just denying all of them outright."

"You'll need to do a lot better than that, Hastings," Baxter grunted. "I discovered that years ago."

"You did, sir?"

"Absolutely, Hastings. Why do you think they pay me the big bucks here at Blue Star? We'd have to pay their crosstown rival Swedish Hospital three times more for the same medical care we get from UW Physicians. You can bank on

94

UW being our preferred provider for years to come."

"That's truly brilliant, sir. I guess I've still got a lot to learn about this business."

That e-mail created quite a guffaw among my fellow chairs. McKenna missed the e-mail until one of the chairs pointed it out to him. Then, he denied it was true; he always did.

One of my biggest irritations with UW Physicians was that the physicians virtually never received feedback about their billings (as documented by H. Richard Winn, MD, in the judge-mandated article he authored).

Winn H.R. Errors in compliance with federal rules and regulations relating to healthcare benefits programs: The University of Washington Department of Neurological Surgery experience. Journal of Neurosurgery. 2004;100:47

Medicare, Medicaid, and private insurance provider rules are complicated and constantly changing, with convoluted modifiers and different levels of service to be billed, depending on the components of the examination provided, whether the patient is new or returning, and many other factors. When claims are rejected or reimbursement amounts decreased (they were never increased) for a particular examination or surgery, the physician should receive direct feedback—but almost never did at UW. Thus, all of us would go on making the same mistakes without knowing. To make matters worse, the UW Physicians billing specialists who worked with ophthalmology were constantly changing during the time I was at UW, so the physician and specialist who might help him or her correct errors rarely knew each other well. I pointed out how the system worked at the Cleveland Clinic at one of my early meetings with Brian McKenna and one of his staff members. The billing specialists in Cleveland actually work in the department and physicians find out immediately if they make an error. McKenna responded that such a system would "be too expensive." Time and experience have, however, proved just the opposite to be true for UW.

In my last year at UW, after McKenna was forced to step down, UW Physicians ran a pilot study using just the type of system I'd suggested, with the billing specialists actually in the clinic in several departments. The system must have worked well because all departments were given the option of implementing this change just before I left UW, with the billing specialist's salary being shared by the department, the hospitals, and UW Physicians. Even then, it wasn't a perfect system because UW administration had smaller departments and different hospitals sharing the specialists, meaning there would be less than optimal direct contact with individual physicians. It was, however, far better than what had been the norm. (For more on this subject and the policies of the medical insurance companies that compounded the problems, see Appendix 2.)

I put enormous effort into improving research and its funding in the department. When I arrived at UW, two of our most senior PhD investigators had ridiculously low salaries around $45,000 per year—far below the national average for this caliber of scientist—even though most of their salary was paid from the scientists' own NIH grants! I immediately doubled their salaries and set out trying to find ways to improve research support for them and other vision researchers inside and outside of the ophthalmology department at UW. I became the principal investigator for the Vision Core Grant funded by the National Eye Institute, renewed it for another five years,

Steven E. Wilson, MD

and then applied successfully to have the yearly budget increased from $320,000 per year direct costs to $500,000 per year. This grant funded core laboratories that could be used by all vision researchers at UW, providing instruments and technical expertise for specialized methods such as confocal microscopy, electron microscopy and monoclonal antibody production. I also applied successfully to have the department restored as a Research to Prevent Blindness (RPB) awardee, bringing between $110,000 and $200,000 per year in critical research support to the department and vision researchers at UW. With help from UW, I was also successful in obtaining over $500,000 in funding from a private foundation for a new state-of-the-art multi-photon confocal microscope for vision researchers and other scientists at UW.

I began a long-term effort to improve the relationship between the Washington and Idaho Lions Clubs and UW Department of Ophthalmology. At one time, there had been a very close affiliation, as there is between the Lions Clubs and many ophthalmology programs across the U.S.A. The Lions supported an eye bank and pathology laboratory in facilities at UW School of Medicine for many years. However, with the departure from UW of a faculty member specializing in corneal transplantation a few years earlier, there had been a near severing of the relationship. The Eye Bank moved away from the medical school and established a new facility at the Northwest Lions Foundation for Sight & Hearing. With the support of Fred D. Minifie, PhD, Monty Montoya, and other Lions, I managed to forge a renewed relationship with the Lions, obtaining additional support for the research of faculty members in the department.

After I'd been in my chair position for a year, I decided it was time to exercise my option to change administrators. The prior administrator was viewed as a divisive influence by a number of faculty members and was definitely resistant to change. By that time, I'd come to understand most of the critical financial complexities of the position and hoped to find a partner to continue restructuring, improving, and building the department. The dean's office agreed this was important, and within a few weeks a highly competent "roving troubleshooter" administrator was brought in to help me during the transition. The longtime administrator I inherited was moved into a position in the dean's office and a search was begun.

The operations of a clinical department with major efforts in medical care, teaching, and research are exceedingly complex, especially in a system that had grown in piecemeal fashion with revenues and expenses coming from so many different sources—faculty practice plan, dean's office, hospitals, grant funding, endowments, etc. Even for the experienced administrator, it was like stepping into a minefield. For the uninitiated, it was almost certain disaster. Couple this with the need for exceptional people skills required to interact with medical school and hospital administrators, demanding faculty and unionized departmental staff, not to mention a demanding boss, and you're looking for a needle in a haystack. The biggest obstacle was finding competent candidates who were willing to accept the salary dictated by the remuneration structure at UW School of Medicine. The maximum salary that could be offered to the head administrator of a department at UW was rigidly controlled based on the size of the department. There could be no variation from the set guidelines; otherwise, there would be mass uprising by other administrators since everyone knew what everyone else was making. Thus, the salary we were allowed to offer, approximately $85,000 to $95,000, was woefully inadequate to attract outstanding candidates in an expensive city like Seattle where the university had to compete with other employers such as Swedish Hospital, Virginia Mason Medical Center, Microsoft, Boeing, Starbucks, Amazon, Adobe, and twenty or thirty other attractive employers. Good administrators in other academic ophthalmology departments or large group practices were earning double or triple that amount. Other chairs at UW were having similar difficulties hiring qualified head departmental administrators, including the former Chair of the Department Obstetrics and Gynecology, Stephen G. Gabbe, MD, who eventually left UW to become Dean of the School of Medicine at Vanderbilt University.

After a long search, in which several good candidates were excluded due to "excessive" salary demands, and against my better judgment, the dean's office (because they had at least equal say) settled on a candidate. Unfortunately, this new administrator was a disaster right from the beginning. She never could grasp the financial complexities of the department and frankly was just too nice. Many of the departmental employees—faculty and staff—ran over her. She became increasingly frustrated, and even desperate, as the months went by. She was all but buried beneath a pile of spreadsheets, university policies, and complaints. The final blow came about six months after she was hired when I'd asked her to manage a transfer from departmental reserves to cover remodeling expenses. I got a frantic call from her later that evening while attending a function at the UW Faculty Club.

"There are no reserves, Dr. Wilson," she cried out, nearly hysterical.

"Just calm down," I replied. "Of course there are reserves."

"The dean's office just told me there are no reserves," she gasped, suddenly bursting into tears.

I called one of the dean's assistants and resolved the crisis, and we both agreed that the current situation wasn't working. Fortunately, the poor woman resigned the next day and another search was begun almost immediately. Once again, I had a succession of temporary administrator fill-ins while we interviewed a series of internal and external candidates. Each time a new fill-in was assigned by the dean's office, I had to spend hours of time reviewing the intricacies of the departmental accounts and affairs. The first new search failed to yield a candidate that the members of the search committee could agree on. At that point, a fiscal specialist (an accountant of sorts) who'd been in the department of ophthalmology for less than a year expressed interest in the position, but after consultation with key faculty and dean's office administrators, the search committee decided he didn't have sufficient experience with the duties of a head administrator. He'd spent all of his time working with spreadsheets and placing orders for supplies and equipment. I would find out nearly a year and a half later how fortuitous that decision had been when the young man, chafing under the new administrator's supervision, leveled false charges that a faculty member was misusing grant funds and quit the department in a juvenile rage. At that point, over two years into my chairmanship and still without suitable administrative support, another search was launched to fill the position.

Scores of additional candidates were screened until finally, almost in desperation, we turned to a candidate who had prior administrative experience in another school at the University of Washington. She worked hard to master the intricacies of the department and, for a time, it seemed there would finally be stability in this critical position. However, once again, it was not to be.

Steven E. Wilson, MD

Chapter 10
The Warning Tremors

In the late fall of 1999, more than a year had passed since I took my position as chair of ophthalmology. Several new faculty members had been hired, or were being recruited, and we were in the midst of trying to make accommodations to include clinical faculty in operating room and clinic schedules to enhance revenues and improve the resident educational experience. As I detailed earlier, the head administrator position in the department was up in the air. On the bright side, the refractive surgery program was progressing rapidly—far beyond our expectations for the first year. Not only were the deans of several colleges at UW my personal patients, but I was also operating on the cream of the Seattle business and social ladder, including a number of people who are household names throughout the world. The refractive program was busting at the seams in the modest space it occupied at UW Medical Center. The space we utilized was also not the best for our cash-paying patients, who expected not only the highest level of medical care and technology, but also an esthetically pleasing environment and superior service.

The clinical space where the UW Refractive Surgery program was housed in UW Medical Center had at one time been devoted completely to ophthalmology. However, a few years earlier, the hospital administrators had taken one of the rooms and converted it into a gastrointestinal diagnostics lab that primarily supported the practice of Carlos A. Pellegrini, MD, Chair of Surgery at UW. This GI lab was directly across the hall from our refractive surgery laser suite and next door to one of our exam lanes and the noises that emanated through the walls—a continuous stream of gasping, coughing, belching and farting—were a constant source of embarrassed amusement and distraction.

"What in the hell is that?" one of my VIP patients asked during a clinic one day when I was examining his eye. "Can't they put that in the basement or someplace else?" he asked, after I sheepishly explained its source.

Robert H. Muilenburg, Executive Director of UW Medical Center, was the first person from the hospital to mention the idea of building a UW Refractive and Cosmetic Surgery Center to house the esthetic surgical services at the medical school. There had actually been discussions about a cosmetic surgery center predating my arrival at UW among Bryan Sires, MD, PhD, cosmetic and orbital surgeon in ophthalmology, Ernest A. Weymuller, Jr., MD, Chair of Head and Neck Surgery, John Olerud, MD, Professor and Head of Dermatology (father of John Olerud, former American League baseball batting champion), and Dr. Pellegrini, Chair of Surgery, along with the plastic surgeons in his surgery department. These discussions had never progressed far, primarily due to inter-specialty jealousies regarding cosmetic surgery—who should be doing it and who had the right to call themselves "plastic surgeons." These "turf battles" have been fought throughout the medical world for decades, but in this case had blocked the development of a center at UW and pitted the Department of Surgery against the Departments of Ophthalmology, Head and Neck Surgery, and Dermatology.

Finally, with the support of Mr. Muilenburg and Dean Ramsey, we decided to have another go at organizing a UW Refractive and Cosmetic Surgery Center. Meetings were held between the chairs of the four departments, along with key surgeons from each department. Yet again, turf battles reared their ugly heads, with the Department of Surgery opposing the others, primarily because of the recalcitrance of the chief of plastic surgery at UW—a faculty member in surgery. Once again this faculty member occupied hours of the committee's time arguing about who should be called a "plastic surgeon." Most of his beef was based on a lack of understanding about the other subspecialties of medicine. In ophthalmology, for example, he assumed, and told his chair, that ophthalmologists doing plastic surgery had merely completed an ophthalmology residency, when in reality ophthalmic plastic surgeons like Dr. Sires had completed two additional years of training devoted exclusively to plastic and orbital surgery of the eye in highly selective fellowships approved by the American Society of Ophthalmic Plastic and Reconstructive Surgery (ASOPRS).

Futile planning and negotiation meetings continued for nearly a year until finally Carlos Pellegrini, MD, Chair of Surgery, notified the dean, the hospital, and the other interested chairs that he was "washing his hands" of the joint program. With the roadblock cleared, the other three department chairs worked with the UW Medical Center to create the new UW Refractive and Cosmetic Surgery Center in beautifully remodeled space at UW Roosevelt, a few miles away from the medical school campus. Ironically, prior to the opening of the center, the department of surgery's director of plastic surgery resigned to move into private practice in the Seattle area, a move he'd likely been planning while he was sitting at the table attempting to block formation of the new UW center—with which he would soon be in competition. Predictably, after the new center designed to accommodate faculty from the three collaborating departments opened, the Department of Surgery hired a new faculty member who was eager to participate in the venture. The only problem was the center hadn't been built with sufficient space or designed to accommodate the expanded service that would now include total body plastic surgery. A compromise was reached, but the entire experience was frustrating, to say the least, to the chairs who had amiably collaborated on the project from the beginning.

Suddenly, in November of 1999, alarming rumors swept the medical school that agents from the Federal Bureau of Investigation and U.S. Department of Health and Human Services had seized records from the UW Physicians and CUMG faculty practice plan offices. Totally in the dark about what was happening, most of the department chairs received scant information from the medical school administrators, including the dean, other than nebulous announcements at the monthly meetings of the Medical School Executive Committee (MSEC). At the time, none of us realized this was the igniting spark of an inferno that would destroy the careers of several prominent faculty members, engulf the entire medical school, and threaten to shake the institution to the ground. What few of us knew for more than a year after the FBI raid was that Mark Erickson, an employee involved in billing and compliance at UW Physicians and CUMG, the faculty practice plans directed by Brian McKenna, filed a whistle-blower lawsuit in the summer of 1999.

_____

https://www.plainsite.org/dockets/22whhizwu/washington-western-district-court/us-ex-rel-erickson-v-university-of-wa-phys/

_____

This occurred shortly after the U.S. Attorney's Office received funding for a full-time prosecutor to pursue health-care fraud. UW was to be the first victim—uh, I mean target—of this erstwhile Federal government plan to "wipe out Medicare fraud that's rampant in medical schools throughout America," according to one U.S. government official.

As the month wore on, a feeling of foreboding permeated the chairs and their departments, as rumors of trucks filled with documents being taken from UW Physicians and CUMG offices, as well as from the hospitals and some departments, filtered through the UW School of Medicine. None of these rumors was ever confirmed. All most of us ever learned about the growing crisis from medical school administration was from vague updates from the dean and his lieutenants at the Medical School Executive Committee meetings, including announcements of decisions about covering the mounting costs of reproducing documents and providing legal defense for the medical school and the faculty practice plans. Those expenses would be borne by all of the departments, regardless of whether or not they were a target of the growing investigation, from the funds derived from physician clinical fees normally used to cover departmental expenses, faculty salaries, and nonexistent faculty incentive payments. Some chairs undoubtedly received more information, but all I knew was the fact there'd been no communication between the FBI and any member of the department of ophthalmology—including me. At these same monthly MSEC meetings, the chairs soon began getting advice about whom to contact in case the FBI appeared at their front door to ask questions, including a hotline phone number where we could reach UW legal counsel twenty-four hours a day—even on weekends and holidays. I remember sitting in stunned silence listening to a briefing from one of the medical school's attorneys and thinking to myself, *What in the hell have I gotten myself into?*"

Despite the uncertainty and ongoing difficulties with the departmental administrator position, departmental finances, disgruntled faculty, and other pleasures of chairmanship, Jennifer, the twins, and I settled into our home on Juanita Bay. We developed great friendships with several of our neighbors and enjoyed boating on Lake Washington and in the San Juan Islands in the Puget Sound during my vacation time. We also socialized with UW friends and families both inside and outside the department of ophthalmology, including Bryan Sires, Kris Palczewski, Bob Kalina, Bruce Ransom, and Dick Winn.

Jennifer and I went out to dinner or joined parties with Dick and Debbie Winn several times during those first three years. One recurring theme stands out clearly from those gatherings. There wasn't a single occasion when Jennifer and I socialized with the Winns that Dick didn't take a long phone call from one of his residents or faculty members to discuss a seriously ill patient, often leaving for the hospital to perform surgery. It must have happened at least a dozen times during those first three years and I remember feeling twinges of guilt because my life was so much more predictable and serene by comparison. I can say bluntly that Dick Winn is unequivocally one of the most dedicated and talented surgeons and teachers I've ever known.

I'm certainly not the only one who felt that way—not by a long shot—I've spoken to scores of people inside and outside of UW who feel the same way.

It's not that Winn didn't have his detractors; he most certainly did. Chief among them were several tenured faculty members in his department of neurosurgery who moaned about everything he'd done for many years—similar to the deadwood I dealt with in my own department. Dick was a quick-witted, no-nonsense kind of guy with a sharp tongue. As such, he at times rubbed people the wrong way, especially those who were envious of the accolades and stature he enjoyed locally, nationally, and internationally because of his prodigious clinical, research, teaching, and administrative skills.

***

UW was hit with a staggering tragedy in early 2000. Robert H. Muilenburg, executive director of UW Medical Center for over two decades and the man who turned the fledgling UW hospital into a nationally-rated medical center consistently ranked among the top institutions in the country, suffered the sudden onset of neurological symptoms early one morning after he arrived at work. A medical workup and surgery revealed a malignant brain tumor and, despite treatment, he suffered a shockingly rapid decline. It was a devastating blow to the UW Medical Center, UW School of Medicine, and to me personally. In the short time I'd been at UW, I'd come to know Rob Muilenburg as an incredibly kind, but insightful, no-nonsense partner in the further development of the ophthalmology and refractive and cosmetic surgery programs, along with David Jaffe, Executive Director at Harborview Medical Center. Now the UW Medical Center had lost its rudder or as Paul Ramsey, Dean of UW School of Medicine, said, "Its heart and soul." Mr. Muilenberg died on September 20, 2000, and it was one of the saddest days of my medical career.

***

Around this time, administrators from the dean's office contacted me about including ophthalmology in a new venture to establish a specialty clinic on the "Eastside" of the extended Seattle metropolitan area. Lake Washington separates downtown Seattle, the University of Washington, and "Westside" neighborhoods like Madison Park, Capitol Hill, Queen Anne, and Magnolia from Eastside communities such as Bellevue, Kirkland, Issaquah, and Redmond. The Eastside is separated from UW Medical Center and Harborview Medical Center by the I-90 and Highway 520 floating bridges, and is the home of Microsoft and many other thriving Seattle businesses. The Eastside is also served by several UW primary care clinics and is an area of tremendous population growth. Many "Eastsiders" were unwilling to cross the bridges for services on the west bank of Lake Washington due to traffic, inadequate parking, or other inconveniences.

The plan, conveyed to several chairs of clinical departments at the medical school, was to concentrate several procedure-oriented clinical subspecialties in a convenient location. To me it was a no-brainer, the medical school obviously needed to have a strong presence on the Eastside. The only problem was the business plan. For the most part, the new clinic would be funded by "investments" from the participating departments' reserves and there would be no participation by UW Medical Center, even though it stood to benefit enormously from the patients who needed surgical care, all of which would be performed at the medical center. The stated reason was that the medical center was already over-committed to other projects, such as the building of the Surgical Pavilion on the main campus of the medical school. I was wary of the venture because ophthalmology participation would require dedication of enormous resources for a department of our size, primarily because, unlike many departments, we could not share clinical spaces with other subspecialties. The expensive and bulky slit lamps, ophthalmoscopes, and other dedicated instrumentation used in eye lanes for diagnosis and treatment precluded other services from sharing our exam rooms. I, however, as a relatively new chair at UW, felt pressured by the medical school to participate and, besides, the business plan created such a rosy picture for the participating departments.

First of all, clinical revenues generated at the center would be exempted from the twelve percent dean's tax for several years. Then, there was the "windfall revenue" that would be generated by the new CT scanning and radiology unit to be included in the specialty center. The projections of Eastside need indicated the CT scanner would support the stakeholders through the startup and beyond. Supposedly in short supply in the Seattle area, the plan projected the CT scanner to be oversubscribed almost immediately with business from the UW primary care network and, therefore, to have a key role in the success of the project.

Despite my lingering reservations, I decided the ophthalmology department needed to have an Eastside presence now and in the future. My concerns were partially assuaged when an ideally-located facility was leased in Bellevue, and remodeling designs included a prominently located ophthalmology suite with five examination rooms, perfect for one or two busy eye surgeons.

I involved myself directly in the operations of the new ophthalmology center at the 'University of Washington Physicians Eastside Subspecialty Center' (a long awkward name I opposed, but to no avail), making sure that we had highly skilled, patient-friendly technicians and desk attendants. I hand-picked the faculty members from my department who would have clinics on the Eastside to make sure we had the very best in bedside manner and skill. I even scheduled myself a half-day of refractive surgery clinic each week.

Finally, the sparkling center opened in 2001, but rather than the glorious event the launch could—and should—have been, it soon became the sounds of silence. Despite assurances to the contrary, there was no marketing program to announce the arrival of the new clinic to Eastside patients. For months, the only marketing strategies performed were notifications to the physicians at the UW primary care centers sprinkled around the Eastside community about the new center, but that brought only a trickle of patients. I was appalled to discover, during the first week the center was open, that a patient couldn't even phone the information operator to get the phone number for the UW Physicians Eastside Subspecialty Center. Instead, they'd be given the number for the UW Physicians billing offices! I immediately notified the administrators in charge of the venture and continued calling them every week for a couple of months before this egregious oversight was rectified.

UW Medical Center was supposed to encourage its Eastside patients to utilize the facility, but the staff at the hospital only paid lip service to our increasingly desperate pleas for help. Rob Muilenberg wasn't there anymore and the hospital administrators now in charge saw the fledgling center as a threat, rather than a partner. Eventually, it became clear that the lack of marketing for the center was active rather than passive. Chairs of departments who were not involved in the center were concerned that high-profile marketing of the new center would alienate Eastside physicians who referred to them and pressured medical school administration to keep the efforts subdued. Belatedly, the center administrators agreed to put up a billboard on busy Highway 520 for a month or two, in addition to placing some advertisements on Eastside buses, but it was too little too late. The signs were so obtuse nobody could understand them. I even scratched my head about the message, and I knew what they were supposed to promote. The sign could have simply said, "UW surgical specialty care now available in Bellevue!" with the phone number. Instead, they were so ineffectual the firm that handled marketing for the medical school and UW Physicians was summarily fired. The administrators who approved the marketing plan should have been fired, too—but they weren't.

Even worse, the CT scanner that was supposed to anchor the center turned out to be a financial albatross. Rather than a flood of new patients beating down the door, there was only a dribble of patients needing advanced imaging referred from the UW Eastside primary care clinics. I recall the pain I felt when reviewing the monthly reports on patient numbers and revenues. The economic picture became so bleak that the stakeholder departments were forced to ante up more seed money—effectively throwing good money after bad—to keep the project afloat. But still the patient numbers remained a fraction of what were needed to make the center successful. Worst of all, there was no prospect for an improvement; nobody in the Eastside Seattle suburbs even knew the facility existed.

Finally, less than two years after the opening, ophthalmology was forced to withdraw from the venture and absorb further losses to sell off the equipment that had been obtained through long-term lease. The department lost over a million dollars in the ill-fated scheme, wasting sorely needed funds that could have been used for additional faculty recruitments and remodeling. In the end, UW Medical Center bought out the specialty center, but ophthalmology recovered only a fraction of the expended funds. Not surprisingly, once the medical center became the primary stakeholder, a reasonable marketing plan was approved, and even the name was changed to a more lucid "UW Medicine: Eastside Specialty Center." But these changes were much too late for several of the founding departments of the center, leaving a bitter taste in all of our mouths and leaving us wary of any future "great ideas" floated by the dean's office. Getting involved in this ill-fated enterprise was my biggest mistake as a chair.

***

On a sunny Wednesday afternoon in June of 2000, while I was seeing patients in the UW Refractive Surgery Center on the first floor of UW Medical Center, an unspeakable tragedy occurred in the basement of the hospital. Dr. Jian Chen, a recently naturalized U.S. citizen from China and a struggling resident in UW's world-class pathology program, let himself into his mentor Rodger Haggit's office and locked the door behind him.

http://articles.latimes.com/2000/jun/29/news/mn-46184

Chen, who at forty-one years of age began his residency in the summer of 1999, had once seen the program as his "golden opportunity" to make a mark in academic medicine. But, almost immediately, he'd run into trouble and, clearly in over his head, by August of 1999 had been told his work was not up to par. Finally, in November of 1999, he was informed that the pathology training program planned to let him go on July 1, 2000. Pathology department faculty, including world-renowned pathologist and researcher Haggit, tried to help him find another, less rigorous, residency. However, as the months passed and no other opportunity appeared, Chen became depressed and likely desperate about his failure and thoughts of losing face with his family and friends back in the Fujian Province of China. His erratic behavior increasingly troubled those around him, culminating in a fellow resident making an alarming discovery on Chen's desk: the yellow pages opened to the gun store section and an internet map on his computer screen showing driving directions to one of the stores. UW officials, including the university police, questioned Chen, but they were powerless to do anything since he claimed he was only interested in a gun for personal safety. Chen subsequently purchased a Glock .357 pistol at a Bellevue gun shop and, after the mandatory waiting period, picked it up on June 12.

A suicide note found in Chen's backpack, contained a note to Haggit that included the missive, "I will die...You will live," seemed to make it clear, at least when he stepped into his mentor's office, Chen only intended to take his own life. For whatever reason, however, events took a different turn once he was inside the office. People outside, in the hall, reported hearing loud voices, followed by several gunshots. Professor Haggit died from four gunshot wounds to the body, while Jian Chen died from a self-inflicted gunshot to the head.

UW School of Medicine was plunged into deep mourning and despair by the murder-suicide. A poignant memorial service followed at the medical school a few days later. Feelings of fear and anxiety persisted among UW faculty and employees for months after the tragedy. Several ophthalmology faculty members told me they'd become afraid to write critical comments in resident and fellow evaluations.

We all struggled to put the tragedy out of our minds and go on with the responsibilities to our patients and trainees. After the hiring of my third head departmental administrator in a little over three years, however, there was increasing malcontent among support staff members, including fiscal specialists, secretaries, and others who'd gotten used to working with little or no supervision the previous two years. I'd worked with unionized employees before at LSU Eye Center and UT Southwestern, but the combination of university policies and union lunacy at UW was unbelievable. It was virtually impossible to get rid of anyone at the medical school, even if they didn't show up to work. One example will illustrate the magnitude of the problem. At one point, we hired a new secretary and, after just a few weeks on the job, he didn't show up for work. Several days passed without contact of any kind—no telephone call, nothing. Since the employee was new to UW and still in his probationary period, we contacted the human resources department about getting a replacement. About two weeks later, we were informed that our employee, who unbeknownst to us turned out to be a HIV-infected drug abuser, would be returning to work the following week. My administrator informed me that human resources said we'd have to take him back in the department. Dismayed, I called the head of human resources myself to ask just what the meaning of the 'probationary period' was if we were precluded from terminating a new employee who didn't show up for work for two weeks and failed to notify us. She told me we had to follow UW policies and the contract with the union. Needless to say, I was beside myself with annoyance and frustrated with a system that prevented me from removing someone who just disappeared without calling or otherwise notifying the department.

***

Somehow, despite all of the time-consuming duties of being chairman and maintaining a busy clinical practice, I also managed to stay on track with my personal academic career. In addition to renewing and increasing the budget for the *Vision Research Center Core* P-30 NIH grant for UW, I also renewed my own R01 NIH grant *Corneal Epithelial Growth Factors and Receptors* for another five years. The latter grant received a score around the fifteenth percentile in the VISC NIH study section. In addition, I submitted another R01 grant *Keratocyte Apoptosis in the Cornea* that focused on the role of keratocyte apoptosis as an initiator of the wound healing response in the cornea and, possibly, involved in the pathophysiology of a progressive corneal ecstatic disease called keratoconus. Despite strong preliminary data suggesting a role for chronic ongoing keratocyte apoptosis in keratoconus and two rewritings of the grant, it never received a fundable score in the VISA NIH study section and the work was abandoned. A colleague who served on VISA at that time told me years later that I'd been just one of many victims of a bloc of reviewers whom fellow study section members referred to as the "Mafia," a group of half a dozen or so section members who undermined grants that focused on areas related to their personal research interests.

I was elected to the Refractive Special Interest Group Executive Board (that later became ISRS-AAO) of the American Academy of Ophthalmology for a five-year term in 1999. In 2001, I was also elected to a five-year term as Corneal Section trustee for the Association for Research in Vision and Ophthalmology, the largest vision research organization in the world with over ten thousand members. I view this as one of the highest honors of my career, since election by my peers in research, both MD and PhD, was an indication of the esteem with which they viewed my contributions in vision research. In addition, in 2002, I was elected to the American Ophthalmological Society, an honorary society of ophthalmologists.

During my time in Seattle, I continued serving on the editorial boards of several peer-reviewed journals, including *Investigative Ophthalmology and Visual Sciences* (*IOVS*) and *Experimental Eye Research*, the two premiere vision research journals, and *Cornea* and *The Journal of Refractive Surgery*. I became Chief Medical Editor of *Review of Refractive Surgery*. My service to *The Journal of Refractive Surgery* and the journal *Cornea* continues to the present.

On the clinical side, I was named a VISX Star surgeon in 1999, and acknowledged by Best Doctors to be in the top two percent of refractive and corneal surgeons in the U.S., as selected by my peers. My refractive surgery staff and I worked hard to make the UW Refractive Surgery Center one of the top refractive surgery programs in the country.

Combined with my duties as Chair of Ophthalmology at UW, these academic pursuits and my responsibilities to my young children and wife kept me exceptionally busy. I used to jokingly tell friends that my position at UW was 50% administrative, 50% research, and 50% clinical.

***

Almost immediately after the UW Refractive Surgery Center opened in 1998, I began seeing large numbers of patients who'd had serious complications after refractive surgery. Most of these patients came from high volume discount LASIK centers like Lexington Eye Institute in Vancouver or ICON Laser Centers in Seattle. The worst problems by far, however, were seen in patients operated on at Lexington, with preoperative and postoperative care performed by an optometry group in Bellevue, Washington. The complications included irregular ablations with a German excimer laser that never received approval for use in the U.S.A., severe flap striae (wrinkles) and epithelial in-growth beneath the LASIK flap from the corneal surface. I was willing to see these unfortunate patients and told each of them I'd do what I could to help, but I made it clear I would not participate in lawsuits. The patients who came to me for a second opinion included three sisters who had serious problems with vision quality, as well as glare and halos at night. I examined each of the women; unfortunately, two had problems that could not be treated. The third had severe striae in one of her eyes. I tried to remove them by lifting the flap and stretching out the flap, but little if any improvement was noted. All three sisters eventually filed a lawsuit against Lexington and the Bellevue optometrists in U.S. courts, with a judge ruling that Lexington surgeons were practicing medicine in the United States since they arranged for their patients to have preoperative and postoperative care in Bellevue, Washington. The three sisters and several other Lexington patients honored my request not to be involved in legal proceedings, but the attorneys for the optometrists in Bellevue, as well as their insurance company, subpoenaed me for depositions and trial testimony and harassed me with phone calls and unwarranted demands for irrelevant information. The attorneys for the optometrists went so far as to serve me with subpoenas to appear for depositions during my own clinics at UW

105

Refractive Surgery Center—in an unsuccessful attempt to embarrass me in front of my own patients, even though I'd never failed to provide records or appear for depositions when I received written notice. As I pointed out to the lead attorney for the optometrists, it really didn't take a rocket scientist to figure out that it was probably not a good idea to antagonize a treating physician who was a potential witness in the case, but the harassment continued. By the time the sisters' trial and that of another patient occurred, I was only too happy to testify on behalf of the patients. Each of these cases was eventually settled in 2002. The awards received by the patients were not disclosed.

***

In September of 2000, UW began having mandatory compliance meetings—purportedly to instruct physicians how to bill properly. All physicians at UW were required to attend, but the fact is that most of my clinical faculty had already been attending yearly Medicare billing courses put on by organizations such as the American Academy of Ophthalmology or the Washington Academy of Eye Physicians and Surgeons (WAEPS) to stay abreast of the constantly changing Medicare and Medicaid regulations. I'm not sure, but I believe it's likely that faculty in other departments were doing the same.

At that point, most of the other department heads, at least those I spoke with frequently, were as totally in the dark about what was going on with the federal investigation into Medicare and Medicaid billing as I was. I don't remember ever speaking with Dick Winn about the investigation. We always seemed to have other things to talk about. In retrospect, I saw less of Dick after my first two years at UW, both socially and at the university, but I thought nothing of it. We were both extremely busy with our departmental, clinical, and research activities. The little information I received was at those monthly Medical School Executive Committee (MSEC) meetings, including private discussions with UW attorneys, but the information was superficial and for the most part continued to focus on what to do in case the investigators came knocking on your door and discussions regarding the escalating departmental share of costs for UW Physicians and UW School of Medicine defending themselves. All of these expenses were being paid from our clinical revenues needed for departmental operational costs and faculty salaries. At that point, we didn't have to worry about faculty incentives, since these increasing costs tipped us into the red and it was necessary to dip into our reserves just to balance the departmental books.

The shocking news that a grand jury had been empaneled to review the case came in 2000. I first read about it in the *Seattle Post-Intelligencer* while drinking my morning coffee and preparing to leave for work. This event raised the stakes to an entirely different level, indicating that criminal charges could be brought against employees of UW School of Medicine. Subsequently, numerous subpoenas were served on University of Washington to demand production of millions of documents relating to claims filed for services provided by UW faculty physicians. In addition, numerous subpoenas were served to compel the appearance of witnesses, including UW Physicians employees, UW School of Medicine employees, UW School of Medicine faculty, and even resident physicians in training. Some e-mail announcement was sent to the clinical department chairs, and eventually clinical faculty, indicating that the medical school was confident that any errors were inadvertent and attributable to the complex and changing Medicare and Medicaid regulations. In addition, the U.S. Department of Justice and the U.S. Department of Health and Human Services began a related civil investigation around this time.

I distinctly remember the Medical School Executive Committee meeting that followed the announcement regarding the grand jury. The room was filled with approximately forty people, including departmental chairs, medical school administrators, and UW Physicians leaders. The atmosphere was very different—much more subdued than usual—prior to the beginning of the meeting. The meeting began with several housekeeping agenda items, and then everyone left the room but the dean, the clinical chairs, a few dean's office administrators—and the attorneys. It was made clear at that point that the rest of the meeting would be confidential and protected by attorney-client privilege and no minutes would be taken. Dean Paul Ramsey said a few words about the grand jury and expressed his confidence that in the end there would be no criminal charges; that the investigation would reveal that there had merely been some mistakes. Then, the team of attorneys gave us a sketchy synopsis about what was happening in the investigation. I'm fairly certain that this meeting was the first time we were told that the investigation at UW was based on a whistleblower lawsuit filed by a UW Physicians employee *who was still working in the office*. The name of the whistleblower had been unwittingly revealed to UW and its attorneys in documents provided by the federal prosecutor. All eyes in the room turned to Brian McKenna, sitting mute near the head of the table. Still, we received no information regarding which departments were involved in the investigation. I felt certain that ophthalmology wasn't involved, since I'd heard absolutely nothing about the case outside of the announcements at the MSEC meetings.

At some point in mid-2000, with begrudging UW Physicians assistance, my departmental administrator and I reviewed several hundred random patient charts and billings, including twenty or so sets of documents from each of the clinical faculty members in ophthalmology. The purpose of this project was to get an idea of where ophthalmology stood with its billing and compliance. We did find some errors, but the majority were actually "down-coding" errors in which the physicians were billing less for service than was actually provided. In fact, there was one faculty member who consistently underbilled nearly every patient. When this was brought to the faculty member's attention, he admitted he'd been doing this intentionally to "make sure he didn't get caught up in the investigation." After reviewing our billing tendencies, I couldn't help wondering whether the feds hadn't already accomplished one of their primary goals at UW— decreasing medical costs, even if it meant the physicians were billing less than they were rightfully due. I also recalled what happened at the University of Pennsylvania after the federal investigation at that medical school. Total billings actually went up in the years following the investigation when measures were instituted to make sure that there was neither up- nor down-coding.

In the late summer of 2001, I had the third of five one-on-one meetings with Dean Paul Ramsey, MD, during my tenure at University of Washington. Yes, we met only five times during my five years and each meeting was less than thirty minutes. The 2001 meeting was prompted by a memo I sent the dean outlining the progress we'd made in ophthalmology the prior three years—increasing the number of clinical and research faculty members in the department, increasing NIH funding, and increasing clinical revenues. I also pointed out that the new space I'd been given and remodeling in the department was fully committed to new and existing faculty and that the department needed additional space if the clinical and research programs were to continue to grow. I specifically asked for more support for faculty recruitment and the remaining three thousand square feet of space still occupied by neuropathology on the eighth floor of the RR building, seventy-five percent of which was already occupied by ophthalmology labs. It was a cordial meeting, with Ramsey complimenting the job I'd done in reorganizing and invigorating the department, and especially in dealing with testy senior faculty in the department—without a permanent, skilled administrator to help out.

"I hope you don't think I misled you during your recruitment about the situation in the department?" he asked at one point.

We also discussed the problems I'd faced in finding a suitable departmental administrator, and he assured me that medical school administrator Marlow Key and Associate Dean of Management and Administration Bob Gust would redouble their efforts to recruit an outstanding professional. Finally, Dr. Ramsey let me know that, for the foreseeable future, there would be no additional funds or space for ophthalmology because there were other projects and chair recruitments that would tax his resources. I must say it was what I expected. For small departments like ophthalmology, it's rare for a chairman, or even a faculty member, to obtain additional resources beyond what they are able to negotiate during their recruitment. I left the meeting that day knowing I needed to decide if I'd be interested in staying at UW and merely maintaining the department of ophthalmology in its current, albeit improved, state for the next ten to fifteen years. Frankly, it wasn't a very attractive prospect.

Chapter 11

Fending Off the Demons

Jennifer and I took off from the Seattle-Tacoma airport in the late afternoon of September 10, 2001, headed for Amsterdam. It was the beginning of a two-week lecture trip and we'd decided to spend a day in Amsterdam to visit the Rijksmuseum before going on to clinical meetings in Milan and Helsinki. The day started inauspiciously, with us missing our direct flight to Amsterdam after being delayed by Seattle traffic. We were diverted to Memphis and arrived at Schiphol Airport in Amsterdam on the afternoon—European time—of September 11, and took a cab to the Hotel de L'Europe on the edge of the Red Light District. After making our way to our room, I sat on the edge of the bed watching the news on CNN, while Jennifer soaked in the Jacuzzi bathtub. Fighting to keep my eyes open, I watched normal programming for a few minutes, before a viewer alert announced that one of the World Trade Center towers in New York was on fire, after apparently being hit by an airplane. Calling Jennifer into the room, I mused aloud how the automated guidance system could have gotten so screwed up to fly a plane into the tallest building in Manhattan. Then, the second plane hit and I turned to Jennifer. "We're at war," I said solemnly, realizing it was no accident.

We immediately called KLM Airlines and moved our flights to Milan back one day and made reservations for a second night at the De L'Europe. This was a fortuitous decision since thousands of travelers were stuck in the Schiphol Airport for days, or even weeks, after the tragedy. We telephoned Jennifer's parents to let them know we were safe and talked to our children before sitting down to watch the dreadful 9/11 events unfold. It was the beginning of two of the most memorable weeks of my life, at once tragic and euphoric. Tragic because of the deep sorrow we felt for our fellow Americans who perished in the cowardly attacks and because we really wanted to be back home with our children and countrymen. Euphoric because of the outpouring of sympathy and support we experienced everywhere we went in Amsterdam, Milan, and Helsinki over the next two weeks. It was truly an amazing, awe-inspiring experience that reminded us just how wonderful it was to be Americans.

We watched the non-stop television coverage of the calamity for several hours. Finally, after seeing the first building collapse, we decided we couldn't bear to watch anymore and made our way down to the street. We spotted a pub a few blocks from the hotel and decided to stop to eat dinner. As soon as we pushed through the door, we realized the obvious—all of the televisions in the pub were tuned to coverage of the terrorist attack. A Brit in the back of the smoky, dim-lit room yelled out, "Hey, are you Americans?" I acknowledged we were. A chill ran up my spine and tears welled in my eyes as everyone in the pub broke into loud applause and cheering. Several patrons approached to speak to us. It would be much the same everywhere we went in Europe for the next two weeks.

We made it to Milan two days later and stayed with our equally gracious Italian colleagues for nearly a week. Several other American speakers didn't leave early for the meeting and never arrived in Milan. Jennifer and I flew back to Amsterdam after the meeting was over, so she could catch a plane back to the States and I could continue on to Helsinki. Jennifer's scheduled flight to Seattle ended up being one of the first allowed back into the United States after the terrorist attack. My reception in Helsinki was even more supportive than it had been in Amsterdam and Milan—just because I was an American. To this day it gives me goosebumps to think about it.

I spent quite a bit of time on airplanes and in hotels during those two weeks and I decided to begin writing my second novel, an adventure story beginning just a few months prior to 9/11 in a Northern Alliance enclave outside of Taloqan, Afghanistan. I managed to finish the first few chapters of *Winter in Kandahar* before I arrived back in Seattle. The novel was published in late 2003, and became a finalist for the *Benjamin Franklin Award* for 2004 in the category Best New Voice in Fiction.

An intense feeling of homesickness swept over me when my plane touched down on the tarmac in Seattle on September 25, 2001. The world had changed forever over the two weeks since I'd left—and so had Seattle.

The immediate effect I noticed, not surprisingly, was a sudden drop-off in the demand for refractive surgery. Patients who'd scheduled surgery prior to the al-Qaeda attack cancelled and the telephones stopped ringing in the UW Refractive Surgery Center. We weren't alone. A dense fog rolled across refractive surgery centers throughout the United States and Canada—a fog that would take two years to lift. The direct effect of this downturn was diminished revenue for the department of ophthalmology, making an already precarious situation suddenly worse. The meager biannual incentive payments for clinicians, already amounting to at most a few thousand dollars for even the most productive physicians, dried up completely. My salary was not based on incentive, but that did little to alleviate the angst I felt for my faculty—or that they felt for themselves and their families, since most were already paid one third to one half of what they could have earned in private practice. As dedicated academic physicians, most of them never complained, at least to me directly. The outstanding faculty members in the department—those who deserved these incentive payments—clearly weren't in academic medicine to make money, but for the privilege of caring for patients, teaching medical students, residents, and fellows, and pursuing research.

The precipitous U.S. stock market decline also had a devastating effect on our department and other departments in UW School of Medicine—since UW Physicians had invested the bulk of departmental reserves in stocks. I remember having an irrepressible sense of foreboding during those months, as did many Americans, while U.S. Special Forces and jets from the Navy and Air Force swept through Afghanistan in search of Osama bin Laden, Mullah Omar, and their henchmen.

In November of 2001, came the stunning news that Brian McKenna had been forced to step down from the positions of Executive Director of UW Physicians and Children's University Medical Group he'd held for seventeen years—in my opinion about fifteen years too late. Amazingly, he was given a new position in business development at UW School of Medicine, where I once again encountered his meager administrative skills when dealing with the UW Eastside Subspecialty Center fiasco. Eventually, the deputy director the UW Physicians retired, likely stepping aside under pressure. I sensed the federal investigation was intensifying, but like the majority of department chairs, I remained in the dark, gleaning little solid information from the monthly Medical School Executive Committee meetings or stories in the Seattle newspapers. The rumor mills were churning, however, and I began hearing snippets about neurosurgery being involved in the inquiry. Upon hearing these whispers, I recalled I'd been seeing less and less of Dick Winn, both at the medical school and socially, during the prior year. I never, however, asked him about the rumors, figuring he'd say something if he wanted to discuss it with me.

In the fall of 2001, I also learned a malpractice lawsuit—the first of my career—had been filed by my patient who had laser correction surgery for six diopters of farsightedness (hyperopia)—shortly after the VISX excimer laser was approved for treatment of this condition. After significant regression of the correction, a retreatment was performed and the patient ended up with significant irregular astigmatism, limiting both his uncorrected vision and vision correctable with glasses. For a time, the patient did well with gas-permeable contact lenses, but eventually had a worsening of the vision in the eye that had been limited to 20/40 since birth by a preexisting condition called amblyopia. I offered the patient corneal transplantation at University of Washington, but he elected to have the procedure done nearer to home in eastern Washington and, unfortunately, ended up with very high astigmatism in the eye after the sutures holding the transplant were removed, as commonly occurs following corneal transplantation.

I knew in my heart I'd done nothing wrong in providing the original treatment of farsightedness for the patient. I'd applied a new treatment that had been approved by the FDA and I had relied on this approval as confirmation that the procedure was safe and effective. However, in the only two patients I treated for farsightedness over 5 diopters, the outcomes were poor—an unacceptable outcome incidence of 100% rather than a typical rate of far less than 1% in eyes within the range from +4 diopters of hyperopia to -7 diopters of myopia. I subsequently discovered that the data submitted to gain FDA approval of the VISX laser for corrections over +4 diopters were generated in Canada rather than the United States. After seeing the results from these patients, and others I treated, and hearing similar reports from other surgeons who treated high farsightedness after the FDA approval, I decided that correction over +4.5 diopters of farsightedness should never have been approved by the FDA in the first place. Nevertheless, the University of Washington and I were the only ones named in the lawsuit, for me based on the "Captain of the Ship" doctrine. Thus, regardless of how flawed the information was I relied on to make the decision that to treat this level of hyperopia with the VISX laser was safe, and likely to be effective, I was ultimately responsible since I was the surgeon who performed the procedure. I really couldn't blame the patient. I probably would have filed a suit myself if I had to have a corneal transplant in one of my eyes, but hopefully, I would have identified those who were truly to blame.

I met with a defense attorney provided by the University of Washington for the first time on November 30, 2001. The patient initially hired an attorney who had no clue about ophthalmology and refractive surgery. Eventually, however, likely after realizing their limitations, the plaintiff linked up with an aggressive attorney who'd cut his teeth on several radial keratotomy cases performed in the proceeding decade by infamous radial keratotomy (RK) surgeon Herschell Boyd, who'd mysteriously vanished (probably to Liechtenstein) after nearly one hundred lawsuits were filed against him. It took two years for the case to proceed to the point at which the patient's deposition was taken. My own deposition wasn't taken until July 29, 2003, just before I left Seattle. I also had to respond to a litany of written questions posed to me every few months by the plaintiff's attorney—questions like "Convert this plus cylinder eye glasses prescription to the equivalent minus cylinder prescription"—that could have been answered by merely looking in any basic text on ophthalmology. The questions weren't really posed to me to gain information for the patient's team as much as they were intended to keep up a steady stream of harassment, hoping we would tire of the aggravation and agree to settle the case.

The claims in the case were typical of those I've seen in other cases where I served as an expert witness—i.e., it was alleged that the patient didn't really give informed consent, even though I documented in the chart that I'd personally discussed the patient's high farsightedness correction, potential complications, and the uncertainties about correcting that level of refractive error despite the FDA approval, in addition to providing the patient with written and videotaped materials regarding potential complications. The patient also claimed he had "suffered severe ridicule from his friends about his glasses" even though he admitted that friends had teased him and called him "Mr. Magoo" from an early age. He also asserted he couldn't participate in usually pleasurable activities, even though my attorney ascertained during his deposition that the gentleman was regularly playing golf at his country club and maintained a low handicap that was as good or better than it had been prior to LASIK surgery.

To add insult to injury, another patient, one who had a poor outcome after LASIK to correct very high myopia (nearsightedness) of approximately -12 diopters shortly after the FDA approved the VISX laser for LASIK treatments up to -14 diopters, found the same aggressive plaintiff's attorney. Thus, I was forced to sit through depositions on two cases with this attorney improperly attempting to get information for one case during deposition for the other. Of course, my attorney didn't allow it. The patient's problems from LASIK came down to the very high –12 diopter correction, inducing aberrations that degraded vision quality. We weren't aware of higher-order aberrations when the FDA approved high myopia corrections. The patient claimed he wasn't a candidate to begin with, since we would only be able to partially correct his -17.5 diopters of myopia, however, our discussions of this fact were detailed in the chart, along with the patient's understanding that he would still need to wear -5 to -6 diopter glasses (approximately one third the thickness of his original glasses). Also detailed in the chart was his desire to proceed, with that understanding. He also claimed he hadn't given informed consent, again despite documentation in the chart that the patient received written, video, and verbal information regarding potential benefits and complications directly from me. Finally, the attorney asserted that "microstriae" in the cornea I "should have removed" were the source of the patient's problem. Every cornea with a correction over -6 diopters of myopia has microstriae— even those with 20/20, or better, uncorrected visual acuity and no visual complaints, because of disparity between the posterior surface of the LASIK flap and its underlying bed that has been ablated with the excimer laser. All of the claims were complete and utter nonsense, and my attorney and I were prepared to prove it in court.

The proceedings for both cases dragged on into 2004, long after I'd left the University of Washington. The plaintiff's attorney used the same "hired gun" Beverly Hills "expert witness" for both cases. This journeyman ophthalmologist, of whom I had never heard, derived a significant proportion of his income from plaintiff witness work that he sought through advertisements on the internet and via expert witness lists for which he paid for inclusion. Clearly, the plaintiffs couldn't find any real expert refractive surgeons willing to testify. I was totally opposed to settlement of the cases, firmly believing I'd done nothing wrong and welcoming the opportunity to present my side of the stories in court, especially regarding the high corrections for hyperopia and myopia that had been approved by the FDA, but which were very shortly thereafter abandoned by most knowledgeable refractive surgeons (farsightedness corrections above +4.5 diopters and nearsightedness corrections above -10 diopters). The University of Washington, however, had other plans. The risk management officials decided they wanted to settle the lawsuits because they'd "changed malpractice insurance carriers" and they didn't want "to risk a high jury award." Since I unwaveringly opposed this, UW agreed with the plaintiffs to dismiss me as a defendant on both cases and subsequently settled. I have no idea what damages were paid to the plaintiff in either case, having only received an e-mail message indicating that both cases had been "closed, having been resolved for a moderate, confidential amount." I subsequently sent a note to the Associate Dean for Clinical Affairs at UW, pointing out that settling such lawsuits rather than fighting them in court if necessary, only encouraged pettifogger plaintiff's attorneys to file more cases against the physicians of UW in the future. Of course, I received no response.

I don't blame the FDA for what transpired with the two LASIK cases performed for very high levels of farsightedness and nearsightedness shortly after approval. Ultimately, it was the VISX Corporation's responsibility to see that the data they provided to the FDA advisory panel truly supported the efficacy and safety of the proposed indications for their medical device—the VISX excimer laser. The FDA advisory panel, composed for the most part of appointed physicians and scientists, also bears some responsibility for recommending FDA approval for too high a range of treatment based on flawed data with limited numbers of patients which, in the case of treatment for farsightedness over +4 diopters, wasn't even generated in the United States, but in Canada, where regulations governing clinical trials are far less rigorous. All too often, approval is recommended for procedures using medical devices that are ill-advised and potentially dangerous, based on data with insufficient patient numbers, too short of follow-up, or some other limitation. Other examples include too high of corrections approved for other brands of excimer lasers, laser thermokeratoplasty (LTK) for hyperopia (plagued with irregular astigmatism and regression of the effect of surgery), and intrastromal corneal rings for correction of myopia (instability, corneal deposits, neovascularization and induction of astigmatism). Both patients and physicians must be able to rely on the safety and efficacy of devices and indications that receive FDA approval. My two patients and I, as well as many other patients and their surgeons, learned a hard lesson about the reliability of the FDA's blessing. Ultimately, I believe *both* the patients and I were the victims of treatments that should never have been approved and yet remain FDA-approved procedures even today—despite the widespread acknowledgement of experienced refractive surgeons that levels of correction of farsightedness much beyond +4.5 diopters and nearsightedness beyond -10 diopters are associated with unacceptably high rates of serious complications with laser vision correction. (For more information on this subject and the medical malpractice crisis, see Appendix 3 and Appendix 4.)

Chapter 12
A Tsunami Sweeps over the UW School of Medicine

February 2002, brought another shocking development in the federal investigation of billing practices at UW Physicians and UW School of Medicine. UW announced that Richard Winn, MD, chair of the Neurosurgery Department, William Couser, MD, Belding Scribner Professor of Medicine and Head of the Division of Nephrology at UW, and Arthur B. Fontaine, MD, head of Interventional Radiology, all in leadership positions at UW for many years, had been forced to step down. I, like many of my fellow chairs, was devastated by this unexpected announcement, and a pall fell over the entire medical school. At the next Medical School Executive Committee meeting it became clear that the federal prosecutors were considering *criminal* charges! Dr. Winn wasn't at the meeting, but I remember looking around the table at several other grim-faced chairmen, and shaking my head in disbelief. Once again, however, the other chairs and I received only superficial information about the allegations against our fellow leaders. Really, all we were told was the legal expenses were continuing to mount and that we would be allowed to use reserves—at least what was left of them—to pay our departments' shares of the expenses.

I didn't know Dr. Couser or Dr. Fontaine well, but in the case of Dr. Winn, the response within the institution was predictable. The neurosurgery department was divided between those who supported Winn and felt his stepping down was a tragedy to both the department and the institution, and those who exuberantly applauded his departure. In my experience, most of the latter individuals were longstanding faculty who had opposed Dick Winn and the changes he'd brought to neurosurgery as he built the internationally-famed department. I couldn't help thinking about the similar backbiting faculty I had nipping at my heels—similar to those faced by every other chairman of an academic medical department in the United States. The same divided response was evident among the UW School of Medicine department chairs. Many, like me, supported Dick Winn and were aghast at what transpired, but some seemed pleased, or at least indifferent, about his demise.

Several months passed as rumors flew, and the only hard information most of us got was from articles published in the *Seattle Times* or the *Seattle Post Intelligencer*. Then, in June 2002, came the unimaginable announcement that Brian McKenna, the former head of the disorganized and incompetent UW Physicians faculty practice plan at the heart of the billing crisis, along with one of his billing administrators and several other staff members, had been granted immunity in exchange for cooperating with federal investigators on the case. According to a March 19, 2003, article published in the *Seattle Times*, immunity was granted, despite the U.S. Attorney's office discovering evidence that McKenna and other leaders of UW Physicians and Children's University Medical Group actively destroyed audit reports that revealed billing irregularities. It was totally inconceivable to me, and many of my colleagues, that all the chickens were dead and the fox had been granted immunity from prosecution. Why did this happen? It's clear to me the U.S. Attorney's office decided to focus their investigations solely on leading physicians in order to make an example of them.

Finally, on July 16, 2002, the last shoe dropped. In what was described by the *Seattle Post Intelligencer* as an "eleventh hour plea bargain reached with federal authorities," Richard Winn, MD, agreed to plead guilty to a single felony charge, not for Medicare or Medicaid fraud, but for "obstructing the communication of information to a criminal investigator." Dr. Winn, who was sixty years old at that time, also agreed to resign his position at UW. The details of the plea agreement struck me as strange from the moment I read them. Winn did not lose his medical license and would be allowed to practice medicine elsewhere. In addition, he would not serve time in jail, but receive probation. He was required to provide one thousand hours of service to indigent patients—which he subsequently performed in Nepal—and to publish an article in a medical journal warning other doctors to comply with federal regulations. This article was subsequently published in 2004, in the *Journal of Neurosurgery*, after being submitted to the prosecutors and the presiding judge.

Winn H.R. Errors in compliance with federal rules and regulations relating to healthcare benefits programs: The University of Washington Department of Neurological Surgery experience. Journal of Neurosurgery. 2004;100:47

In addition, Dr. Winn was required "to pay" $500,000 as restitution to government programs serving the poor and elderly. How this amount was derived is unclear, since it was not based on any financial forensics. Originally, the government presented a figure of a $100,000, but the UW attorneys suggested *raising* the amount to $500,000. As reported by the Seattle Weekly, in October 2006, the University paid this amount in full.

---

http://www.seattleweekly.com/news/unimpressed-whistle-blowers/

The eagerness of the University to pay more than amount demanded by the prosecutors was presumably to signal the government that the University was willing to cooperate. For the University, the hope was that the prosecutors would relent in their focus on the University. For Dr. Winn, it meant he was about to be sacrificed.

A review of the court documents reveals that the $500,000 was a global restitution for all billing errors for all members of the Department of Neurosurgery, and not just for Dr. Winn. The press repetitively and incorrectly reported this amount as a "fine." Actually, the fine was $2000—which was the lowest possible amount that the court could impose. The $500,000 represented less than 2% of the total neurosurgery departmental billings during the period of the governmental investigation, which is below the accounting threshold, according to most auditing standards (again, see Dr. Winn's Journal of Neurosurgery article in 2004).

Finally, in return for Dr. Winn agreeing to plead guilty to the felony count, and resigning his tenured position on the faculty, UW agreed to cover all of his past and foreseeable legal and insurance costs, and clinical bonuses, as well as to pay him up to $3.7 million dollars (and possibly more) over a six-year period following the agreement—minus salary that he earned if he took another position during that period. I'm certain UW officials were not amused by Dr. Winn's acceptance of a rather low-paying research position at a prominent East Coast institution, mandating that they shell out nearly all of the agreed-upon settlement.

Of all the chairs in the medical school, why did the prosecutors focus on Dr. Winn? A review of the history of the neurosurgery department can provide some answers to this question. Because of the similarities between the status of the neurosurgery department and my department, Dr. Winn shared many of his experiences with me during and after my recruitment. Thus, I had a good understanding of what transpired during the federal investigation.

According to members of the search committee that brought Dr. Winn to the UW at age forty, the department prior to his arrival was "asleep" and below academic, clinical and financial national norms. The faculty members in the Department were dispirited and in disarray. The previous chair, Arthur A. Ward, Jr., MD, had been in place for 38 years. As outlined by one of his former residents, Ward was a cold and remote individual, and clearly a product of a different era.

---

http://alphaomegaalpha.org/pharos/PDFs/2017-1-Rapport.pdf

Dr. Ward was unrelentingly opposed to Dr. Winn becoming his successor. On the national scene, he bad-mouthed Dr. Winn widely for years after Dr. Winn became his successor.

Three of the senior faculty members, all Ward acolytes, envisioned themselves as the future leader of the Department, but the search committee, and the medical school dean at that time, were determined to go outside of the UW for the new chair. Within a short time after Dr. Winn's arrival, the department's clinical, academic and financial performance dramatically improved. He recruited multiple new young faculty members, who were routinely met with hostility by these senior faculty members. Over the next two decades, many of these young faculty members eventually went on to assume leadership positions around the U.S. as departmental chairs and section heads. These institutions include University of California at San Francisco, UCLA, Washington University (St. Louis), University of Pennsylvania, University of Iowa, The Cleveland Clinic, Ohio State University, Duke University, Stanford University, University of North Carolina, University of Massachusetts, University of Illinois, University of Connecticut, University of Texas (Houston), Columbia University (NYC), Mount Sinai (NYC) and Methodist Hospital Houston/Cornell Medical School, to mention a few.

Dr. Winn was committed to resident education, and to his residents, and soon the department became the most sought after neurosurgery residency in the U.S. His superlative teaching of medical students was recognized by several awards from the medical school and the University.

Under Dr. Winn's leadership, the department soon became the number one recipient of NIH grants and funding for neurosurgery departments in the U.S., and remained so for more than a decade. After his demise, other faculty and residents left the department and sought university positions elsewhere. NIH funding for UW neurosurgery decreased, and by 2016, had sunk to the 13th position.

And despite the success of the department under his leadership, it was widely recognized within the school that the three erstwhile chair candidates never forgave Dr. Winn for depriving them of the position they felt was theirs. On multiple occasions, one of more of these faculty members attempted to initiate investigations of Dr. Winn, but routinely these efforts were evaluated and rejected by a succession of committees, deans and university officials. For twenty years, they waged guerilla war against Dr. Winn—and they finally "got" him—thanks to the perfect storm made possible by the federal investigation, combined with weak leadership of the Medical School and spinelessness of the UW Board of Regents.

Even after Dr. Winn left the UW, these unrequited chair candidates continued their vendetta. A Freedom of Information Act (FIOA) request revealed that they wrote adverse letters to the Washington State Medical Board, which was to consider terminating Dr. Winn's medical license. Their letters suggested that Dr. Winn had harmed patients and committed malpractice, even though the prosecutors and the presiding judge had previously affirmed in court proceedings that no patient harm had occurred and urged that Dr. Winn be allowed to continue to practice medicine. The State Medical Board, with some wisdom and some courage, allowed Dr. Winn to retain his license.

And when the four year federal investigation reached a zenith and forced Dr. Winn into a protective crouch, a recent addition to the faculty, saw his chance and joined in Dr. Winn's demise. Of course the ultimate opportunists were UWP employees and UW administrators, who were accused by the U.S. prosecutors of the destruction documents related to UWP financial audits. Rather than fight the good fight, they chose to sacrifice the UW's Chair of Neurological Surgery.

---

http://community.seattletimes.nwsource.com/archive/?date=20030319&slug=uwprobe19m

---

Within days of the announcement of the plea bargain, there were hundreds of postings on a web site devoted to Dr. Winn, the overwhelming majority being poignant tributes from grateful patients, colleagues, students, friends, and family members. The postings repeatedly reinforced Dr. Winn's compassion for his patients, skill as a physician and surgeon, dedication to his students, and devotion to the University of Washington and his department.

It is important to understand that the charges brought against Richard Winn really had nothing to do with the billing practices that were actually laid out in the *qui tam* lawsuit filed by Mark Erickson or investigated by the federal prosecutors. *Qui tam* is a component of the federal False Claims Act, originally enacted in 1863 during Abraham Lincoln's presidency, which allows any person to bring a lawsuit on behalf of the federal government against anyone who uses government funds in a fraudulent manner. Dr. Winn drew the interest of federal investigators for allegedly using improper billing practices, including billing for surgeries performed by some residents in his department. However, during the course of the investigation—actually, rather far along in the process—the U.S. Attorney's office and the FBI became aware of a signed contractual agreement between the government agency that reimbursed for the medical services provided (Premera Blue Cross), the Health Care Financing Administration, and UW School of Medicine, and its hospitals, covering longstanding UW practices of billing Medicare and Medicaid for the services provided by senior residents in some departments. Unbelievably, in a letter to UW counsel in September 2002, the Medicare fiscal intermediary agreed that the very practice of billing for senior resident doctor services in the Department of Neurosurgery, the practice that was under criminal investigation, had been approved by the responsible government agency and its agent many years earlier. Just imagine the embarrassment of the U.S. Attorney's office and the FBI when, after several years of investigation and subpoena of millions of documents from UW School of Medicine, UW Physicians, individual UW medical school departments, and other agencies, such as the American Board of Neurological Surgery, they finally became aware of this agreement. To add insult to injury, they didn't even find it themselves. Richard Winn's attorney, Cyrus R. Vance, Jr., provided it to them. Wouldn't we all loved to have been flies on the wall at the investigative team's next strategy meeting? Thus, as part of the plea bargain, the government was forced to acknowledge: "the evidence gathered during the investigation is subject to a reasonable and good faith interpretation that although claims for professional services were submitted by the University of Washington Physicians in conjunction with professional services provided by the Department of Neurological Surgery, these claims were not intended by the Defendant to be fraudulent and were instead the product of mistake and confusion as to the meaning and application of the rules and regulations that controlled the submission of claims to the Medicare, Medicaid, and TRICARE programs."

Reread that last paragraph because it is the crux of the injustice perpetrated on Dr. Winn and the other UW physicians charged by the federal prosecutors. Any physician who has dealt with the complex and changing Medicare and Medicaid billing rules will get a knot in his or her gut at the thought of exuberant federal investigators putting the doctor's billing practices under the scrutiny brought to bear against Dr. Winn and his colleagues. And yet, in the end, the prosecutors were forced to admit, I'm sure to their chagrin, that they could find *nothing* Winn did that couldn't be explained away based on the confusion inherent in Medicare and Medicaid regulations (Does that somehow remind you of another investigation being carried out under the direction of the U.S. Department of Justice in 2017 to 2019?).

What were the specifics of the felony charge of obstructing justice to which Richard Winn pleaded guilty? The federal prosecutors alleged that Winn obstructed the investigation by "instructing doctors to lie to investigators and the federal grand jury about potentially incriminating information." According to charging documents, he also provided "false exculpatory information" to doctors and staff so they would lie to investigators. The prosecutors claimed Winn intimidated employees in his department by saying "he had spies" and "heads would roll if witnesses testified in a way that was unfavorable to him." In short, Winn was charged with "creating an atmosphere of fear and intimidation" in the department of neurosurgery at UW with regards to the federal investigation of Medicare and Medicaid billing. I can only smile and shake my head when I read these charges because in my career I've worked under several departmental chairs who clearly, "created an atmosphere of fear and intimidation" in their departments and were considered among the outstanding ophthalmology chairmen of their time. Faculty members and staff are always intimidated by the power of a boss who controls salary, space, and other resources in an academic department. As to the charges that Dr. Winn claimed he had spies and that heads would roll, I believe that Winn, like all departmental chairs, including myself, had enemies within his department who would have said or done virtually anything to rid themselves of him. You show me a successful and powerful chairman who has changed a department and I'll show you a man or woman who has adversaries in their midst.

Some will undoubtedly ask why Richard Winn agreed to plead guilty to the trumped up felony charge. I don't know for sure, but I suspect he was threatened with permanently losing his medical license and probably being charged with multiple felony counts that could have sent him to prison for the remainder of his life. His career had already been destroyed by the unfolding investigation and response of UW School of Medicine. Would anyone reasonably expect him to turn down this settlement offer and face indefinite incarceration and the destruction of his family?

An overriding question remains. *Why did UW agree to the deal?* Why would the university agree to pay Dr. Winn's $500,000 fine and $3,700,000 in compensation? (There were rumors the amount UW paid Dr. Winn was actually far greater). To answer this question, one needs to ponder what would have happened if Richard Winn versus the United States of America had gone to trial. I have personal knowledge from discussions with medical school administrators, and periodic updates at Medical School Executive Committee meetings, that UW School of Medicine leaders irrationally hoped to avoid a large fine similar to those that had been imposed on other schools caught up in Medicare and Medicaid billing scandals, such as the University of Pennsylvania ($30,000,000), University of California ($22,500,000) and University of Pittsburgh ($17,300,000). They clearly hoped that by offering up a few sacrificial scapegoats they could convince the feds to be lenient. This appears to be the intent of a letter written on October 21, 2002, by UW Board of Regents Gerald Grinstein and Daniel J. Evans to the presiding judge Robert S. Lasnik (Appendix 7). But, of course, it would all be for naught. After pouring tremendous resources and their reputations into the investigation, U.S. Prosecutor John McKay, his cronies, and other government officials weren't going to let the university off that easily. In the end, UW was forced to agree to pay the largest medical school fine in history—*$35,000,000.* But, in my opinion, there was likely another, far more ominous, storm cloud the university feared more than the stiff fine. Dean Paul Ramsey said after the plea bargain was announced, "In reaching a settlement with Dr. Winn, the government recognized the harm that could have been done to the public that the UW Academic Medical Center serves." What he really should have said was: "In reaching a settlement with Dr. Winn, the government recognized the harm that would have been done to the leadership of the University of Washington School of Medicine."

Avoiding the trial saved UW School of Medicine and UW Physicians from disgraceful disclosures about how billings for medical care at UW were handled. It also prevented the public from discovering just how in the dark we UW clinical chairs were about bills submitted to Medicare, Medicaid, and insurance companies by UW Physicians, and about what happened to the bills that were initially rejected by the payers. "If Winn had gone to trial," said an unnamed UW physician quoted in a 2005 *Seattle Times* article, "it would have been a bloodbath for the UW." I agree completely with this assessment. If Dr. Winn had not agreed to the plea bargain, I believe his trial would have come to focus on the UW Physicians practice plan, which was under the leadership of its erstwhile executive director, Brian McKenna. Was Dean Paul Ramsey to blame for this unbelievable mess? Clearly he was not the only one who bears responsibility, because the system had been in place for many years before he was named Vice President and Dean of UW School of Medicine. Thus, his predecessors must also bear some of the blame for retaining Brian McKenna in his critical leadership position, despite incontrovertible ongoing evidence that he represented the personification of the Peter Principle. Whenever I ponder this question of blame, however, my mind keeps coming back to that old axiom I learned on my first trip to interview to be the chair of the Department of Ophthalmology at the University of Washington: "Medical School Deans come and go, but Bob Gust is always here." Brian McKenna reported directly to Bob Gust, and truth be told, Gust manipulated his strings like a puppeteer. I believe Gust kept McKenna in his critical position for just this reason: because he could maintain complete control over him. Therefore, Bob Gust must bear a large part of the blame for what ultimately happened at UW School of Medicine. In the end, UW attorneys built a wall around Bob Gust as the investigation intensified and eventually UW administration moved him out of his position of authority, but not before providing him with a *golden parachute* that ensured his silence.

Paul Ramsey and his predecessors, as well as many UW presidents and even the UW Regents, share blame for maintaining an inadequate governance system for UW Physicians. The office of the dean and vice president for medical affairs were one and the same at UW. UW Physicians Officers and UW Physicians Board Members were appointed by the dean/vice president and the board consisted almost exclusively of UW School of Medicine clinical departmental chairs, all of whom served at the pleasure of the dean. There was not a single non-UW School of Medicine member on the UW Physicians board. In addition, decisions of the board were advisory to the dean/vice president. It seems that the leadership of UW School of Medicine was consumed with keeping the affairs of UW Physicians secret from those outside the medical school. I believe this secrecy played a major role in what eventually transpired at UW Physicians.

My own impressions of Brian McKenna and his UW Physicians administrators, along with the bewildering Medicare/Medicaid system being at the heart of the billing scandal at UW, have only been reinforced as more information has become available after the fact. Another former long-term UW Physicians employee, Swannee Rivers (whose real name is actually Renay Bruner), who testified before the grand jury, stated that when a medical record was incomplete, her UW Physicians manager told her, "Just pick a doctor and bill it," according to a June 9, 2004 article published in the *Seattle Weekly*. Rivers, in the same article, also recalled a UW Physicians billing manager giving a co-worker a document and saying: "I don't want you to send this back to the physician because it will take too long, and he probably will never sign it anyway. Just sign his name on the report, and send it to the main office." According to Rivers that's what the UW Physicians employee did. In her 1995 resignation letter, Ms. Rivers stated:

> "What has become of a department when people are too frightened to speak up because of the consequences if you do? Why should employees have to call other workers to see what type of mood the manager is in before they ask her a question? . . . The list of problems are lengthy and just continue on. My objective in writing this letter is not to cause problems and not because I am angry with someone, but I am frustrated. Frustrated by the fact that a manager has been able to get away with so much mis-management over the years. Everything is overlooked or shoved under the carpet."

In her book, *Healthcare Under Duress: An Inside Look at the University of Washington Billing Scandal*, "Swannee Rivers" recounted these and many other examples of outright fraud committed by her supervisor and others at UW Physicians. She provides no evidence whatsoever of physician involvement in fraudulent practices that became routine at UW Physicians, including signing of documents, doctoring of documentation required for reimbursement, and not returning overpayments to patients, insurance companies, or Medicare.

Clearly, these are examples of UW Physicians employees perpetrating fraud without any involvement by physicians. In the June 2004, *Seattle Times* newspaper article, she also admitted telling Mark Erickson, the whistleblower, when he came to work at UW Physicians, "There is the right way, and there is the UW Physicians way." Erickson, who secretly began recording meetings with UW Physicians officials in 1999, stated that he didn't see Richard Winn and William Couser as fall guys. "I don't feel they meet the true definition of scapegoats," he said in the *Times* article, "as they clearly were aware of what was transpiring in their departments." Well, I'm here to tell you that none of my faculty, nor I, had any clue what UW Physicians was doing with the billing documents that were submitted to them from the clinics or operating rooms, or what they were doing when claims were denied by Medicare, Medicaid, or private insurance companies. I agitated to get more detailed information from Brian McKenna and his lieutenants during the entire time I was a chair at UW and didn't begin receiving these details until a new UW Physicians Executive Director was finally named in 2003. I only had the opportunity to work with the new director a short time before I left Seattle, but he seemed to be a knowledgeable and vigilant administrator—just the type of professional UW Physicians should have had for the past twenty-some years. I hope he and others who followed have truly made a difference in the time that has passed since I left UW School of Medicine.

Eventually, on March 26, 2003, Dr. Couser was also forced to plead guilty to a single felony count of "*mail fraud*"—admitting, also under duress, that he falsely claimed to be present during a dialysis treatment billed for $124 by UW Physicians. Couser agreed to pay $100,000 in restitution, an amount also paid from UW Physicians funds earmarked for clinical faculty salary and incentive payments, even though the agreement noted that, "the United States acknowledges that a significant portion of this sum did not directly benefit the defendant financially." So, once again, UW covered the cost of the restitution. In a prepared statement, Dr. Couser stated:

> "I also want to emphasize that in all cases of possible billing errors identified by the government, the patients involved underwent the dialysis treatments billed for, all treatments were supervised by highly qualified attending physicians . . . and no significant financial benefits came to me, or any other member of the division, as a result of these errors."

Kim Muczynski, MD, a nephrologist at UW, said after the plea agreement was announced: "I think it is quite clear that Couser is a scapegoat. We have the federal government saying the best academic physicians in this country should be under investigation for billing errors." I applaud Dr. Muczynski's courage in pointing out publicly what has become all too obvious to many of us.

Dr. Couser retired from clinical practice in 2004, and his NIH funding also ended. He also lost his Belding Scribner Chair, but continued on to the present at UW as "Affiliate" Professor of

Medicine. The esteem with which his worldwide colleagues hold him was signified by his winning the David Humes Award from the National Kidney Foundation in 2007, an award "bestowed upon an individual who exemplifies outstanding scholarship and humanism in the field," the Joel Kopple Award from the International Federation of kidney Foundations in 2012, an annual award "for contributions to nephrology," and the John P. Peters Award from American Society of Nephrology in 2018, an award given for "substantial research contributions to the discipline of nephrology and to those who have sustained achievements in one or more domains of academic medicine including clinical care, education, and leadership."

Arthur B. Fontaine, MD resigned from UW School of Medicine shortly after he was asked to step down as head of Interventional Radiology at UW and took a position at Group Health Cooperative in Seattle, a non-profit healthcare organization. He was never charged in the UW case. He currently practices at Bakersfield Heart Hospital in Bakersfield, CA.

The fallout from the investigation and settlements was hardly over with the resignation of H. Richard Winn, MD. On December 21, 2004, Ramsey was asked by the UW Faculty Senate to provide a more detailed explanation of the medical school's handling of the scandal. The members of the faculty senate expressed doubts about the legality of using UW funds for the Winn settlement and questioned why funds available to the dean were not used rather than funds available to pay clinicians salary and incentive. Some asked why such a large settlement was made to secure the resignation of a faculty member whose alleged conduct would have justified termination for cause, if proven. *Why, indeed?!* It appears that many faculty members at UW, even those who are not chairmen in the medical school, perceive the thinly-veiled truth. Other questions asked about the transparency of organization, governance, and avenues for remedies in the medical school and called for an examination of the culture in the medical school, which some faculty said was intimidating. This stain on UW and the UW School of Medicine would not soon fade, certainly not before Brian McKenna and the other UW Physician and UW School of Medicine administrators who aided and abetted him faced their own reckoning.

In June of 2004, Dean Paul Ramsey ordered an "independent review" to determine "the lessons to be learned" from the federal investigation. The review committee was initially to be headed and organized by Dennis Okamoto, Chairman of the UW Board of Medicine, who said Dr. Ramsey's own performance wouldn't be a subject of the review. I would think a truly independent review of this situation would not have limited its scope before it even began. All six members of the review committee also serve as members of the UW Medicine Board. The results of this review were released on July 20, 2005, and at the time of the release, the six-member committee was headed by Seattle attorney William Van Ness Jr. Among the findings and suggestions of this review committee, released in the ninety-nine-page report entitled "Achieving Excellence in Compliance," was that there should be more direct oversight of the UW School of Medicine by the UW Regents and the president of the University of Washington. The report concluded that "ultimate accountability" rested with Paul Ramsey, MD, Dean of the UW School of Medicine, but that "blame must also be shared by those who intentionally over-billed the government and other administrators who failed to exercise adequate oversight." After reading the report, I was still left with many questions regarding UW's overall response to the crisis that were not addressed by the committee. For example, the roles of Brian McKenna and Bob Gust were barely mentioned. At one point the report states, "An informal review undertaken by the Chair and Committee staff concluded that, of the eighteen School of Medicine clinical Departments subjected to the Federal billing investigation," there were varying levels of interest on the part of the government in the billing practices of specific departments at UW School of

Medicine. The report then lists departments where there was no known interest, minimal interest, minor concerns, some concerns, significant concerns, and major concerns on the part of the federal government. In this section, the report states that, "Minor concerns were raised by the government at four other Departments (Family Medicine, Medicine, Ophthalmology, and Psychiatry)." *Oh really?* I can unequivocally state that at *no time* did any administrator of UW Physicians or the UW School of Medicine inform me that the federal government had any concerns whatsoever regarding billing practices in the Department of Ophthalmology. Therefore, I am left to wonder about this informal review. I am also concerned that the review committee apparently did not make any effort to interview Richard Winn, MD, or William Couser, MD, before issuing its report. I believe this was a major deficiency limiting the value of the committee's findings and that final report.

As this book was finalized in 2019, Paul Ramsey, M.D., remained CEO of UW Medicine, executive vice president for Medical Affairs and dean of the UW School of Medicine. Paul and UW have seemed to flourish despite the heavy fine levied by the federal government.

And what of dedicated federal prosecutor John McKay, the man charged with hunting down and punishing the crooked physicians who roamed the halls of Washington's esteemed medical schools and hospitals? "We believe a national message has been sent," U.S. Attorney McKay said at the news conference where Dr. Winn's settlement was announced. In saying this, McKay only confirmed my impression that making an example of one or more prominent physicians at UW was the intention of the feds all along. There but for the grace of God go I. Mr. McKay, by hunting down and punishing these evil academic physicians, undoubtedly thought he'd set himself up for a run at a seat in Congress, a leadership position in the Department of Justice, or at least some other high governmental post. Bravo, Mr. McKay! Patients in need of skilled emergency brain surgery and renal dialysis in the Northwestern United States salute you. However, imagine his surprise when he was fired by the George W. Bush administration in 2006 for "performance-related issues related to policy, priorities and management." Oh, I would have loved to have been there to see his face when he got the news. He protested his firing. CBS News quoted him. "I am disappointed with the president," says John McKay, former chief prosecutor for western Washington state. "I am disappointed with the attorney general. I asked for the reasons that I was being asked to resign and I was given no reasons." Mr. McKay thought there were political reasons he was fired. I think I know why you were fired, Mr. McKay…it's referred to as *karma*. You're the real Darth Vader of this saga, Mr. McKay. Dark Lord of the Sith and Master of the Dark Side. Or maybe the detailed letter I sent to the Attorney General and President Bush detailing the ignoble affair upon my departure from UW found receptive readers. I notice there's nary a mention of Mr. McKay's involvement in this sordid affair on numerous postings of John McKay's biography on-line, most of which he probably provided himself—including on Wikipedia. Could it be Mr. McKay isn't so proud of his involvement in this witch-hunt he perpetrated on the University of Washington School of Medicine and some of its most storied physician-scientists? No, I don't think that's possible. That would require him to have a conscience.

John McKay is currently a faculty member at the Seattle University School of Law, where he teaches "Constitutional Law and National Security Law, as well as courses on *ethics* and leadership." Interestingly, his biography on the Seattle University website makes no mention of his role in taking down the evil physicians at UW School of Medicine. But he was the first author on a piece entitled, "Congress Should Stop Messing With Rod Rosenstein," published in Politico Magazine on July 9, 2018. I guess I don't need to point out the obvious irony.

And what about whistle-blower Mark Erickson, the individual who filed suit under the False Claims Act and netted $7.25 million? Some may feel he should be applauded for exposing the mismanagement and corruption at UW Physicians and UW School of Medicine. I'm among those who believe he did not carry out his actions because he was selflessly searching for the high road, but because he saw an opportunity to make the millions of dollars he received as stipulated under the False Claims Act. Erickson carefully recorded conversations, *illegally* sold and copied UW Physicians' documents to support his claims, and contacted whistle-blower.com to pursue his lawsuit. He has made statements that many more clinicians were involved and that the fine paid by UW should have been far higher. Why would he think otherwise when he personally stood to gain a cut of any increased fine? Don't misunderstand me; it was high time that the leadership of UW Physicians received their due. The organization at UW Physicians and the UW School of Medicine will be better as a result of the changes that have come. However, I don't believe Mr. Erickson was in a position to ascertain whether Dr. Winn and the other "felon" was complicit in the billing scandal. The statements by "Swannee Rivers" and others, along with my personal experience with the disorganized UW Physicians administrators, provide ample evidence that UW Physicians officials should have borne the brunt of the blame and confirmed that these lower-level UW Physicians employees served as unwitting pawns, helping the culpable parties to escape unscathed from the federal investigation. Mr. Mark Erickson, and to an extent Ms. Swanee Rivers (Renay Bruner), should be ashamed of the parts they played in damaging the careers of three outstanding academic clinicians and for allowing the blame for UW Physicians wrongdoing to be misdirected away from the true culprits. (For more on this subject, see Appendix 6.)

It is important to consider just what UW lost as a result of the Medicare and Medicaid Fraud investigation and subsequent settlements. A first blush assessment shows that at least $25,000,000 was spent for the legal expenses of the school of medicine, UW Physicians, and the charged faculty members. Several million dollars more were likely spent in responding to federal requirements—such as establishing compliance programs and improving the management of UW Physician—expenses that in any case should have been incurred years earlier. Then, there was the approximately $4,000,000, or more, to settle with Dr. Winn. Add to that an all-time record $35,000,000 fine paid to the federal government, and one is left with the staggering sum of *at least* $65,000,000. However, I would make the case that there are other incalculable losses to UW that burgeon this sum at least two- or three-fold. How many physicians, like me, decided to leave UW after coming to the decision that the university and its leaders had turned their back on faculty members to save their own behinds? What value can be placed on the loss of reputation in Seattle, the state of Washington, and throughout the country? What has been lost from teaching, research, and clinical care programs that had to be trimmed or abandoned in the face of these enormous financial penalties?

Some faculty members at UW blame H. Richard Winn, MD, for the expenses and penalties paid by the school of medicine, but most of these people were not chairs and, therefore, were not in a position to know what was really going on at UW Physicians and the UW School of Medicine. I would ask these faculty members to consider the simple question I posed earlier: Why would UW agree to the settlement offered to Dick Winn? Other chairmen resented Winn and his success, or just seem to ignore the truth about what really happened. I, on the other hand, feel only deep sorrow about what happened to Dr. Winn. I see the final settlement and the admission of the U.S. Attorney's Office that they could uncover no evidence of billing fraud as his vindication, but am reminded of former Secretary of Labor Ray Donovan, who, during the McCarthy Era of the 1950s, asked, "Where do I go to get my reputation back?" Where, indeed, *could* Dr. Winn go? Fortunately, there were many outside of UW who saw his guilty plea for what it was.

After completing his required service in Nepal, Dr. Winn found a home in New York at Mount Sinai Medical School—as a tenured Professor of Neurosurgery and Neuroscience, and Director of Research for the Department of Neurosurgery. As at the UW, where he won several awards for teaching, he remained dedicated to education, and uniquely for a surgeon, was selected by all four Mount Sinai medical school classes for the yearly Distinguished Teaching Award. He continued as Editor-in-Chief of the 5000 page text book, Youmans and Winn, *Neurological Surgery*, which the Journal of the American Medical Association (JAMA) called "The Bible of Neurosurgery."

He also remained active in research in his new position in New York, despite road blocks from the UW. Just after the Dean Ramsey asked Dr. Winn to relinquish his position as chair, the National Institutes of Health (NIH) approved Dr. Winn's basic science research grant (RO-1) focused on brain blood flow—at a very high level (2.3 percentile). With this approval, Dr. Winn extended his grant support into three continuous decades, a remarkable achievement for an active clinical neurosurgeon. Incredibly, Dr. Ramsey and the acting chair of neurosurgery, without any consultation with Dr. Winn, asked one of Dr. Winn's junior associates to write to the NIH and offer to displace Dr. Winn as the principal investigator. However, the junior associate refused, despite his untenured position and considerable pressure from the acting chair.

The Society of Neurological Surgeons, the oldest neurosurgery organization in the world, chose Dr. Winn for the Distinguished Service Award in 2005, and then in 2006, the Society established and endowed *The H. Richard Winn Prize in Neuroscience Research* in his honor. This prize, a yearly international prize for outstanding neuroscience research by a neurosurgeon, is considered by many neurosurgeons to be the Nobel Prize in neurosurgery.

My own conclusions about culpability in the scandal were confirmed by the book by Swannee Rivers, *Healthcare under Duress,* published in 2004 (iUniverse, Inc, NY, ISBN 0-595-32008-2). In this book, Ms. Rivers detailed the outright fraud that was being perpetrated over many years by staff within UW Physicians. It is also clear from reading this account that physicians had nothing whatsoever to do with the illegal activities of UW Physicians' employees. Certainly, federal investigators and prosecutors had access to all this information during the investigation at UW. That makes the outcome and the immunity from prosecution given to many of the principals involved even more upsetting.

There is one blatant error that must be set straight in the book account by Ms. Rivers. She recounts seeing an incentive check for a surgeon for $10,000 and mentions that the physicians received such checks on a monthly basis. This is patently false. As was previously detailed in Chapter 8 of this book, incentive payments at UW School of Medicine, that, in actuality, constitute a portion of the annual compensation for established physicians at UW—who, on average, receive tens or hundreds of thousands of dollars less salary than their national peers—have always been provided to physicians every six months . . . if available departmental funds collected by UW Physicians allow. Thus, this incentive payment Rivers wrote about in her book represented $1666.66 per month beyond the base salary paid to the physician by UW. That puts the amount received in a far different light.

It has been over fifteen years since my departure from the University of Washington. The first search for a permanent successor lasted nearly a year and a half, and failed in January of 2005. A second search to fill the chairmanship also failed. The first acting chair of the department, Bryan Sires, MD, PhD, a UW faculty member who was also Chief of Ophthalmology at Harborview Medical Center, had very limited powers to hire new faculty, promote faculty, or perform other critical functions. He essentially served as an overseer until a permanent chair could be named, and in frustration, decided to step down after a year and a half, and not become a candidate for the permanent position. He subsequently left UW for private practice in the Seattle area. In April of 2005, Kris Palczewski, PhD, the brightest research star in the department, with multiple NIH grants and several publications in Science, announced he was leaving UW to take a position at Case Western Reserve in Cleveland. In 2006, David Saperstein, MD, an outstanding retina clinician-scientist, left the medical school for private practice. Finally, in 2008, five years after I stepped down, Russell N. Van Gelder, MD, PhD, an outstanding retina and uveitis clinician-scientist, was hired to become Professor and chair, Boyd K. Bucey Professor and Director of the UW Medicine Eye Institute. I happened to have dinner at a table with Dr. Van Gelder during a meeting at the University of Southern California Department of Ophthalmology in May of 2017. He told me he was doing well and mentioned a number of new faculty members he'd hired into the Department of Ophthalmology at UW School of Medicine. He mentioned a new Retina Center will occupy a floor of an eight-story clinical and research facility, slated to open in January 2019, at UW Medicine at South Lake Union. I couldn't help myself and asked him, "Are you still straddled with that archaic UW Physicians reimbursement system, with its "departmental incentive pool?" He smiled and said, "Yes."

Just one example will highlight the damage this situation wrought in the Department of Ophthalmology at UW School of Medicine. A year and a half after my departure from UW, in January of 2005, the Department of Ophthalmology and the vision research program at UW began to lose $110,000 to $200,000 dollars per year, depending on individual scientist research awards that might have been granted from the organization "Research to Prevent Blindness" (RPB). RPB is one of the largest supporters of vision research in the United States. Funding from RPB allows ophthalmology departments to foster research, support the early careers of scientists and clinician–scientists (I myself was a RPB William and Mary Greve International Research Scholar as an assistant professor at UT Southwestern and received an RPB Clinician-Scientist Award in 2006), and augment the research funding of more senior scientists, both MD and PhD. The loss occurred because an ophthalmology department supported by RPB loses its funding the year following a permanent chairman's departure and the support could only be re-established once a new permanent chair was named and an application for reinstatement was accepted. The loss of these funds by the Department of Ophthalmology at UW only added to the pressures and feelings of despair in the financially strapped department. I hope that has now been remedied.

Unfortunately, the long-term absence of a chairman of ophthalmology was by no means restricted to the University of Washington. According to the Association of University Professors in Ophthalmology (AUPO), an association of ophthalmology department chairmen and residency program directors, at any one time there are ten to twenty unfilled ophthalmology chairmanships in the United States. This has been an ongoing problem for years. For an ophthalmology chairman search to end in failure has become the rule rather than the exception. Some highly sought-after chairmanships, such as the Massachusetts Eye and Ear Infirmary at Harvard University or Wilmer Eye Institute at Johns Hopkins University, filled rather quickly. Others, however, languish due to issues such as lack of funding or other problems that hinder academic accomplishment. Some chairs eventually fill, only to be abandoned a few years later by capable academic physicians who've become disillusioned by financial pressures, regulations, and other albatrosses inherent in academic medicine today. It's also important to point out that these problems are by no means restricted to ophthalmology. Similar troubles in attracting chairs and other physician faculty members permeate all specialties of medicine in the United States today.

Within a week of the July 2002 announcement of Richard Winn's plea bargain and settlement, I decided I couldn't stay at the University of Washington. I felt, and still feel, that UW turned its back on Dr. Winn and the other physician faculty members involved in the investigation in order to try to avoid, or at least limit, the severe financial penalties that inevitably followed. I believe UW pulling back its support for its physicians was a fully deliberated decision—as it was in the case of football coach Rick Neuheisel's dismissal for betting on basketball pools when memos from UW superiors clearly indicated he'd been told betting in pools did not violate NCAA policies. In that case, it was an attempt to avoid NCAA sanctions on the university. Coach Neuheisel eventually settled his wrongful termination suit against UW and the NCAA for $4.5 million, close to the amount Dr. Winn received.

https://www.seattletimes.com/sports/uw-huskies/settlement-reached-in-neuheisels-lawsuit/

Upon learning about yet another settlement, my wife teased me that I hadn't made nearly enough of a ruckus when I left UW School of Medicine.

The medical school case was made all the worse by the final admission by the federal prosecutors—as a part of the settlement—that they could find nothing Dr. Winn did that couldn't be attributed to confusion inherent in Medicare and Medicaid regulations. Dr. Ramsey's comment in the newspapers, parroted by several of his minions in e-mails sent to UW School of Medicine faculty stated that, "UW School of Medicine will not tolerate the actions to which Dr. Winn has pleaded guilty." These comments made me clench my teeth in anger, since I knew all too well that Dick Winn had pleaded guilty to this single trumped-up felony count under threat of imprisonment and complete destruction of his career, including loss of his license to practice medicine.

Once I'd decided to leave UW, I'm afraid I became a bit too vocal in my criticism of some of the goings-on at the medical school, including the response to the federal investigation, the debacle at the UW Physicians Eastside Subspecialty Clinic, and changes that UW Medical Center had decided, without consulting me, to make in the business plan for the UW Refractive Surgery Center. Dean Paul Ramsey asked to meet with me and we had our fifth and final meeting in his office on October 31, 2002. I always thought it appropriate that our final meeting took place on Halloween. After a few niceties, Dr. Ramsey told me he and others in the UW administration had hoped that I would have a long and productive career at UW, but that from reports he'd received from some of his subordinates in UW School of Medicine administration, he felt I should pursue anger management counseling. Smiling, I replied, "Thank you for your concern, Paul, but sometimes anger is an appropriate response." I nonetheless took the card on which he'd written the contact information for a psychologist, said goodbye, and left. That was the last time we spoke, other than briefly at the small ceremony they held for me at my last Medical School Executive Committee meeting just before I left UW—where I was given the customary engraved chairman's chair—that still resides next to the piano in our home library.

I began looking across the country at other chairmanship opportunities—which wasn't too difficult since there were twenty-five ophthalmology chairmanships available at that time in 2003. During the next six months, I became a "short list" candidate at Vanderbilt University, Louisiana State University, and University of Wisconsin, but soon came to realize that none of these ophthalmology programs or chairmanships was any better off than those at the University of Washington. All were suffering from limited resources to recruit new faculty and to foster research and teaching. The dean at one program gave me an impressive speech about his school's intention to build "one of the top ten ophthalmology departments in the country." I pointed out that this would be a very expensive proposition, considering his department's current ranking among other programs and the enormous resources and facilities that were in place at institutions that were in the top ten—like Jules Stein Eye Institute, Bascom Palmer Eye Institute, and Massachusetts Eye and Ear Infirmary. He asked me to develop a detailed ten-year plan—and I did, estimating conservatively that it would cost between $100 and $200 million to accomplish this goal. Of course, that was the last time I heard from him.

I awoke one sunny early spring Seattle morning in March of 2003, and taking a deep breath, said, "Honey, I don't want to be a chairman anymore."

"Really?" she replied with surprise, as she handed me a cup of coffee.

"Yes. I've decided I only want to treat patients, pursue my research, and teach residents and fellows. I don't want to spend any more time on endless meetings, depressing spreadsheets, and medical school administrative responsibilities."

It was one of the happiest mornings of my life, that just happened to coincide with that rare sunny day in springtime Seattle. Once I'd made my decision, I felt a yoke had been lifted from my shoulders. Jennifer and I took the kids on a ferry to Friday Harbor in the San Juan Islands, and I couldn't stop smiling. These feelings lasted for months and left little doubt that I'd made the right decision.

I withdrew my applications for those chairmanships where I was still active and contacted a few programs I thought might be interested in my clinical and research skills. I'd gotten quite far along in negotiating with one of these programs when Hilel Lewis, MD—my former chair at the Cleveland Clinic—telephoned me.

"Steve, I've heard you're looking at non-chairman positions."

"Yes, Hilel," I replied. "I've decided I want to spend my time doing the things I really love—caring for patients, research, and teaching residents and fellows."

"Then why don't you come back to the Cleveland Clinic?"

"Well, Jennifer and I would certainly consider it. We loved living in Shaker Heights and we both miss our friends and colleagues."

"Okay, why don't we arrange a visit for you and Jennifer? Meanwhile, I'd like you to send a letter detailing what you'd need from me to come back."

It felt very strange to suddenly be on the other side of negotiations again. But I prepared the letter, visited Cleveland, and within two months, agreed to return to the Cleveland Clinic. I sent a note to Paul Ramsey giving him several months of notice, with an intended departure from UW in August of 2003, and informed my laboratory coworkers (most of whom decided to accompany me back to Cleveland) and my Department of Ophthalmology faculty members. Notifying the faculty members who had supported me at UW, especially the ones I'd hired into the department, was one of the hardest things I ever had to do.

Word of my resignation spread quickly in the ophthalmology and vision research communities, with many of my friends and colleagues sending bewildered e-mails and letters. Upon hearing of my resignation, Robert Maloney, MD, a prominent refractive surgeon in Los Angeles and former faculty member at Jules Stein Eye Institute at UCLA, sent me an e-mail message that encapsulated many of the others. He said, "It speaks volumes when probably the most promising academic ophthalmologist of our generation decides he doesn't want to be a chairman anymore." Others wrote they couldn't believe I'd just give up a department chairmanship, tenured professorship, and endowed chair at a major university at only fifty-one years of age "without good reasons." Of course, there were good reasons, but I chose not to expound upon them at that time—except with my closest friends.

Fall was especially beautiful in Cleveland Heights in 2003. I felt happy and at peace with my decisions. I looked forward to resuming my career in clinical medicine, research and teaching, with no spreadsheets to examine but my own, fewer purposeless hours consumed in medical school meetings, and the horrors of my five years at UW becoming a distant memory. I think my oldest daughter, who was six years old at the time, summed it up best when she said, "Daddy, you seem so much happier now that you aren't the boss anymore." And, of course, she was right.

Chapter 13
Renewal

I'd hoped that my departure from Seattle would be a new beginning...an opportunity to forget about the angst, heartbreak, and umbrage that had besieged the five years I'd spent as Chair of Ophthalmology at the University of Washington, and to devote my working hours to what I loved most about medicine—caring for patients, pursuing my basic and clinical research, and teaching fellows and residents the intricacies of ophthalmology and refractive surgery. But sadly, it was not to be.

First came a fall on poorly-maintained, iced-over sidewalks at a hotel in Vail, Colorado, where I'd been invited to speak to the Colorado Ophthalmological Society in late January of 2004. The multiple displaced fractures of my lower tibia and fibula required rods, plates, and screws, and left me seeing patients and operating in a wheel chair for six months. Nerve damage in the leg morphed into a disorder called Reflex Sympathetic Dystrophy (RSD), also called Complex Regional Pain Syndrome (CRPS), that left my leg with permanent pain, numbness, and swelling—which severely limited my mobility and changed my life forever. Activities I'd taken for granted—such as seeing dozens of patients in clinic, operating, traveling to lectures, or even helping with the yard work or playing with my children—became exceptionally difficult or impossible. Just as I was managing to get on with my life, however, another wave threatened to crash down on my career as a physician–scientist, the career I'd worked all of my life to establish.

The worst crisis began inauspiciously enough in early 2004, with a less than favorable review of the application I submitted to renew my NIH RO1 grant, "Corneal epithelial growth factors and receptors." Typically this had been nothing to be too concerned about. Many NIH-funded scientists and physician–scientists endure a cycle of critique, revision, and resubmission before his or her NIH grant was finally restored. However, the revised grant received an even worse score—despite the reviewers on the study section lauding the progress we had made in the previous funding period and our response to the previous grant review. In my opinion, the low score was based on critical errors made by the primary reviewer in the second review that proved, beyond a doubt, that he or she was completely ignorant of the field. So it goes these days with many grant reviews provided by NIH's Center for Scientific Review (CSR), leading many of my colleagues inside and outside of vision research to refer to this division of NIH as the *"Center for Shameful Review."* I appealed the review to the overseeing body, the National Eye Advisory Council, based on the errors and the importance of the work to patients who develop corneal opacity and other complications after corneal surgery, but the Council declined to take up the matter. So, once again, and for the last time (based on NIH rules then in effect), I revised and resubmitted my grant in February of 2005—fully convinced that my career as a physician–scientist was over, since the funding level at the National Eye Institute had slipped from over 40% to only 17% of grants submitted in the years since the "War on Terrorism" had burst forth. I was so convinced, I began applying for positions in private and group practices as I awaited the *coup de grace.*

Some might say, at age fifty-three and in the prime of my research life, I gave up too soon—that I should have come up with another area of research, and submitted a completely new grant—if this one weren't funded. I certainly thought about it, but in the end decided not to continue "beating my head against the wall." Why should I, when we'd been so productive, made so many contributions, and submitted three grants that I felt were truly outstanding? No, there wasn't a reason to struggle on, when all around me other prominent vision scientists and physician–scientists were suffering similar fates, brought on by a combination of damaging peer reviews in study sections and falling NIH funding levels.

After more than twelve years of continuous NIH funding and making numerous discoveries and contributions to vision science and ophthalmology, particularly in cornea and refractive surgery, and experiencing so much triumph and jubilation, it would have been devastating to be forced to say goodbye to colleagues who'd worked with me for years and to watch other scientists cart off instruments and unused supplies from my laboratory at the Cleveland Clinic.

But, it turns out, I was to be one of the lucky ones. On its final review, my NIH grant received a 2nd percentile ranking, ensuring I would be able to continue for another five years before once again holding my hands to the fire. One would have thought I'd have shouted with joy when the e-mail came from a National Eye Institute grants administrator, graciously informing me of my score, but instead I quietly bowed my head and thanked God.

The next time I had a competing renewal, in 2010, my grant flew through study section with a fundable score. But once again, in 2015, my RO1 grant was not funded with a ranking of 12th percentile! I resubmitted the grant again, a process taking over nine months, while NEI provided limited "bridge funding" and I was supported by The Cleveland Clinic, along with my clinical practice. This second submission received a 5th percentile ranking and was funded for five years beginning June 1, 2016. So, I'll need to start working on another competing renewal of that grant in about one year from now, and submit it well in advance of the expiration of my current funding period.

My return to the Cleveland Clinic has, for the most part, been a happy one and the past fifteen years have definitely been a time of renewal—for me personally and for my career. Daniel F. Martin, MD, a physician-scientist himself, became Chair of the Cole Eye Institute at the Cleveland Clinic in 2008, and he has been very supportive of me and my research program. Unfortunately, however, the Cole Eye Institute building I helped design is out of space, and I will soon move my laboratory to a different building in the Cleveland Clinic for the fourth time since my return in 2003. The research space has been more than adequate, but we lost valuable time on each occasion I had to move my busy research program. I may need to move my lab yet another time after the 2019 move. That would be, as planned, when the Cole Eye Institute builds its second building that will include more laboratory space. That's a move I'll enjoy making!

Steven E. Wilson, MD

Despite these nuisances, with the support of NIH, Research to Prevent Blindness and the ophthalmology department, my laboratory continued to make important contributions to understanding corneal physiology since I arrived back in Cleveland in 2003. These include:

1. **Corneal stromal surface irregularity is directly related to the development of stromal opacity.** [Netto MV, Mohan RR, Sinha S, Sharma A, Dupps W, Wilson SE. Stromal haze, myofibroblasts, and surface irregularity after PRK. Exp. Eye Res. 2006;82:788]

2. **Mitomycin C blocks haze generation by inhibiting the proliferation of myofibroblast precursor cells.** [Netto MV, Mohan RR, Sinha S, Sharma A, Gupta PC, Wilson SE. Effect of prophylactic and therapeutic mitomycin C on corneal apoptosis, proliferation, haze, and keratocyte density. J. Ref. Surgery, 2006;22:562]*

3. **Myofibroblasts disappear from the cornea by late apoptosis.** [Wilson SE, Chaurasia SS, Medeiros FW. Apoptosis in the initiation, modulation and termination of the corneal wound healing response, Exp. Eye Res. 2007;85:305]

4. **Myofibroblasts undergo development in the cornea to express vimentin, alpha-smooth muscle actin and desmin.** [Chaurasia SS, Kaur H, Medeiros FW, Smith SD, Wilson SE. Dynamics of the expression of intermediate filaments vimentin and desmin during myofibroblast differentiation after corneal injury. Exp Eye Res., 2009;89:133]

5. **TGF β and IL-1 having opposing regulatory effects on myofibroblast viability in the corneal stroma.** [Kaur H, Chaurasia SS, Agrawal V, Wilson SE. Corneal myofibroblast viability: Opposing effects of IL-1 and TGF beta-1. Exp. Eye Res. 2009;89:152].

6. **Bone marrow-derived cells differentiate into myofibroblasts in the cornea.** [Barbosa FL, Chaurasia S, Cutler A, Asosingh K, Kaur H, de Medeiros F, Agrawal V, Wilson, SE. Corneal myofibroblast generation from bone marrow-derived cells. Exp. Eye Res., 2010; 91:92].

7. **Implantation of AcuFocus Kamra inlays triggers transient stromal apoptosis.** [Santhiago MR, Barbosa FL, Agrawal V, Binder PS, Christie B, Wilson SE. Short-term cell-death and inflammation after inlay implantation in rabbits. J. Refract. Surg. 2012;28:144].*

8. **Injury to the epithelial basement membrane and defective regeneration underlies the development of anterior corneal fibrosis.** [Torricelli AAM, Singh V, Agrawal V, Santhiago MR, Wilson SE. Transmission electron microscopy analysis of epithelial basement membrane repair in rabbit corneas with haze. Invest. Ophth. Vis. Sci. 2013:54:4026].

9. **Transepithelial ribroblavin-UV crosslinking likely has at least equal efficacy to epithelium-off crosslinking, depending on the agent used to break down epithelial barrier function.** [Armstrong B, MD, Lin M, Ford M, Santhiago MR, Singh V, Grossman G, Agrawal V, Roy A, Dupps WJ, Wilson SE. Biological and biomechanical responses to traditional epithelium-off and transepithelial riboflavin-UVA crosslinking techniques in rabbits. J Ref Surg. 2013;29:332].*

10. **Stromal keratocytes in the cornea produce epithelial basement membrane components after corneal injury.** [Santhanam A, Marino, GK, Torricelli AAM, Wilson SE.

Epithelial basement membrane (EBM) regeneration and changes in EBM component mRNA expression in the anterior stroma after corneal injury. Mol. Vision. 2017; 23:39].

11. **Regeneration of the epithelial basement membrane in corneas with scarring (fibrosis) results in myofibroblast apoptosis and restoration of stromal transparency.** [Marino GK, Santhiago MR, Santhanam A, Lassance L, Thangavadivel S, Medeiros CS, Torricelli AAM, Wilson SE. Regeneration of defective epithelial basement membrane and restoration of corneal transparency, J. Ref Surg. 2017;33:337].

12. **The corneal scarring (fibrosis) that occurs after Pseudomonas keratitis is due to injury to the epithelial basement membrane and Descemet's membrane.** [Marino GK, Santhiago MR, Santhanam A, Lassance L, Thangavadivel S, Medeiros CS, Bose K, Tam KP, Wilson SE. Epithelial basement membrane injury and regeneration modulates corneal fibrosis after pseudomonas corneal ulcers in rabbits. Exp. Eye Res. 2017; 161:101].

13. **The process leading to corneal stromal scarring in persistent epithelial defects is myofibroblast-mediated fibrosis.** [Wilson SE, Medeiros CS, Santhiago MR. Pathophysiology of corneal scarring in persistent epithelial defects after PRK and other corneal injuries, J. Ref. Surg. 2018;34:59].

14. **Damage to corneal endothelial cells produces posterior stromal keratocyte apoptosis.** [Medeiros CS, Lassance L, Saikia P, Wilson SE. Posterior stromal keratocyte apoptosis triggered by mechanical endothelial injury and nidogen-1 production in the cornea. Exp. Eye Res. 2018;172:30.]

15. **The bone marrow-derived cells that migrate into the cornea after injury and develop into myofibroblasts are fibrocytes.** [Lassance L, Marino GK, Medeiros CS, Thangavadivel S, Wilson SE. Fibrocyte migration, differentiation and apoptosis during the corneal wound healing response to injury. Exp. Eye Res. 2018;170:177].

16. **The Descemet's layer basement membrane in the posterior cornea also regulates fibrosis by modulating aqueous humor TGFβ access to keratocytes and fibrocytes to drive myofibroblast development.** Medeiros CS, Saikia P, de Oliveira RC, Lassance L, Santhiago MR, Wilson SE. Descemet's membrane injury-related posterior corneal fibrosis, Invest. Ophth. Vis. Sci., in press

17. **Injury and defective regeneration of basement membranes, resulting in high tissue levels of TGFβ, may underlie the development of fibrosis in other organs such as the skin, lung, heart, and kidneys.** [Wilson SE, Marino GK, Torricelli AAM, Medeiros CS. Corneal fibrosis: injury and defective regeneration of the epithelial basement membrane. A paradigm for fibrosis in other organs? Matrix Biology 2017;64:17].

*Three of these papers won post-doctoral fellows in my lab the prestigious Troutman Award from ISRS of the American Academy of Ophthalmology. All the papers from my lab can be reviewed at https://www.ncbi.nlm.nih.gov/pubmed/?term=Wilson+SE+cornea

A major focus of our recent work has been on our discoveries that injury and defective regeneration of both the epithelial basement membrane, that the epithelium (skin) in the anterior cornea is attached to, and Descemet's basement membrane in the posterior cornea, that the corneal endothelium is attached to, underlies scarring (generally referred to as fibrosis) of the corneal stroma that results in vision loss after injuries, infections, surgery, and some diseases. Defects in the generation of the basement membrane results in the growth factor transforming growth factor (TGF) β penetrating into the stroma from the tears, epithelium, and/or aqueous humor (fluid in the front of the eye) at sufficient concentrations to drive the development of myofibroblasts (the cells that produce scarring) from both resident fibroblastic "keratocytes" in the stroma and cells that circulate in the blood from bone marrow called fibrocytes—that penetrate into the cornea after injuries. Eventual repair of the basement membrane(s) by the tissues, or through surgical transplantation, reestablishes the control on TGFβ penetration into the corneal stroma, and leads to programmed cell death (apoptosis) of the myofibroblasts and disappearance of the scarring through the actions of keratocytes in reabsorbing and renewing the collagens and other matrix materials in the corneal stroma. We hypothesize that similar injury and defective regeneration of basement membranes leading to dysregulation of TGFβ, and possibly other growth factors, leads to fibrosis in most organs of humans and other animals.

Wilson SE, Marino GK, Torricelli AAM, Medeiros CS. Corneal fibrosis: injury and defective regeneration of the epithelial basement membrane. A paradigm for fibrosis in other organs? Matrix Biology 2017;64:17.

Saikia P, Medeiros CS Thangavadivel S, Wilson SE. Basement membranes in the cornea and other organs that commonly develop fibrosis. Cell and Tissue Research. 2018;374:439.

I owe a huge debt of gratitude to the postdoctoral fellows, clinical fellows and residents who've worked with me in my laboratory. Many of them were American citizens or permanent U.S. residents who were part of my Clinical Refractive Surgery Fellowship at University of Washington or the Cornea and the Refractive and Corneal Surgery Fellowship Victor Perez, MD and I began at Cole Eye Institute shortly after my return to Cleveland in 2003 or resident physicians at Cole Eye Institute, including special people like Mark Walker, MD, Rosan Choi, MD, Laura M. Periman, MD, William J. Dupps, MD, PhD (who is now a faculty member at Cole Eye Institute and succeeded me as clinical fellowship director), Andrew Esposito, MD, Brian Armstrong, MD, Edgar Espana, MD, Viral Juthani, MD, Naveen Mysore, MD, PhD, J. Martin Huer, MD, PhD, and many others. I've also had amazing PhD and MD researchers in my laboratory, including Rajiv Mohan, PhD, Vivek Singh, PhD, Harmeet Kaur, PhD, Shyam S. Chaurasia, PhD, Abirami Santhanam, PhD, Paramananda Saikia, PhD, Manasvee Kapadia, MD, Woo-Jung Kim, MD, Jong-Wook Hong, MD, PhD, Jong-Soo Lee, MD, PhD, and many others. But I would be remiss if I didn't make special mention of the incredible contributions made to my career by my "Fellows from Brazil." Beginning in 1995 with Marco Helena, MD—and really even before that when I was a young assistant professor at UT Southwestern with James McCulley's fellow Carlos M. Mafra, MD—it has been my honor and privilege to have a long line of truly outstanding young postdoctoral fellow MDs and PhDs from Brazil ("What a country!") work with me for two to three years in my laboratory, clinics and surgery. These brilliant and hardworking people have included Renato Ambrosio, Jr., MD, PhD, Marcony R. Santhiago, MD, PhD, Marcelo V. Netto, MD, Andre A. M. Torricelli, MD, PhD, Marcella Q. Salomão, MD, Fabricio Witzel de Medeiros, MD, Maria Regina Chalita, MD, Flavia Barbosa,

PhD, Gustavo K. Marino, MD, Luciana Lassance, PhD, Carla S. Medeiros, MD, and Rodrigo Carlos de Oliveira, MD. Hopefully, many more of these exceptionally talented people will find their way to my program in the years to come. Many of them have become like sons and daughters to me over the years. Many of these Brazilians have risen to become leaders in Brazilian ophthalmology and refractive surgery. I'm so proud of them all! If you search my publications on PubMed.com, you will see that I owe all of these professionals a debt I can never repay for the contributions they have made to my career—and to my life.

I also want to thank my many collaborators over the years, with special thanks to Stephen D. Klyce, PhD, Jerry W. Shay, PhD, George R. Stark, PhD, James D. Zieske, PhD, Timo Tervo, MD, James V. Jester, PhD, William M. Petroll, PhD, David M. Meisler, MD, Alexander V. Ljubimov, PhD, Yaron S. Rabinowitz, MD, William J. Dupps, Jr, MD, PhD, and Marcony R. Santhiago, MD, PhD.

The biggest problems I've encountered with research have been dealings with the Investigational Review Board (IRB) and the Institutional Animal Care and Use Committee (IACUC). Most of this likely relates to pressures these committees feel from federal, state and local authorities—and even the public at large.

For the IRB, it was never the board itself that caused me headaches and cost me time. It was the bureaucrats associated with the IRB. This culminated in a study in which I got IRB approval to work with Arun Singh, MD, our ocular oncologist, to obtain the normal corneas from patients who were unfortunately undergoing enucleation because of a severe choroidal melanoma that were not treatable with a radioactive plaques. In some cases, these eyes had topical anesthesia applied and an epithelial abrasion produced with a scalpel up to 30 minutes prior to the enucleation, and this was included in the IRB approval. This study was set up so that these patients provided written informed consent, but when the cornea left the operating room, the cryofixed cornea was no longer associated with any protected health information—no names, no clinic numbers, no sexes, no ages, nothing—because these were not important to our cell biological studies performed using these normal corneas. The signed consent forms were retained in a locked file cabinet at my office—as was required by the IRB—but even these signed forms could not be associated with a particular tissue block in my lab freezer. Two years into the study, we had obtained a handful of corneas that were used in various experiments confirming the expression of specific epithelial basement membrane components in the stromal cells of human wounded corneas but not human unwounded corneas. Then one day, along came the helpful bureaucrat to my office. She wouldn't believe, as the original IRB application laid out in detail, that I was not keeping any protected health information related to the donors of these research corneas. I explained to her—in precise detail—that we didn't need that information, and once each cornea left the operating room, there was no way to tie it to the original patient, or go back to a patient chart even if we wanted to. She still didn't believe me, and insisted on searching my office computer, and then insisted that I bring in my laptop computer and two external hard drives from home so she could search those, too. I told her when she was done, after her unnecessary intrusion into my time and unwillingness to accept my word, I would never do anymore human research, even chart review research—which I'd used for dozens of studies in the past involving Cole Eye Institute residents and fellows. And I never did.

For the IACUC, our problems usually revolved around what was an acceptable number of mice or rabbits for a group at each time point. Let me say at the outset that I'm an animal lover!

Steven E. Wilson, MD

My two dogs are full members of the family. I love all animals, and insist that our laboratory mice and rabbits (which are the only research animals I've ever used), that are raised exclusively for research by FDA-regulated suppliers, are treated with utmost care—according to the guidelines of the FDA, NIH, ARVO, and every other reasonable organization that expresses interest in the well-being of research animals. Many of the experiments we perform have a direct relationship to human healing abnormalities and disorders involving interactions between corneal cells, nerves and cells carried in the blood vessels, for example. At present, there is no way to simulate these interaction in test tubes or cell cultures. When we do perform these experiments, for example in mice, the last thing we want to have happen is the study end up with results that are equivocal because the number of mice at each time point did not allow the result to reach statistical significance. I constantly spar with the IACUC about decisions they enforce on us. For example, in several important studies, only three animals were allowed at each time point. It was a pilot study—with no prior variability information, so power calculations were not possible. Predictably, even though the results were significant without statistics, high-level vision research journals we submitted the paper to were reluctant to accept these manuscripts because "too few mice were included at each time point." I reviewed the data with a biostatistician at the Cleveland Clinic, and the first thing he said to me was, "Why did you only use an n of 3 mice at each time point for the study? I recommend using at least five or six mice at each time point." I replied, "Tell that to the IACUC, FDA, and NIH!" But truthfully, the IACUCs themselves are under tremendous and constant pressure from the three federal agencies that regulate animal research—the U.S. Department of Agriculture's Animal and Plant Health Inspection Service (APHIS), the Food and Drug Administration (FDA), and the National Institutes of Health (NIH). Inspectors from these organizations constantly try to enforce the 3Rs of animal research—Replacement, Reduction and Refinement. Thus, investigators and the IACUC at each university hospital strive to **replace** animals with in vitro experiments in tissue culture, the test tube, etc. That seems reasonable, but many complex cellular interactions such as those between the cornea, bone marrow-derived cells and corneal nerves cannot be meaningfully simulated in tissue culture or the test tube. Similarly, the investigators and IACUC should endeavor to **refine** experiments so that fewer animals are used. This is very reasonable, and we always have this in mind when designing experiments. Finally, the investigators and IACUC should do their best to **reduce** the number of animals used in a particular experiment. We always do that, too. But when these efforts to reduce the number of animals are excessive, and result in experiments that are not scientifically sound, then all of the animals used in the experiments could end up being wasted—since other scientists reviewing the study for publication or reading the study after publication may discount the work as statistically invalid. Thus, IACUCs must work with research investigators to find a proper balance of achieving scientific validity, while at the same time using the minimum number of animals. The devil is in the details, and it is often difficult for the investigator and IACUC members to agree on what constitutes an adequate number of animals, especially for pilot studies where no prior variance is available to allow power calculations to be performed. This is a constant source of angst for research investigators who must use animals to study complex processes, as well as IACUC members who are constantly harried by the responsible federal agencies. This ongoing struggle drives research investigators—MD and PhD—crazy.

A few years ago, an online application mechanism for animal studies called esirus was adopted at Cleveland Clinic. It was such a disorganized mess that researchers began calling it "are you serious." It was a prime example of how something adopted "to make researchers or clinicians lives easier," profoundly complicated our professional lives. Dozens of sections must be filled out completely—with some important details, but also lots of trivial nonsense—before the animal research protocol is reviewed by the IACUC. Then, after the review, invariably changes need to be made on many of these sections, before the protocol is accepted and the experiments can proceed.

Another example of bureaucracy making our lives difficult is the Information Technology Department doing everything possible to complicate our clinical and research lives. For example, in the past year, the IT department at Cleveland Clinic decided for "security reasons" we could not forward an email (with or without an attachment) from our Cleveland Clinic email address to our private email account, for example, a Yahoo or Roadrunner email account. If we try to do that, the forwarded email simply disappears. Many of us forwarded ourselves such emails to retain important information, such as Award Notices from NIH about our grants, so they wouldn't just drop from our Cleveland Clinic email accounts a few months later when we exceeded our allotted space. To save these important attachments, we were suddenly forced to download them to memory sticks at our work computers to transport them to our laptops, or find ways of saving the documents into our cell phones before adding them to new private account emails we sent to ourselves. Meanwhile, hundreds of spam emails—that we don't want to receive—pour through the system with every kind of scam and phishing attempt imaginable—that we need to screen ourselves as to whether they are real or potentially dangerous. All the email messages in the world to the Cleveland Clinic "Help Desk" about these dangerous emails coming into the system accomplish nothing.

Changes also came to my clinical practice. When I first returned to the Cleveland Clinic, in 2003, my 50% clinical time was totally in refractive surgery. That is what I'd done for the prior eight years and it was what I knew best. However, with the downturn in the U.S. economy in 2008, and the fact I was now not the Medical Director of Refractive Surgery—Ronald Krueger, MD, whom I helped Cleveland Clinic identify as my successor when I left in 1998 was in that position (and welcome to it!)—the number of patients coming to me for refractive surgery dropped with the economy. To counter this, I voluntarily returned half of my clinical time to cornea, and once again began performing corneal transplants, including the new Descemet's Stripping and Automated Endothelial Keratoplasty (DSAEK) surgery. I continued with this combined refractive surgery-surgical cornea practice for three years, until 2011, but then decided the "surgical cornea" would become "medical cornea" because of my frustrations with inefficiencies in the operating rooms, that were seriously cutting into my research and family time. At that time, I was scheduled to operate on cornea patients on Wednesday afternoons at 12:30 pm, but often—because the morning surgeons constantly ran over—I wasn't getting started until late afternoon or even early evening and, then, operating into the night. Dr. Martin graciously accepted the rearrangement of my clinical activities. I still saw many of the same patients, but if one of them needed surgery, I referred them to my younger clinical cornea colleagues, who loved operating late into the night! I still continued to perform laser vision-correction LASIK and PRK, and therapeutic PTK, but only two or three half-days a week, depending on the week during a month. Since I'm no longer performing corneal surgery, my medical cornea practice has transitioned into more of a medical comprehensive ophthalmology practice—with a few cornea and external disease patients sprinkled in. This too may be changing as of January 2019—since one of my refractive surgery colleagues just announced his departure to the University of Nebraska—but at this point I'm not sure how that will impact me. I may get busier in the operating room, at least for a while.

The introduction of EPIC electronic medical records also impacted our lives in immeasurable ways. Once we at least partially mastered this system—after two to three years—most of us actually came to view it as a useful tool to record our patient visits, fill prescriptions, obtain test results, communicate with patients, communicate with other doctors, etc. But the constant changes made in formatting of pages and required minutiae added to the history, physical, assessment, etc. remain the bane of our existence. I always pity new residents, fellows, and faculty who must learn to use EPIC for the first time—they often can be seen pulling at their hair at one of the computers in an examination room.

Finally, the biggest changes came to my teaching opportunities at The Cole Eye Institute. I was the Cornea and Refractive Surgery Fellowship Director at Cole Eye Institute from 2003 to 2017. These fellows are in the Ophthalmology Match Program. In 2017, faculty who worked with me in this program decided that a substantial portion of the training should occur at a Cleveland Clinic satellite clinic. This change would substantially reduce the refractive surgery experience for fellows in the one year program, that was already substantially less than cornea. I did not agree with this change but since the other faculty were in favor, I stepped down as fellowship director and no longer have these fellows on my clinical service or in research (which had steadily declined since Victor Perez, MD and I had formed the fellowship in 2003). Thus, at this point, I only have international postdoctoral fellows with me for a small portion of their time in my medical cornea or refractive surgery clinics or operating time.

Similarly, with the large number of clinical faculty at Cole Eye Institute, I no longer have residents with me in clinics or surgery. Thus, the only time I have with residents at Cole Eye Institute is one hour lectures I give three to four times a year.

It's been quite a change since I was both the residency program director and cornea/refractive surgery fellowship director at University of Washington. Fortunately, I still have my MD postdoctoral fellows, mainly from Brazil. It's ironic that I now spend far more of my time with young Brazilian doctors than I do with young American doctors.

My old mentor, Herbert E Kaufman, MD, used to say, "Nowhere is perfect, or we'd all be there." I myself tend to think back to the old Meat Loaf rock song, "Two out of three ain't bad." For now, I have my research program and I have clinical care of my patients. I guess, after all these years, I can live with only my postdoctoral research fellows and a few medical and undergraduate students to teach. The Brazilians seem to appreciate it, based on the number of times I get invited to Brazil each year to give lectures!

Afterword

It would be easier to accept the upheaval in my career at University of Washington, and later when I returned to Cleveland Clinic the temporary loss of NIH research funding for over a year, if what happened to me was an isolated event. But the landscape of academic medicine in America is littered with the remains of promising physician–scientists—outstanding physicians who finally abandoned careers in research after enduring years of struggle to maintain funding and needing to convince their leaders to support them during the lean times—people who finally gave up the fight and devote all their time to the clinic and operating room.

The continuing decline in physician–scientists will be highly detrimental to the future of medicine in the United States. These professionals are frequently said to "bridge the gap" between the laboratory and clinic, bringing new methods for diagnosis or treatment to the patient. These are not just idle words. Physician–scientists are typically in the best position to recognize clinical problems, syndromes, and complications—and begin bench research to understand the underlying pathophysiology or develop new treatments. They also serve as role models for medical students, residents, and fellows who might not otherwise consider careers as physician-scientists in academic medicine. They are also much more likely to remain in academic medicine than pure clinicians, who often eventually leave for the perceived rewards of private or group practice. Physician–scientists therefore provide critical continuity in medical departments.

It is important to point out how very difficult it is to develop a true physician–scientist. In my experience, only about one or two percent of those who set out during their training with a goal of becoming a physician–scientist actually succeed. Most aspiring physician–scientists fall by the wayside along the long, treacherous path, unable to compete for funding or otherwise to be promoted after five to seven years in their first academic position. Most top universities have rules that dictate that a physician–scientist must be promoted within five to seven years of beginning as an assistant professor, as decided by their senior faculty members, chairman, and/or dean, or they are required to leave the university. Those who do make it, tend to be the cream of the crop in terms of academic potential. Even then, many fail.

In my opinion, physician–scientists also make the best chairmen for academic departments and deans of medical schools, since they are in the best position to understand and sympathize with the needs and problems of both clinicians and scientists. As fewer and fewer physician–

scientists are available for leadership in medical schools, more chairman and dean positions are filled by pure clinicians, some of whom obtained MBA or other non-medical ancillary degrees at weekend or evening programs. These chairs and deans tend to surround themselves with accountants and attorneys, who concentrate on the business or legal side of medicine, and in many cases, ignore what's really important to build and maintain a strong, well-rounded academic department or medical school. My view is that you are asking for trouble when you have an attorney in a role so critical to the growth and wellbeing of the medical school. I, myself, have experienced the paralysis—the hesitancy to do what's right—when, for example, dealing with disruptive or unproductive faculty members. One falters when the details are left to a lawyer who surrenders on every point, even when the department is clearly in the right, out of paralyzing fear that the faculty member will file a lawsuit.

A medical school department chairman's main job is to facilitate the teaching, medical care, and research activities of his or her faculty by smoothing bureaucracy, obtaining grant and endowment funds, and perhaps most importantly, empowering the faculty to make their own career choices. The question, 'How can I make it easier for my faculty members to succeed?' should be on the top of every day's list of things to accomplish. Some chairmen seem to think it's their main job to micromanage and make life difficult for their faculty members. I thank God every day I don't work under one of *those* chairmen. I don't think I could, at least for long.

Unfortunately, the situation isn't much better for pure clinical physicians in America today, whether in academic departments, group practices, or private practices. As earlier chapters and the appendices pointed out, these doctors are beset by declining reimbursement for services provided, insurance companies that strategize to limit reimbursement by denying claims that *they* deem medically unnecessary, Medicare/Medicaid/private insurance dictating which drugs or treatments can be utilized for individual patients, confusing and changing Medicaid and Medicare regulations, non-physician "*quality assurance*" administrators who also decide what treatments a patient should receive or when a patient is medically stable to leave the hospital, ambulance-chasing malpractice attorneys, legislation allowing other professions medical or even surgical privileges, and increasingly burdensome regulation by federal, state, and local bureaucracy. Then, if all of that isn't enough, we have over-zealous federal prosecutors trying to establish names for themselves by making examples of physicians who err (I'm not referring here to real fraud).

Some people who read this book will undoubtedly dismiss all of these grievances as more unending whining by pampered and overpaid physicians who already enjoy an exalted position in society. Are doctors really deserving of the esteem and adulation, even reverence, some people in America bestow upon them? I believe most physicians are worthy. Most of these devoted professionals are unbelievably hardworking, sacrificing their personal and family time for the well-being of their patients, and in the case of physician–scientists, struggling through governmental and academic minefields to discover new diagnostic methods, medications, and treatments that will ease the pain and suffering of those afflicted with the hundreds of diseases and injuries that affect the quality and longevity of our lives. After all, with the exception of true love, isn't good health the main prerequisite for a happy and fulfilling life? Many hold the profession as a whole in contempt, but revere the individual physician who saved his or her life, health, hearing, or sight—or that of a family member or dear friend. Most physicians aren't in it for the money. These bright people could make far more money spending the countless hours they contribute in other pursuits. In any case, they are not deserving of the onslaught of bullying, legal attacks, and regulation they must endure from governments, insurance adjusters, managed care companies, accountants, prosecutors, and attorneys.

So what should be done to improve the present situation? How do we stem the onslaught that is driving more and more physicians from medicine and making the physician–scientist an endangered species? First, federal and state legislators and executive branch leaders must enact reasonable and meaningful national tort reform—including provisions that make sure it's the *patient* who receives most of the settlement or award when one is really justified. Also, if a jury or panel finds in favor of the physician, then all expenses of the physician, including time spent reviewing records and depositions and responding to queries from the plaintiff's attorneys should be compensated fairly. Clients and attorneys who bring frivolous lawsuits must suffer financially for doing so. Medical insurance companies and health maintenance organizations should be brought to task for the unfair policies they use in dealing with physicians. This will likely require further ongoing litigation on the part of physician groups. Those who establish and administer Medicare and Medicaid reimbursement rules must make sure they are consistent across the United States and easier for both physicians and administrators to understand. Federal, state, and local governments should strive to make sure there is no more bureaucracy and paperwork in place than is actually necessary. Our governments should also make sure the ramifications of any policy, such as HIPPA (For more information, see Appendix 5), are fully understood, so that clinical practice and medical research are not unduly hindered or blocked. When billing issues are discovered, prosecutors and grand juries should take into account the complexity of the constantly changing statutes governing Medicare and Medicaid reimbursement, and until proven otherwise, assume that errors were related to mistakes and not criminal activities.

Obviously, prosecutors should make sure they discover any agreements between physicians and Medicare/Medicaid intermediaries so they don't waste taxpayer and medical school funds pursuing unwarranted criminal charges against physicians. They must be careful not to get themselves into situations where they're so far down the road on an investigation that they must find *some* charge to bring or risk losing face. These prosecutors must also realize that low-level employees within a billing unit of a large medical institution are usually not in position to determine whether wrongful billing is physician-driven or administrator-driven. They must also understand that, within any department or medical school, there are individuals who are disaffected with their leaders and willing to say or do virtually anything—even commit perjury—to get rid of them.

Finally, legislators and governmental executives, as well as the leadership at NIH, must enact new policies and programs to foster the careers of successful mid-career physician–scientists. The first break that needs to be fixed is to restructure the grant review process so it is fair, more meaningful, and less prone to errors. Hopefully, we can quickly make progress to prevent the loss of more valuable professionals in the next decade.

The medical profession in America is definitely in serious trouble and what is, or is not, done to remedy the crisis in the next decade will determine the quality of medical care that is available in this country over the generations to come. Will the United States continue to have the greatest medical care in the world or will the quality of this care gradually diminish over time? Will the medical research performed in America continue to lead the world? Will the physicians and physician–scientists who are currently in practice feel good enough about their profession that they will encourage the best and brightest, even their own children, to pursue careers in medicine? These are worrisome questions that loom before us. We can insure these queries will be answered in the affirmative if physicians, medical institutions, insurance companies, and government work together to seek what is really in the best interests of patients. I am reminded of an aging emeritus professor at UC San Diego School of Medicine who came to speak to the members of my medical school honor society. With a tear in his sagging eyes, the kindly physician lamented how lucky we medical students were to have our whole careers ahead of us. I can only hope I feel the same way when I reach the end of my career as a surgeon-scientist.

It is my hope that some high school, undergraduate college and graduate students who dream to be physicians or physician-scientists will read this book. If there is one piece of advice I could give these students, it's DON'T GIVE UP ON YOUR DREAM! Like me, if you're an undergraduate student who is not accepted to medical school, go to graduate school and earn an advanced degree to better yourself and apply again. If you're not accepted then, do something else for a couple of years that better prepares you for medical school—like teaching college science classes—and apply again. Of course, your undergraduate and graduate grades and MCAT scores must be at a realistic level, but if they are, don't give up. Persistence is appreciated and rewarded by medical school admissions committees.

Appendix 1
Trainee Abuse—Attempts at a Solution and Meaningful Progress

For years there has been increasing realization that excessive hours are detrimental to patient care and young physician training. There was, however, great resistance to change because hard work during early training had always been a part of the cultivation of physicians and surgeons. Also, it's not difficult to imagine the economic consequences to hospitals of having to replace trainee house staff members who work from 100 to 130, or more, hours a week—for salaries that amount to little more than two to three dollars an hour—based on decreasing dollar values in the 2000s. There is a litany of pertinent opinions, lawsuits, and regulations that could be detailed here, but I will confine myself to some of the important events that influenced meaningful reform.

The first physicians' union began in the U.S.A. in 1934, with formation of the Intern Council of Greater New York. The Council negotiated for the first stipends ($5 per month) for house staff in U.S.A. history. These early efforts at house staff unionization collapsed during World War II and the Cold War, and anti-union sentiments of the McCarthy Era.

Some of the earliest efforts to revive collective representation of house staff were brought about by the Committee of Interns and Residents (CIR) founded in New York City's public hospitals. In 1958, CIR managed to negotiate the first collective bargaining agreement for house staff anywhere in the U.S.A. By the late 1960s, members in the private sector started organizing and joining CIR. A dispute over resident working hours led to a three-day strike, led by CIR in New York in 1975, and CIR won contractual limits for on-call schedules of one night in three. In 1989, CIR helped shape New York State's groundbreaking regulations that set maximum work-hour limits for house staff, but still real progress in addressing abusive hours and patient loads was slow because the regulations applied only in New York, and in some cases, hospitals merely ignored the regulations because few victims reported infractions. Even if they did, there were paltry penalties for violators.

The power of house staff members, interns and residents alike, to organize and bring about change for better working conditions would seem to have been ensured by passage of the National Labor Relations Act in 1974. However, in 1976, shortly after enactment of the Health

Steven E. Wilson, MD

Care Amendments to the act, a majority of the National Labor Relations Board members [223 NLRB 251 (1976)] agreed with the Cedars-Sinai Medical Center (*of all places!*) position that interns, residents, and fellows were not employees, but students, and therefore the hospital's interactions with the house staff were not governed by the Labor Relations Act.

In 1977, the National Labor Relations Board clarified the Cedars-Sinai decision in its St. Clare's Hospital & Health Center decision [229 NLRB 1000] by stressing that the decision was one involving students. In this decision, the majority set forth four categories of cases involving students and concluded that hospital house staff fell within the fourth category "in which students perform services at their educational institutions which are directly related to their educational program," reasoning that house staff serve primarily as students, not as employees, and that their relationship with their institution is predominantly academic rather than economic. Thus, the majority believed the interests of the house staff were not "readily adaptable to the collective-bargaining process." In effect, hospitals were free to treat their house staff as they saw fit, and interns, residents and fellows could not use the National Labor Relations Act to protect themselves, if they were to organize against egregious offenders.

In 1993, the State of New York Hospital Code incorporated provisions to protect patients from medical errors due to sleep-deprived and overworked physicians by limiting the working hours of physicians in hospital residency training programs to no more than eighty hours per week over a four-week period and no more than twenty-four consecutive hours. These regulations also mandated close supervision of medical residents by attending physicians.

Cousins wrote an article criticizing the hardships of internship as a hazing ritual that had long since outlived its usefulness, prompting numerous commentaries supporting long work hours for interns to promote responsibility, self-reliance, and confidence.

Cousins N. Internship: Preparation or Hazing?" *Journal of the American Medical Association.* 1981;245:377.

I personally agree with the comments that Michael J. Green, MD, M.S., wrote in his article.

Green, MJ. What (If Anything) Is Wrong with Residency Overwork?" *Annals of Internal Medicine.* 1995;123:512.

"If the primary non-cognitive training objective for residency is to promote virtue and professionalism in a physician's interaction with his or her patients, then long work hours must be measured against this goal. In this regard, several observations are appropriate. First, patients value humanistic traits in their physicians but believe that physicians lack such attributes. Second, compassion in medicine appears to have declined as technological medical care has increased. Third, the physician-patient relationship tends to become increasingly negative during the internship, even though medical schools have tried to enroll students who have humane core values. Fourth, residents report that sleep loss hurts their relationship with patients. Although many factors contribute to these trends (including information overload, lack of free time, inadequate role models, and new responsibilities for patient care), the effects of sleep deprivation on attitudes and values should not be underestimated. For many residents, fatigue cultivates anger, resentment, and bitterness rather than kindness, compassion, or

empathy. Embittered physicians may still be able to accurately analyze chest radiographs, and they may do procedures with technical proficiency, but we would not say that they are virtuous . . . sleep deprivation can contribute to attitudes that differ from those admired by the profession."

Green also brought to my attention an extraordinarily honest entry made by a resident in an intensive care unit diary.

Groopman, LC. Medical Internship as Moral Education: An Essay on the System of Training Physicians. *Cult Med Psychiatry,* 1987;11:207.

"One A.M. and I'm ready to go to bed: one should never be ready to go to bed in the ICU— you'll always be disappointed. Anyway, I'm on my way to the EW . . . when there's a code (cardiac arrest). Get up there and find (a resident) trying to intubate a lifetime asthmatic who is as blue as this ink. I keep thinking—he's blue enough to go to the ICU. I keep hoping he's going to be too blue to go anywhere. Probably a nice man with a loving wife and concerned children, but I don't want that SOB to make it because I've got one special who is going to keep me up 2 more hours. I don't need an intubated, blue, pneumothoraceed SOB coming to my unit . . . I don't want the asthmatic SOB to live if it means I don't sleep. I don't want the special to live if it means I don't sleep. I just want to sleep."

More than any other piece I've ever read, this honest diary entry encapsulates what overwork and lack of sleep can do to the thinking of even the most empathetic and moral human being. If you don't think you're capable of such callous thinking, that somehow you're above such heartlessness, then I can only advise you to spend a year in an internship where you're on all-night call every two or three nights and where many of those days last thirty-six hours without sleep. At some point, you'll be shocked at the thoughts that creep into your consciousness . . . even if your moral fiber leads you to dismiss them a moment later.

A major case that raised public consciousness of the problem of house staff overwork was the case of Libby Zion, an eighteen-year-old patient who died unexpectedly within twenty-four hours of admission to New York Hospital in 1984.

Asch, D.A., & Parker, R.M. "The Libby Zion Case: One Step Forward or Two Steps Backward?" *New England Journal of Medicine*, 1988;318:771.

Some felt strongly Miss Zion's death could have been avoided if residents caring for her had not been overworked and sleep-deprived. A Manhattan grand jury did not find the physicians or hospital at fault, but did issue a critical report that led to the establishment of the Ad Hoc Committee on Emergency Services, also known as the Bell Commission, in 1987. The recommendations of this commission led to legislative reform of medical resident work hours in New York State. Jurors issued a verdict in the civil lawsuit *Zion vs. New York Hospital* in February 1995, in which they found New York Hospital was not responsible for Ms. Zion's death, but they concluded that the hospital was negligent in assigning an intern too many patients, even though this negligence was not found to be the proximate cause of her death. They also concluded that the hospital was not negligent with regard to the manner in which its house staff was supervised. It is my belief that Libby Zion did not die in vain, because this case benefited countless other patients by shining the bright light of public opinion on the issue of house staff work hours.

Report Finds Abuse of N. Y. Residents Rules; Hospitals Say No," *The New York Times*, 16 January 1995;A5.

Organized medicine fell on both sides of the house staff organization issue. The Resident Physician Section of the American Medical Association (AMA) supported resident physician rights to form collective bargaining organizations. However, the American College of Physicians-American Society of Internal Medicine (ACP-ASIM) Associates Council opposed it, cautioning that collective bargaining could "adversely affect the learning and mentoring environment." The Association of American Medical Colleges (AAMC) also opposed collective bargaining by physicians-in-training and objected to the formation of collective bargaining units for residents, maintaining that interns and residents were primarily *students* and that collective bargaining would "interfere with the educational objectives of graduate medical education programs."

On November 26, 1999, the National Labor Relations Board issued decision1-152 on BOSTON MEDICAL CENTER CORPORATION AND HOUSE OFFICERS' ASSOCIATION/COMMITTEE OF INTERNS AND RESIDENTS, PETITIONER Case 1-RC-20574. With one dissenter, who, in my opinion, merely rehashed old arguments of gloom and doom for the profession in the event of house staff organization, the board concluded that "the legislative history amply demonstrated that Congress, to the extent it considered the question, thought house staff to be statutory employees." Therefore, the decisions of the prior board based on the Cedars-Sinai Medical Center, 223 NLRB 251 (1976), where the decision that house staff were to be considered students was forwarded, was reversed. Thus, house staff were governed by the National Labor Relations Act and could organize to negotiate with hospitals and clinics.

On April 30, 2001, Public Citizen, a consumer and health advocacy group that claimed 150,000 members, the Committee of Interns and Residents, the American Medical Student Association (AMSA), Bertrand Bell, MD, Professor of Medicine at Albert Einstein College of Medicine and author of New York State Health Code 405 restricting resident work hours, and Kingman P. Strohl, MD, Professor of Medicine and Director of the Center for Sleep Disorders Research at Case Western Reserve University, petitioned the Occupational Safety and Health Administration (OSHA) to implement regulations on medical resident and fellow work hours: *"with the primary intent of providing more humane and safe working conditions for medical residents and fellows, which will result in a better standard of care for all patients."* The petitioners requested: 1. A limit of 80 hours of work per week, 2. A limit of 24 consecutive hours worked in one shift, 3. A limit of on-call shifts to every 3rd night, 4. A minimum of 10 hours off-duty time between shifts, 5. At least one 24-hour period of off-duty time per week, and 6. A limit of 12 consecutive hours on-duty per day for emergency medicine residents working in hospitals receiving more than 15,000 unscheduled patient visits per year.

These petitioners provided impressive documentation of the detrimental effects of long hours of work. They also acknowledged, and effectively dismissed, the arguments others had made against implementing limits.

These included:

"(1) continuity of patient care will be disrupted, (2) long hours are necessary in order to sufficiently train physicians, (3) training under conditions of fatigue and sleep deprivation

prepares residents to function should these conditions arise in future practice, and (4) long hours promote favorable character attributes in physicians, such as discipline, endurance, responsibility, self-reliance, confidence, collegiality and humility."

These petitioners also noted that other countries had implemented far stricter limits on resident physician work hours, including:

- **Australia**: 75 hours/week (Western and Victoria), 70 hours/week (Tasmania), 68 hours/week (South), and 24 consecutive hours for a shift (Capital Territory).

- **Denmark**: 45 hours/week, 11 hours between shifts, although it can be reduced to 8 hours under certain circumstances.

- **United Kingdom**: 56 hours/week averaged (cycle time not specified), 72 hours maximum/week, 14-16 total hours/regular shift, 16-24 consecutive hours for a shift, 32 consecutive hours on weekdays and 56 consecutive hours on weekends when on-call.

- **European Union**: 48 hours/week, including overtime; night work must not exceed 8 hours on average, 11 consecutive hours/day maximum.

- **Germany**: 56 hours averaged/week over 24 weeks, 7.5-10 hours/day in addition to 12 hours on-call or 24 hours on-call when off-duty, 24 consecutive hours maximum, guaranteed 10 consecutive hours off after duty >7.5 hours, 12 consecutive hours off when on-call.

- **Netherlands**: 48 hours averaged/week over 13 weeks, 60 hours maximum/week, 15 hours total/day, although can be extended up to 3 hours, 9.5 hours for a night shift, 24 maximum consecutive hours, 5 shifts worked consecutively/week for a maximum 13 weeks out of 26 weeks,10 consecutive hours between shifts, 1 off-duty Sunday in every 13 when on an on-call schedule, 9 hours rest after a shift <15 hours or 24 hours rest after a shift >15 hours, in addition to 1 off-duty Sunday in every 13.

In September of 2001, the Island Peer Review Organization (IRPO) of New York, an independent party engaged to conduct annual reviews of the state's 115 teaching hospitals began unannounced inspections lasting several days and nights to ascertain whether the institutions were in compliance with the "Bell Regulations." Sixty-two percent of the programs were inspected, and by June of the following year, IPRO reported that "at least one" of the programs they had visited had been cited. CIR Associate Director Eric Scherzer stated, "The majority of programs in New York appeared to be in compliance," although, predictably, IPRO found that at least one residency program at many of the hospitals was in violation. In addition to making these unannounced inspections, IPRO was also charged with investigating complaints reported to the Department of Health from individual residents, their family members, and anonymous callers—and dozens were received. Veronica Wilbur, IPRO's Director for Hospital Compliance also noted that during some of the annual inspections IPRO inspectors noted "residents who appeared to have been coerced into giving false or inaccurate statements about their work hours." *Imagine that!*

As of June 2002, IPRO reported that in New York, *"of the residency programs cited for having residents work greater than 80 hours per week: 63% were in Surgery; 16% in Family Practice or Internal Medicine; 16% in OB-GYN; 4% in Pediatrics and 1% in Anesthesia. Of those cited for working greater than 80 hours per week: 45% were interns; 19% were postgraduate year (PGY) 2; 15% were PGY 3; 12% were PGY 4; and 9% were PGY 5 or more. Of those programs cited for working more than 24 consecutive hours: 43% were in Surgery;*

42% in Family Practice or Internal Medicine; 8% were in Pediatrics; 5% were in OB-BYN; and 2% were in Anesthesia."

One must remember that this was data only from New York State, where the greatest scrutiny of training programs was occurring.

To my knowledge, only one hospital in New York has received a fine and none has been shut down through loss of accreditation. St. Vincent's Hospital and Medical Center was fined for violating resident work hours after health department inspectors discovered during a September 27, 1998, survey:

- All of the hospital's 20 surgical residents were working in excess of 85 hours per week;
- All 20 surgical residents worked 30 to 36 hours straight in violation of the 24-hour maximum shift rule;
- Residents "on-call" during night shift hours were not resting due to frequent interruptions for patient care responsibilities;
- Continuous assignments for residents that included night shift "on-call" duty are not followed by a required non-working period;
- In 12 of the 25 medical records reviewed, documentation of oversight of residents by the senior resident or supervising attending physician was not evident;
- The hospital failed to appropriately limit the duties of medical students. Thus, medical record entries were not countersigned within 24 hours and medical students were permitted to write medical orders, including orders for controlled substances;
- Seven of nine medical records reviewed did not contain documentation to indicate that telephone orders for the administration of drugs were personally authenticated by the prescribing doctor.

And what was the fine that St. Vincent's hospital received in December of 1998 for these blatant transgressions? A paltry $20,000—ridiculous when one considers that the hospital bill of a single hospitalized patient is often much greater than this amount.

Sentiments to limit house staff work hours, by federal legislation if necessary, snowballed across the country and finally, in July of 2003, the Accreditation Council for Graduate Medical Education (ACGME) issued national regulations that mandated:

- Residents could not work more than 80 hours per week.
- Residents could not work more than 30 hours (24 hours patient care + *6 hours didactics*) consecutively in the hospital. [bold italics added to note a gaping loophole for abuse].
- Residents should have at least 10 hours off between hospital shifts.
- Residents must have at least one 24-hour period off per week (out of the hospital and free of clinical duties).

Debate continues within the medical community itself, with some abhorring the new guidelines and others strongly supporting them.

Charap, M., "Reducing resident work hours: unproven assumptions and unforeseen outcomes," *Annals of Internal Medicine,* 2004; 140:814-5)

Schroeder, S.A., "How Many Hours Is Enough? An Old Profession Meets a New Generation," *Annals of Internal Medicine,* 2004; 140:838-9

Why the enormous chasm in thought? I believe Dr. Schroeder best encapsulated the debate in his article when he wrote:

"How can the same phenomenon engender such different responses? One reason is that residency itself has changed dramatically in the past 4 decades; thus, physicians from different eras recall vastly different experiences. In effect, while the length of the residency week decreased (from an every-other-night schedule to every fourth night or less), the work became more stressful—modern diagnostic and therapeutic technologies greatly expanded what we can do and to whom we can do it, business pressures forced less acute care out of the hospital setting, and constant paging interruptions disrupted workflow. The result for residents is heightened intensity of patient care, less control over time, and lower margin for error—all inherently stressful. Another reason is the changed composition of residents. Medicine has evolved from a dominantly male profession to one equally represented by both sexes. Because many female residents are considering becoming or already are parents, their home responsibilities add an extra dimension to their lives and create a stronger pull away from the residency than occurs for most men. Furthermore, few residents—men or women—have the home support that a traditional "wife" provided in years past."

In my mind, the argument that there is no evidence that medical errors, some deadly, follow from excessive hours, is hollow. Anyone involved in any demanding activity understands that their capacity for flawless performance declines the longer they perform the activity without adequate rest. It doesn't matter whether that activity is truck driving, interpreting medical data, or fighting in battle. Errors increase the longer one continues without rest.

So how effective have the ACGME regulations been in improving the lot of interns and residents? On July 28, 2004, the Associated Press New Service released an article titled "Young Doctors Working Less Hours." However, during the intervening year, the ACGME had reviewed 2,019 programs—about a quarter of the total—and cited five percent on-duty hour violations: nearly half cited were breaking the eighty-hour week limit. According to the Associated Press article, the ACGME has already allowed some seventy-five surgical programs to extend resident work hours to eighty-eight hours a week. Although over one hundred doctors filed complaints between the date the ACGME regulations went into effect and 2008, officials from the American Medical Student Association believe that violations are markedly underreported due to fear of reprisals, including weak letters of recommendation that could affect job searches after completing training, and concern that their program could lose accreditation.

In my opinion, federal legislation that includes meaningful penalties and protections is needed to stop the abuse once and for all. The danger to patient safety is eminent. I support the Patient and Physician Safety and Protection Act of 2003, introduced by Senator Jon Corzine (S.952) and Representative John Conyers (H.R.1228), and reintroduced in 2005 after dying in Congress, only to die again in committee, which would enforce work-hour regulations through civil penalties rather than a loss of accreditation, make available needed funds for hospitals to hire auxiliary staff needed to replace diminished intern and resident work hours and provide whistleblower protection to resident physicians who report violations. Importantly, the civil penalties must be meaningful. I suggest $500,000 for the first infraction by a program, $2 million for the second, with additional $1 million *increase* in the penalty for each infraction thereafter. I guarantee this level of penalty would result in compliance.

Predictably, the ambulance chasers have gotten wind of the controversy. I guess I'm like most physicians who abhor the plaintiffs' attorneys who boldly advertise on radio, television, the phone book cover, and just about anyplace else. I don't dislike attorneys groundlessly. In fact, there are many—plaintiff and defense—whom I respect and admire. In my mind, however, there are clearly a large group of plaintiffs' attorneys—certainly larger than among physicians (although we also have our misfits)—who have no apparent redeeming qualities. For example, see the thinly veiled website Injuryboard.com—"Your source for personal injury news, attorneys and information" of Napoli, Kaiser, Bern & Associates.

For the most recent information on this subject see:
https://www.acgme.org/What-We-Do/Accreditation/Clinical-Experience-and-Education-formerly-Duty-Hours/History-of-Duty-Hours

Appendix 2
The Insurance Industry and Managed Care

The billing offices at UW, or for that matter in any practice, can't be blamed for all of the problems that hindered physicians from obtaining fair reimbursement for services they provide. Unfortunately, health insurance companies have a long history of abusive, and in some cases, fraudulent business practices designed to limit payments for medical care. Finally, after getting fed up with years of futile haggling over denied claims, confusing regulations and unreasonable fee schedules, some physicians and their organizations have filed lawsuits in both federal and state courts over the last few decades alleging that insurance companies exploit dominant market positions to engage in fraud, extortion, and racketeering. Some of these lawsuits have been consolidated into federal cases certified as class action suits that include many, or all, of the 713,800 physicians practicing in the United States in 2018, according to the U.S. Bureau of Labor Statistics. For example, one anti-racketeering lawsuit, named *In re Managed Care,* consolidated litigation by physicians and more than twenty medical societies against the who's who in managed care companies—including Aetna, Anthem, Cigna, Coventry, Foundation, Humana, PacifiCare, Prudential, United, and Wellpoint—under the jurisdiction of U.S. District Judge Federico Moreno in Florida. The suit alleged that the managed care companies "engage in systemic attempts to cheat doctors, control medical decisions through non-payment, and manipulate the amount and kind of necessary care provided," according to attorney Archie Lamb, Esq., the lead co-counsel for the physician plaintiffs. "For the first time, the nation will see exactly what these companies have been doing to doctors and their patients—and it's not been the management of care," added Rocky Wilcox, general counsel for the Texas Medical Association, a party to the lawsuit. David Cook, general counsel for the Medical Association of Georgia, said, "We have tried for years to resolve our concerns with the plans through endless discussions, on a case-by-case basis. Subsequently, we sought resolution through state legislation and active enforcement of those laws and even petitioned the United States Congress. We have arrived at this federal courthouse in Florida—after futile and lengthy attempts to fix a mounting problem—as a last resort." This lawsuit—only one of many brought by physicians and physician groups against insurance and managed care companies alleging outright cheating—went to trial in September 2005. The parties settled the lawsuit in 2005, but many more followed.

See https://www.leagle.com/decision/infco20140618121 for examples.

Several large insurance companies, in an attempt to ward off higher court-ordered awards and even more future lawsuits, offered settlement proposals providing more favorable reimbursement policies and procedures that physicians had sought unsuccessfully for years through negotiated contracts and legislation. For example, Independence Blue Cross and Aetna, Inc., proposed extensive changes in their coding and reimbursement practices that included cessation of bundling and down-coding practices, disclosure of fee schedules, and reimbursement coding protocols. Both companies also promised to establish new mechanisms for physician reimbursement appeal. Aetna agreed to reimburse physicians retroactively, on a pro-rated basis, for wrongfully denied claims—in addition to investing in electronic measures to expedite physician billing and reimbursement activities. Amazingly, Aetna also offered to define "medical necessity"—an important concession that physicians have sought for many years. Cigna Healthcare offered similar reforms. It may seem outrageous that physicians would have to resort to litigation to induce health-care companies to provide fee schedules for medical services provided, but that is the medical reimbursement environment that has existed in the United States for many years. It's difficult to comprehend the enormous amount of time and money physicians, their staff, and physician groups like UW Physicians, wasted over the years trying to get insurance and managed care companies to pay rightful claims for medical care.

The settlement offered by Aetna and accepted by the courts October 23, 2003, deserves special mention. It included provisions for payments for wrongfully denied claims in the past. Some of the redresses Aetna agreed to were:

- To make $100 million in payments to physicians divided among three categories—those who received an aggregate payment from Aetna of less than $5,000 during the years 2000, 2001 and 2002—who will receive a base amount; those who received between $5,000 and $50,000 during those three years—who will receive twice the base amount, and those who have received more than $50,000—who will receive three times the base amount.
- To discontinue automatic down-coding of evaluation and management (E/M) codes and agree to a nationally recognized, physician-approved set of rules governing claims coding and grouping procedures, while jointly developing with physicians a claims editing software package that incorporates those procedures.
- To use a definition of medical necessity which is set down in the settlement and that applies medical community-approved standards. Aetna would also disclose the percentage of covered services that they denied on the grounds of medical necessity.
- To eliminate "all-products" clauses from Aetna contracts, while retaining the right to offer higher fee-for-service rates or other incentives to physicians who remain contracted with all of Aetna's products.
- To commit to making payment within fifteen days of clean claims submitted electronically, and within thirty days if submitted on paper forms, while putting into place date-stamping mechanisms for claims receipts and offering interest payments on late reimbursements.
- To invest in systems to increase electronic connectivity and direct Web-enabled access to

Aetna systems to verify reimbursement information and track claims. Each physician would have individualized Web access to Aetna's fee schedule—including all the codes applicable to his or her practice.

- To establish a National Advisory Committee of practicing physicians to provide advice to Aetna on issues of concern to physicians.
- To establish an independent appeals process for physician billing disputes.
- To devote $20 million in initial funding to a newly formed foundation to support initiatives in areas such as eliminating racial and ethnic disparities in health care, improving end-of-life care, reducing and preventing childhood obesity and addressing the problem of the uninsured. Physicians had the option of directing their individual shares of the $100 million retroactive payments to the foundation.
- To make a pharmacy discount card program available for physicians to offer their patients.

Aetna estimated the value to physicians of its business practice improvements over the course of the agreement to be $475 million, not including the estimated $100 million in retroactive payments to physicians. Aetna agreed to abide to these new guidelines, however, for only four years. This was a major sticking point for many physicians who wanted to see permanent agreements put in place. In return for making these concessions, Aetna and the other companies that offered settlements, wanted complete immunity from lawsuits over their business practices up to the date of the settlement and reserved the right to invalidate the agreements if a certain percentage of providers opted out of the settlement. The agreement was eventually approved, but many physicians, especially those in large groups that sustained huge losses attributable to the disputed practices, opted out of the agreement.

The court also approved a settlement agreement between CIGNA and the plaintiffs. That agreement required disclosure of coding edits, adoption of certain CPT conventions, clarification of medical necessity criteria, funding of a charitable foundation, and reimbursement of money to the plaintiff class. It also provided for an overall payment of $55 million to the plaintiffs' attorneys. *As usual, the attorneys were the real winners of the litigation.*

In a recent case in 2018, a New Jersey judged ruled on an orthopedic surgeon's lawsuit against Aetna when it refused to reimburse the surgeon $209,000 for a procedure that he'd received written authorization for prior to surgery—even though he was an "out-of-network provider." The surgeon initially sued Aetna in the Superior Court of New Jersey for breach of contract, promissory estoppel, account stated, and fraudulent inducement. Aetna removed the lawsuit to federal court and filed a motion to dismiss, arguing that it provided coverage to the patient through the Employee Retirement and Income Security Act (ERISA), so Dr. Glastein's state law claims were preempted. The judge, however, decided otherwise, and Aetna was forced to pay for the surgery.

Another issue is insurance companies refusing to reimburse for new treatments and surgeries that are developed for diseases or conditions—typically claiming they are experimental and, therefore, not covered. A good example of this is what's currently happening for riboflavin-UV crosslinking used for keratoconus or ectasia of the cornea. Despite overwhelming evidence in numerous studies that this treatment is effective at halting, or at least slowing the progression of the diseases, insurance providers, including Cleveland Clinic employee insurance, has persisted in refusing to reimburse for the treatment that typically costs between $2,500 and $4,000 per eye. Often, corneal providers have been required to file appeals to pre-authorization denials and set up personal phone calls with the claims adjusters or medical representatives of the providers to get approval for the sight-saving treatment for individual patients. Given the number of patients seen, busy corneal specialists do not have time for this nonsense. There are hundreds of treatments in all subspecialties of medicine that are treated similarly by insurance companies striving to decrease outlays.

Inappropriate insurance company denials also apply to needed drugs that these companies mandate pre-authorization to receive. Some companies routinely force patients to shift a less effective medications that are less expensive, or deny payment outright—despite medical necessity. An example of this in my practice is insurance companies denying an effective antibiotic for a severe corneal ulcer and trying to force the use of a lesser antibiotic to which over 50% of the possible infecting organisms are resistant—threatening severe vision loss. It's appalling how often this happens. Again, the treating physician must typically contact the insurance company and speak to an employee of the company, sometimes a physician who's not experienced with the condition, and who, therefore, knows nothing whatsoever about the disorder or disease—but they often think they do. This type of behavior by insurance company is unacceptable and often threatens the well-being of the patient.

It's gratifying to see physicians and their organizations are finally standing up against the insurance companies who unjustly hold them at bay. Hopefully, at some point, the years of nasty acrimony and squabbling between physicians and insurance companies will be put behind us. I have doubts, however, that there will ever be true peace because memories tend to be short and legions of up-and-coming junior executives will undoubtedly be tempted to enhance corporate profits on the backs of patients, physicians and hospitals.

Appendix 3
The Food and Drug Administration and Patient Safety

Unfortunately, many areas of uncertainty loom in treatments provided today in ophthalmology and other medical specialties. Let me provide one example. On September 10, 2004, the FDA approved the Verisyse/Artisan™ phakic intraocular lens manufactured by Ophtec U.S.A., Inc., Boca Raton, Florida, for correction of nearsightedness from -5 to -20 diopters of refractive error (now updated to +12 to -23.5 diopters). This lens is placed behind the cornea in the anterior chamber of a patient's eye in front of the colored iris. At least theoretically, it leaves the fragile "crystalline" lens of the eye untouched, although the development of a cataract is one potential complication.

http://www.fda.gov/cdrh/pdf3/p030028.html

Just one of the areas of apprehension created by the data submitted for FDA approval concerned loss of corneal endothelial cells in eyes implanted with the lenses. These cells are critically responsible for maintaining hydration and, therefore, normal function of the cornea and vision in that eye. Three-year data from the clinical study indicated a continuing loss of endothelial cells at a rate of 1.8% per year. If the endothelial cell loss continued at this rate, 39% of patients would be expected to lose 50% if their corneal endothelial cells within 25 years of implantation. Human corneal endothelial cells have very limited, if any, potential to replace themselves. If the endothelial cell density falls to a sufficiently low level (less then approximately 250 to 300 cells per mm^2), the cornea fails, leading to blindness in the eye. An endothelial cell transplant is then needed to restore vision. This level of endothelial cell loss might be safe for a 60-year old, based on his or her life expectancy, but what about a 21-year old who would only be 46 years old in twenty-five years? In my opinion, many of these young patient's corneas are destined to fail when they reach their sixties, seventies, and beyond. A careful inspection of the data yields even more concern. The 1.8% loss of endothelial cells per year was based on a cohort group of only fifty-seven eyes and is an *average*. Therefore, some patients lost endothelial cells at even higher rates. For example, Table 1 shows actual data from the study. The average corneal endothelial cell loss from six months to three years was 4.75%, with a standard deviation of 7.3%. Therefore, an eye that was one or two standard deviations from the mean would lose 12.0 % or 19.4%, respectively, of their endothelial cells in just the first three years after the lens was placed in the eye. The data from the study also reveal other alarming trends. The loss from year one to year two after implantation of the lens was -1.12±5.8 %, and from year two to year three was -2.37 ±6.3%. Therefore, the rate of endothelial cell loss appeared to be *accelerating* the longer the intraocular lens was in the eye. With the approval, the FDA rightfully required the manufacturer to provide yearly reports on the endothelial cell loss, data reaching out to five years for the cohort of eyes included in the original study. The approval also mandated a post-approval study out to five years of follow-up to evaluate other vision-threatening complications that might occur following implantation of the lens, including retinal detachment, corneal failure, cataract formation, chronic inflammation in the eye, development of glaucoma, and secondary surgical procedures such as lens removal.

Table 1: Percent loss in endothelial cell density by period
for the Verisyse phakic intraocular lens

Period	% Cell Change ± standard deviation	Lower 95% Confidence level	Number of Patients
0 to 6 months	-0.40 (7.8)	-1.58	139
6 months to 1 yr	-1.17 (6.2)	-2.17	149
1 year to 2 yrs	-1.12 (5.8)	-1.92	198
2 years to 3 yrs	-2.37 (6.3)	-3.22	216
6 months to 3 yrs	-4.75 (7.3)	-6.1	111

In a study published in 2018, 507 eyes of 289 patients received the Artisan Myopia or Artisan Toric intraocular lens for the treatment of myopia with or without astigmatism.

Jonker SMR, Berendschot TTJM, Ronden AE, Saelens IEY, Bauer NJC, Nuijts RMMA. Long term endothelial cell loss in patients with Artisan and Artisan Toric phakic intraocular lenses: 5- and 10-year results. Ophthalmology. 2018;125:486

In that study, chronic endothelial loss was calculated from six months (when endothelial cell loss due to the surgical procedure itself would likely have stabilized) after surgery to the end of the follow-up period. These investigators found an ANNUAL endothelial cell density decline of 48 cells/mm^2 and 61 cells/mm^2 in the myopic and toric (also corrects astigmatism) groups, respectively. This resulted in a total endothelial cell loss of 16.6% and 21.5%, respectively, in these two groups from 6 months to 10 years after surgery. Ten years after implantation, the corneal endothelial cell density in eyes had decreased by more than 25% in 7.9% and 6.3%, respectively, of eyes in the two groups. Also, at only **ten** years after surgery, 3.9% and 4.0% in the myopic and toric groups, respectively, had endothelial cells densities already less than 1500 cells/mm^2. Many of these corneas are likely to fail over the coming decades and require corneal endothelial transplant surgery.

Similar endothelial cell loss has been documented with another phakic intraocular lens, the Visian® TORIC ICL, marketed by the STARR Surgical Company. In a post-FDA approval study of this lens, at 60+ months after implantation surgery 13 of 115 eyes (11.3%) had greater than or equal to 30% loss of the central endothelial cell density compared to the preoperative examination.

https://www.accessdata.fda.gov/cdrh_docs/pdf3/P030016S001b.pdf

Based on these results, and others presented at meeting and published in the literature, I've decided I will not implant phakic intraocular lenses into the eyes of my patients. It is my hope that the epidemic of corneal failures (pseudophakic bullous keratopathy, also called PBK) from faulty intraocular lenses used in cataract surgery in the 1980s to 1990s is not repeated when the Verisyse lens, and other phakic intraocular lenses that have been or will be approved by the FDA, are implanted in hundreds of thousands of patients' eyes, but I must say that I look to the future with considerable trepidation. It is the surgeons and hospitals who will be blamed if widespread problems develop.

Phakic intraocular lenses are only one area of concern in medicine. Many other areas of alarm are clearly present, not only in ophthalmology, but throughout medicine. The scare regarding COX-2 inhibitors, such as Vioxx and Celebrex, a decade ago is one highly-publicized example showing that just because a drug or device receives FDA approval, it doesn't necessarily mean it is safe.

Some surgeons feel that the FDA represents an unreasonable burden to the timely implementation of new drugs and devices, and at times FDA policies are clearly rigid and unthinking. Many rather ridiculous situations where the FDA pointlessly blocks treatments could be cited. However, it's best we remember the lessons learned from thalidomide and the courage of Dr. Frances Kelsey when he prevented the U.S. from having the tragic epidemic of malformed thalidomide babies seen in Canada, Germany, and other countries. Also, let us not forget the Hippocratic Oath—*"above all else, do no harm."*

Appendix 4
The Medical Malpractice Quagmire

The growing medical malpractice crisis is probably the number one issue unsettling American physicians today. It represents a constant, and growing, source of angst and disillusionment within the profession. After previous crises in the 1970s and 1980s, the current medical malpractice crisis appears to be deeper and broader, resulting in physicians abandoning medicine altogether or in some cases restricting their practices to specific areas of medicine. For example, due to the high risk of lawsuits resulting from difficult births, many physicians specializing in obstetrics and gynecology stopped performing baby deliveries. Let me cite one example of this disturbing trend. Twelve obstetricians at the Everett Clinic in the state of Washington stopped performing baby deliveries in 2004, due to jumps in malpractice insurance. Other physicians in high-risk specialties are similarly affected. In one east coast city, physicians were considering putting up a billboard on the freeway that said, "Drive Carefully! Due to skyrocketing malpractice premiums, there are no practicing neurosurgeons within 150 miles." I personally know of ophthalmologists who've decided to stop practicing refractive surgery because the risk of malpractice litigation is higher, including the levels of claims, compared to cataract or corneal transplant surgery. Similar scenarios are being repeated over and over again across the country and throughout medicine.

How high are the increases in malpractice insurance premiums? That depends on the geographical area of practice and the specialty in medicine. The median increase in malpractice premiums throughout the United States ranged from fifteen to thirty percent over the years from 1996 to 2006. However, in some states where malpractice claims are higher, or carriers more limited, the rates increased far more. In Pennsylvania, for example, increases ranged from 26% to 73% in 2003 alone (see *Medical Liability Monitor,* October 2003). In January of 2004, the Congressional Budget Office released a study titled "Limiting Tort Liability for Medical Malpractice." This study found that premiums for all physicians nationwide rose 15%, on average, between 2000 and 2002. However, the increases during that period were even more dramatic for certain specialties, such as 22% for obstetricians (thank you for your contribution, former Senator Edwards!), and 33% for internists and general surgeons. The study also found that the average plaintiff award rose from $95,000 to $320,000 between 1986 and 2002—an annual growth rate of almost eight percent. These trends have continued into the second decade of the 2000s. A 2011 study in the New England Journal of Medicine reported that 75% of physicians in "low-risk" specialties and nearly 100% of physicians in "high-risk" specialties would face a malpractice claim during their careers.

Jena AB, Seabury S, Lakdawalla D, Chandra A. Malpractice risk according to physician specialty. N. Engl. J. Med. 2011;365: 629.

A recent article in Gallagher in December 2017, noted a decrease in the rate of medical malpractice claims paid from 15,000 in 2003 to less than 8900 in 2014, so some progress has apparently been made in health care provided, tort reform and/or other factors.

https://www.gallaghermalpractice.com/blog/post/how-much-does-medical-malpractice-insurance-cost

Increasing malpractice insurance rates can be attributed to a number of factors. Some claim we are just in a tight period in the normal cycling of insurance liabilities and costs. An important parallel factor, however, is the obvious decrease in the number of firms that offer malpractice insurance. Some firms, such as the St. Paul Companies, previously the provider of insurance for more physicians than any other company, abandoned the malpractice insurance industry completely due to high losses. There is also little doubt that insurance award amounts have increased over the last ten to twenty-five years, with one study showing that both jury awards and settlements had more than doubled from 1992 to 2002 (Physician Insurers Association of America (PIAA) data-sharing project. Washington: PIAA, May 17, 2002). Also, the cost of malpractice defense has mushroomed due to increases in attorney fees, expert witness costs, and other expenses. Finally, the increased marketing, and in some cases, unabashed ambulance chasing by plaintiff's attorneys have generated unprecedented numbers of groundless claims. Just log onto any search engine on the Web and insert "malpractice" or "malpractice Florida" (or any other state) and you'll be shocked at the long list of law firms crawling all over themselves to get the attention of patients who had medical care or outcomes that didn't meet their expectations. The same is true of the phone book or television. It's unbelievable how tasteless many of these commercials have become. "My attorney got me $2 million dollars and a new car," said one purported patient on a television commercial I saw in Pittsburgh, followed by missives from several other clients who'd purportedly won big awards or settlements. Is it any wonder that some patients have come to view initiating a malpractice case like playing the lottery?

Many physicians are fed up with the increasing risks and costs of practicing medicine. There were work slowdowns in New Jersey, physician strikes in West Virginia, and temporary closings of hospital services, such as trauma care at the University of Nevada Medical Center, just to name a few. Physicians in other states, such as Connecticut, staged rallies at their state capitol, demanding reform. Other physicians just walked away—closing or selling practices and taking early retirement. In some areas of the country, there are growing shortages of physicians, with many practices taking no new patients, especially in some subspecialties. The number of newspaper and magazine articles pointing to the inability of patients to get medical care at any cost will most definitely grow over the next few decades.

Meanwhile, the citizens of Florida have created their own special crisis that will affect medical care in that state for years to come. In November of 2004, they passed "Amendment 8"

called "Public Protection from Repeated Medical Malpractice," but better known as "The Three Strikes Amendment." The language now added to the Florida Constitution is as follows:
Section 20. Prohibition of Medical License after Repeated Medical Malpractice.

(i)   No person who has been found to have committed three or more incidents of medical malpractice shall be licensed or continue to be licensed by the State of Florida to provide health care services as a medical doctor.

(ii)   The phrase "found to have committed" means that the malpractice has been "found in a final judgment of a court or law, final administrative agency decision, or decision of binding arbitration."

Presumably, a judgment which was entered several years before this proposal passed would be counted and estimates were that as many as eight percent of doctors practicing in Florida could have lost their licenses. In practice, I believe only a handful did lose licenses. This probably sounds like a great thing to most people—"Let's get rid of all the lousy doctors." Who could argue with that? The only problem: in today's medico legal climate, almost all doctors will have claims against them and few will be willing to risk the loss of their career. Therefore, the primary effects of this proposal will without question be:

• Any doctors who have had one or more adverse judgments against them are likely to move out of Florida to avoid the risk of a second or third strike.

• Most young doctors will simply not consider positions in Florida where they could lose the career they've worked so hard to establish.

One effect of the new amendment will be that doctors who have one or more professional liability cases pending, or who have a case filed against them in the future, will be likely to demand that the case be settled rather than tried or arbitrated. Since the language is phrased in terms of final judgments, few physicians will be willing to run the risk of a judgment being entered against him or her. Instead, they will demand the case, no matter how frivolous, whether based on causation, liability, or damages, be settled in order to avoid the risk of an adverse judgment. The malpractice litigation system will now see more of these cases being settled, likely for more than they would have been settled for in arbitration or trial. There will be no effect of such settlements in terms of the three-strikes law, even if ten or twenty cases are settled, but this new reality will undoubtedly drive up malpractice insurance rates in Florida. Opponents of the Amendment, that include the American Medical Association, argue that doctors who practice in high-risk fields, such as obstetrics, neurosurgery and trauma, will be obligated to leave Florida because of the fear of this "three-strikes Amendment," and that newly-trained doctors will elect not to come to Florida to practice. The result will actually be decreased access for patients to quality health care—that will increase over the years. Thus, there are at least two good reasons for doctors to leave the Sunshine State. I know of two ophthalmologist who elected NOT to go to Florida, but instead to go another state, after completing training due to this law. Woe is the state that follows Florida's example.

Another effect of the malpractice crisis is the practice of defensive medicine—ordering tests and consults that are not really justified to protect oneself against litigation. This, in turn, drives up medical costs. Another serious impact is the manner in which litigation by aggressive attorneys can alter the practice of medicine in a negative way. Let me provide one unfortunate example of this. Some low birth weight babies develop retinopathy of prematurity and the only possibility of maintaining vision is aggressive treatment—which in most cases requires surgery. Despite these measures, some of these heartbreaking infants will go blind. A number of lawsuits have been brought against ophthalmologists when blindness has been the final outcome, when blindness likely would have occurred in any case. The result of these lawsuits was increasing reluctance on the part of ophthalmologists to attempt anything—leading to almost certain blindness, even for infants who might have benefited from the surgical treatments. A nationally prominent pediatric ophthalmologist recently told me, "Plaintiff's attorneys are responsible for more childhood blindness in this country than any other factor because of the effect their frivolous lawsuits have had on the willingness of ophthalmologists to treat the most needy low-birth-weight infants." I could cite many other examples where litigation has forced physicians to refrain from attempting to help needy patients. Something needs to be done about this at the federal governmental level.

I have served as an expert witness in a number of malpractice cases, primarily for the defense, because this is who tends to ask my opinion, but also on occasion for a plaintiff. One of the most outrageous situations I've noted has been that many so-called "expert witnesses"—almost always for the plaintiff side—are not expert witnesses at all, but shams found through advertisements on Web sites and in legal trade journals (see https://www.jurispro.com, https://www.forensisgroup.com/expert-witness/medical-malpractice/, or look up "medical malpractice expert witness" with any Web search engine). When one carefully examines the *curriculum vitae* of these "expert witnesses," one commonly finds they are far from expert. Many are laughable imposters with a long curriculum vitae filled with bogus awards, non-peer-reviewed publications, and memberships in fake medical societies. Despite this, they are frequently allowed to participate in depositions and trials. It is, of course, the opposing attorney's prerogative to question the credentials of these charlatans during deposition and trial, but rarely have I seen a judge dismiss an expert witness, however ridiculous his or her qualifications. Another egregious wrong, that occurs all too often, is the courts allowing physicians from the same geographic area—obvious medical practice competitors—to testify for a plaintiff. Often this testimony is retribution for perceived transgressions—like the defendant having a busier medical practice in the community. This is clearly an unethical practice and should not be allowed by the courts or by our medical societies. Even when experts are used, their testimony is often flawed. The prime example of this in refractive surgery is an airline pilot, with a result yielding better than 20/20 uncorrected vision in both eyes after LASIK, who brought suit in Arizona because he claimed he could no longer pilot airplanes at night and won a $4 million jury verdict on the basis of flawed expert witness testimony—by a refractive surgeon who practices in Canada. The plaintiff's witness acknowledged errors in his testimony after the case ended. Despite this stunning admission, motions for retrial, filed all the way to the Arizona Supreme Court, were unsuccessful.

Plaintiff's attorneys recognize that a less than perfect outcome to a surgical procedure is not malpractice, so they frequently file suits claiming, "the patient didn't receive informed consent" or "the patient wasn't a candidate for the surgery to begin with," or other similar nonsense. I've seen many cases where it is clearly documented that the patient saw informational videos, spoke to the surgeon about the risks, benefits, alternatives, and complications, on one or more occasion, with the patient signature indicating that he or she understood there were no guarantees and that serious complications could occur…and still the plaintiff's attorney claims there was no informed consent. It's unbelievable that the legal system in America would give credence to such nonsensical claims, but they often do.

What measures can be taken to ease the current medical malpractice crisis? Clearly, ongoing efforts at tort reform, preferably at the federal level so that physicians are treated equally in different states, is at the top of the list. Some reforms that should be considered in legislation are as follows:

- A cap on non-economic damages in medical liability cases. Some states have already adopted caps that vary from $250,000 to $350,000.
- Provisions for binding arbitration that would reduce attorney and other litigation costs.
- Provisions to encourage early offers that would also get money to truly injured patients more quickly and eliminate the growing costs of trials. Rules requiring the plaintiff to pay defense attorneys' fees if a subsequent judgment is below an earlier offer would also help control costs.
- Requirements that plaintiffs pay *all* costs of the defendant physician, including fees for time lost from clinic and surgery revenues, as well as time spent preparing for trial through the reading of depositions and answering bothersome interrogatories, in the event of a decision for the defendant. This would be an effective deterrent to frivolous lawsuits. Some states, for example, Oregon, have statutes providing for reimbursement of defendant's costs, but none cover all of the costs inherent in a physician defending himself or herself from a lawsuit—and they should.
- Fixed attorney's fees that vary depending on the level of award and how the award is granted. Clearly a 30% fee on a $4 million dollar award granted to a patient is outrageous and not in the interests of the patient. Plaintiff's attorney fees should clearly be less if the case settles early, compared to settlement prior to trial or after a jury decision.

Many polls indicate that the majority of citizens are in favor of tort reform. Then why doesn't it happen? Clearly, the personal injury attorneys and their lobbies are the major factors blocking fair national tort reform. It gives me shivers to think how close a personal injury lawyer experienced in suing obstetricians when babies were born with cerebral palsy came to becoming vice-president of the United States—and the effect that would have had on the prospects for tort reform in this country. Some of the lawsuits brought by the former senator from North Carolina may have been justified, but many were not, and were designed to play on the sympathies of jurors who were not prepared to understand the intricacies of complex medical cases. Edwards' typical case was based on claims that these unfortunate babies would have been spared their brain disorders if only their doctors had performed Caesarean sections—claims that scientific studies have proven false. How could a man who operates like this help solve this serious problem? As the crisis continues to deepen and more and more physicians leave medical practice or decrease their services, and the population ages, the pressure for effective tort reform will mount. We must elect leaders who understand how important this issue is to the wellbeing of all Americans.

Does tort reform work? Absolutely! A study of California's 1975 California Medical Injury Compensation Reform Act (MICRA) by the RAND Corporation's Institute of Civil Justice found a decrease of 30% in the damages doctors and their insurers were ordered to pay in medical malpractice lawsuits. MICRA limits jury awards for pain and suffering to $250,000 and also limits attorney fees. The law also requires plaintiffs' attorneys to bear more of the costs of litigation. Thus, in the study of two hundred fifty-seven plaintiff verdicts, compensation to injured patients declined by 15%, while the fees for plaintiffs' attorneys fell by an impressive 60%. Caps on non-economic damages were imposed in 45% of these trials that ended in a verdict for the plaintiff. This law should be considered a model for federal medical malpractice legislation, and in the absence of federal action, should be adopted in other states. In either case, something needs to be done. The time for ceaseless debate and rumination has ended. Further delay will only deepen the crisis and further compromise the quality of the American medical system.

Steven E. Wilson, MD

Appendix 5
Government regulation—and the Health Insurance Portability and Accountability Act (HIPAA)

Government regulation, federal, state and local, has long been a pervasive burden on private, hospital-based, and academic medical practices throughout the United States. Most universities also have their own rules and policies regulating medical care and research. All aspects of medical care, teaching, and research are governed by overlapping rings of rules, policies, and laws that cover drugs and medical devices, residency and fellowship teaching, laboratory chemicals and radioisotopes, human and animal research, and virtually all other facets of medical care, teaching, and research. Clearly many of these regulations are important for maintaining the quality and safety of medical practice and research, but the mushrooming burden of forms and other paperwork, and annual courses, required to conform to the regulations has generated a labor-intensive compliance industry within the offices, departments, and schools of our institutions. This is not only costly, but hampers innovation and flexibility. My department, just like all the others in every medical school in America, struggled to comply with the regulatory quagmire, but nothing prepared us for the morass created by the Health Insurance Portability and Accountability Act (HIPAA) which was created in 1996 by the Clinton administration and congressional healthcare reform advocates. The goals and objectives of this legislation were to "streamline healthcare industry inefficiencies, *reduce paperwork*, make it easier to detect and prosecute fraud and abuse," and make it possible for people with pre-existing medical conditions or who have family members with health conditions to change jobs without impediments created by health insurance portability concerns. I'm certain the men and women who drafted this legislation had nothing but the best interests of the American people in mind. After all, who could argue with safeguards to protect personal health-care information from those who might use it to determine whether you and I are a suitable employment or insurance risk? However, I'm just as certain that these bureaucrats did not foresee the impact these new regulations would have on clinical practice, teaching, and research. Each and every person in medical care, teaching, and research—and even research industries—had to undergo long hours of HIPAA training—at tremendous cost. The expense of training new staff and monitoring compliance are ongoing, and it is estimated that the cost to date has been between $100 and $150 billion, depending on the breath of costs included—a staggering amount stripped from resources that would have

164

otherwise been available for medical teaching and research.

An immediate effect of HIPAA was to further complicate clinical research. The legislation included sweeping new regulations regarding when, and by whom, individually identifiable personal health information (PHI) could be used and disclosed. Under the new rules, individual authorization to access PHI is required from every study participant, even for minimal-risk research—like a chart review.

Many physician–scientists get their start in research as a medical students or residents doing simple reviews of medical charts. For example, one may evaluate the outcomes of gall bladder surgery in a consecutive series of patients who had minimally invasive laparoscopic surgery compared to traditional surgery. This time-honored tradition often stirred young trainees' interests in medical research, and results from these studies frequently became the impetus for larger multi-center trials. After HIPAA went into effect, these small studies that had previously been covered in our department by blanket Investigational Review Board (IRB) approvals required detailed multi-page applications with an individual review. Clearly, the risks of these studies to an individual patient's privacy were minimal, but nonetheless complex—and time consuming—regulations had to be followed. The result was predictable. Many trainees and faculty, including myself, became reluctant to pursue this type of entry-level research with trainees. Usually, by the time the trainees completed the paperwork (typically requiring several hours) and waited for the IRB to approve their proposal, they were onto another rotation or too late to finish the project for presentation at a medical meeting. One can just imagine the tangle encountered when planning infinitely more complex prospective clinical trials in the HIPAA era. Unbelievably, all clinical research ground to a halt in some institutions while the administrators and faculty struggled to comply with HIPAA regulations, often in a confused, deer-in-the-headlights fashion. For example, clinical research in all of the Veteran's Administration Hospitals stopped for over six months in 2003, while efforts were made system-wide to comply with the new regulations. There had previously been suspensions of human research at individual universities and hospitals over the years due to regulatory compliance issues, but HIPAA paralyzed medical research across the United States and convinced many trainees that medical research was not a viable career option.

Several years later, scrutiny has relaxed somewhat for these simple chart-review studies. But many among us are still wary of the nuisances associated with doing human medical research, including laborious repetitive applications, time-consuming detailed consents for even the most trivial studies, periodic reports about the progress made on the projects, and hours of mandatory on-line course work repeated every three years. The entire medical community has suffered, but not nearly as much as the patients afflicted with diseases and disorders who likely will be denied new treatments, or at least have to wait years longer for effective therapy, because the mechanics of research have become too difficult and expensive. I myself suspended all human research three years ago, primarily due to HIPAA (see Chapter 13) and aggressive bureaucrats. I may someday decide to go back and once again complete the two to three days of CITI program coursework required to participate in human research—so a medical student, resident, or fellow can do a human research project. But then again, I may not.

Appendix 6
Medical School Medicare Audits by the Federal Government

The University of Washington became entangled in its Medicare and Medicaid billing crisis because of a whistle-blower lawsuit filed by a UW Physicians employee, who made several million dollars for his efforts. Many other medical schools and physicians, however, have been ensnared by the U.S. Inspector General's "Physicians at Teaching Hospitals" (PATH) project, that investigates Medicare and Medicaid billing at medical schools and teaching hospitals throughout the country. Settlements have been reached between the government and many medical institutions—with a threat of False Claims Act litigation hanging over them. As Gregory Peaselee, executive director of the University of Pittsburgh Physicians, said, "Arguing with the federal government in a long and litigious manner is not in our best interest, even though we have serious problems with the PATH audits." Jack J. Chielli wrote in *Physician News Digest* in May of 1998, "Many institutions have questioned the legitimacy of the auditing criteria the government is using: guidelines that mandate teaching physician supervision of residents and interns for billing of Medicare services performed by them. The guidelines, they contend, have been vague and inconsistent, and the government has retroactively applied revised guidelines to audit past billing behavior."

At about this time, in 1998, new Evaluation and Management (E&M) Guidelines were put forward by the government, causing outrage among physicians because of the time-consuming documentation they mandated, the increased penalties that would be assessed for errors, and the increased random audits imposed on physicians treating Medicare patients. Is it any wonder that many capable and successful physicians have responded by declining to care for Medicare and Medicaid patients?

In the case of the numerous audits the government has performed on American medical schools, the settlements were not based on specific fines and reimbursements for improper bills, but on negotiated settlements. I see the Office of Inspector General's PATH project as little more than a wildly successful and creative governmental effort to reduce medical costs on the backs of medical schools, and teaching hospitals, and the physicians that work in them—amounting to more than $500 million to date. That is an impressive amount, sure to warm the cockles of the Inspector General and his superiors in Washington D.C. So what if the charges are based on errors in interpretation of Draconian Medicare and Medicaid regulations and the careers and lives of a few physicians and administrators are destroyed? So what if most of these medical schools and teaching hospitals and their departments had just as many "down-codings" as "up-codings"? Clearly there were problems at University of Washington, but I feel strongly that blame was misplaced and many were unjustly punished—not just Drs. Winn, Couser, and Fontaine—but hundreds of other patently honest and hardworking physicians at UW, many of whom were in departments, such as ophthalmology, that had no role whatsoever in the investigation, but nonetheless had to relinquish funds from their already sagging budgets to pay legal costs and the penalties. The effects of the resulting shortfalls on teaching, research, and medical care at UW, and other similarly pillaged institutions, will be longstanding—and will invariably lead to a decline in the availability and quality of medical care, not only in the areas served by these specific institutions, but throughout the country. The most immediate effect will be difficulty in retaining and attracting new faculty members to academic careers in medicine.

How can the innocent medical schools and physicians throughout the United States defend themselves from these attacks? Some in the medical community have chosen litigation as a means of correcting what they see as serious flaws in the PATH project originated by the Clinton Administration. The American Association of Medical Colleges (AAMC) and American Medical Association (AMA) jointly filed a lawsuit in U.S. District Court in California in 1997, seeking to end the way the PATH audits were being conducted. John Parker, an AAMC spokesperson said, "All along, the issue has not been the audits, but the way they are being conducted, particularly the taking of ambiguous standards and regulations and applying current clear standards to a period of time when they were not clear."

The focal point of the clash, detailed in countless pages of documents, is whether, during the 1990s, a teaching physician needed to be physically present at the time of treatment by an intern or resident (themselves licensed medical doctors) to bill for Medicare Part B reimbursement. While Medicare Part A provides a measure of funding to medical schools and teaching hospitals for training these young doctors, the amount received is not nearly sufficient to cover the augmented expenses of running a teaching facility. In any case, the regulations have most definitely been inconsistent and changing. As Harriet Rabb, General Counsel for the Department of Health and Human Services, admitted in a July 11, 1997, letter to the AAMC, "The standards for paying teaching physicians under Part B of Medicare have not been consistently and clearly articulated by the Health Care Financing Administration over a period of decades." This is a gross understatement and I am confident that no institution I've been associated with in my medical career—either in training or as a faculty member—could have withstood the level of scrutiny that UW and other medical schools have borne in this area. The federal government would point to Dartmouth and Yale as institutions that passed Path audits with flying colors, but I would assert that this was most likely due to those institutions being fortunate to have reasonable and empathetic auditors who acknowledged the ambiguity and inconsistency of the Medicare and Medicaid regulations.

The Department of Health and Human Services, despite alleged findings of inappropriate billings, conceded that the positions of the AAMC and the AMA on PATH audit protocols had merit. Changes were subsequently made to accommodate teaching hospitals that didn't receive proper guidance regarding the regulations. Revised PATH guidelines and were outlined in a July 1997 letter to the AAMC from Rabb. The changes can be summarized as follows:

- Henceforth, PATH audits would only be carried out in cases where Medicare and Medicaid carriers issued clear explanations of the rules prior to December 10, 1992.

- The OIG would not approach a hospital to open PATH discussion unless it obtained carrier materials showing that clear instructions on the physical presence issue had been provided.
- Hospitals would have the opportunity to produce materials demonstrating they had received unclear instructions on the physical presence issue from the carrier.
- The OIG would take action only in "egregious cases" of abuse or fraud.
- PATH audits of up-coding violations would not be conducted where the OIG decided not to conduct an audit of the physical presence requirement.

As a result of these new rules of engagement, PATH audits were canceled at a number of medical institutions. Hopefully, future audits will more reasonably consider the level of confusion inherent in Medicare and Medicaid regulations. I am certain there will be occasional physicians who have criminal intent and submit obviously false claims, just as there are criminal individuals in all human enterprises, and these individuals should be prosecuted and punished if they are found guilty. But, in my opinion, there is no place for investigations, such as seems to have been carried out in Seattle, that assume from the very beginning that a physician must be guilty of criminal activity. Anyone who has dealt with voluminous and complicated medical billing regulations that vary even between different insurance companies, or in the case of Medicaid, even with the geographical location of practices, would find themselves wrong on specific points on many occasions without having the slightest intent of defrauding payers.

My hope appears, however, to have been misguided because Medicare/Medicaid fraud investigations have continued, with the most recent to my knowledge being at Duke University Health System, leading to a fine of $1 million in 2014, and at Vanderbilt University Medical Center, leading to a fine of $6.5 million in 2017. I guess, we all should be pleased to see the amounts of the fines are at least decreasing.

If you have some free time on a rainy weekend and want to see the latest victims, you can go to the U.S. Department of Health and Human Services, Office of Inspector General website at https://oig.hhs.gov/newsroom/whats-new/index.asp and review the programs ensnarled in these investigations in 2017 and 2018. Some of these may be justified, but I have a feeling many of them were similar episodes to what happened at University of Washington School of Medicine.

About the Author

STEVEN E. WILSON, MD, a cornea and refractive surgeon-scientist with an international reputation, has published more than two hundred-thirty-five medical and scientific articles and book chapters. Originally from Whittier, California, the author was educated at California State University, Fullerton (B.A. Biology, 1974) and the University of California at Irvine (M.S. Molecular Biology and Biochemistry, 1977). He received his MD degree from University of California at San Diego in 1984, took his residency in ophthalmology at the Mayo Clinic in Rochester, and his fellowship in Cornea and Refractive Surgery at the LSU Eye Center in New Orleans. Dr. Wilson served on the faculties at the University of Texas Southwestern (1990–1995) and the Cleveland Clinic Foundation (1995–1998) and was Professor and Chair of Ophthalmology at the University of Washington (1998–2003). Since 2003, he has been Professor of Ophthalmology, Director of Corneal Research, and Staff in Refractive Surgery and Cornea at the Cole Eye Institute of the Cleveland Clinic Foundation in Cleveland, OH.

Steven Wilson is also the author of novels *Winter in Kandahar*, a Benjamin Franklin Award Finalist for 2004 in the category Best New Voice in Fiction. He also authored *Ascent From Darkness* (2007) and *The Benghazi Affair* (2018), of The Stone Waverly Trilogy. His novel *The Ghosts of Anatolia: An Epic Journey to Forgiveness* published September 2010 was Foreword Reviews Book of the Year Gold Award in Fiction (multicultural category) in 2010 and won the Runner-up Award in General Fiction at the Hollywood Book Festival in 2011.

ALSO BY STEVEN E. WILSON

The Stone Waverly Trilogy

Winter in Kandahar

AFGHANISTAN—the name conjures images of rugged mountains, ancient cities, hardened Mujaheddin, a country rife with regional rivalries, and the eternal struggle between Tajik and Pashtun. Afghanistan comes to life in this epic adventure of love, betrayal, and war. Young Tajik Ahmed Jan's heroic journey begins in the Northern Alliance stronghold near Taloqan just a month prior to 9/11. He is swept away by the chaos that soon engulfs the country before a chance discovery propels him to the forefront of the clash between civilizations. Pursued by both the CIA operative Stone Waverly and al-Qaeda, Ahmed Jan struggles to save his people from obliteration and find the true meaning of life in a land where all seems lost.

Ascent from Darkness

A top CIA agent, Stone Waverly, entrusted with a mission to find weapons-grade uranium in the heart of the Islamic world, becomes a real life "007" who sacrifices family for duty to country when he joins U.S. forces and Iraqi peasants alike in a quest to change the face of the Middle East after the overthrow of the Butcher of Baghdad. Masterfully using known facts of the Iraq war, including where weapons of mass destruction may have been hidden and how Saddam Hussein was top- pled, Wilson creates a rich fiction which takes you through Syria and Iraq in search of stolen Ukrainian uranium, which, if not found, will almost certainly be used by terrorists. This thriller unfolds like a motion picture, complete with forbidden romance, desperate Special Forces operations, and a never-say-die love of country.

The Benghazi Affair

Retired CIA case officer extraordinaire, Stone Waverly, is contentedly caring for his motherless children and teaching precocious middle schoolers, when out of the blue, duty calls once again. Within hours, he finds himself leading a team of covert operators in treacherous revolutionary Benghazi during the Arab Spring. Battling Gaddafi loyalists, and purportedly allied jihadists, he surreptitiously hunts for a terrifying weapon before it can be unleashed on the US homeland. Can he prevail where nothing is as it seems, despite severe injury, unsettling events at home, captivity in a chamber of horrors, and betrayal by a compatriot? The odds are stacked against him and time is running out.

The Ghosts of Anatolia

The Ghosts of Anatolia is an epic tale of three families, one Armenian and two Turkish, inescapably entwined in a saga of tragedy, hope, and reconciliation. Beginning in 1914, at the start of the Great War, confident Ottoman forces suffered a devastating defeat at the hands of the Russians. Pursuing Russian forces drove deep into eastern Anatolia, and the ensuing conflagration, fanned by fear, mistrust, and sedition, engulfed the Ottoman Empire. What happened there is contentiously debated, and to this day remains a festering sore of division. This compelling adventure novel brings these events poignantly to life.

CPSIA information can be obtained
at www.ICGtesting.com
Printed in the USA
FSHW012020180219
55772FS